Along with quotes for the book itself, included here are just a few of the quotes from individuals who have experienced Joys work, which is explained in detail in this book.

What Others Are Saying About Joy's Book and Work

"*Seven Keys to Connection* is a profound work integrating decades of personal growth work with extensive research of what Joy calls "The Great Disconnect". She shines light on the dysfunctional characteristics of our industrialized technological culture, one which greatly influences our collective tendency toward addictive behavior. Joy speaks vulnerably to her own transformative journey and invites the reader to experience self-love and compassion, while taking full responsibility for the lives we create.

This masterful work provides a road map with extensive tools and processes to lead us home to our true nature, free of guilt, shame and dysfunctional patterns. Our energy is then liberated to express our life purpose and contribute to the transformation of our culture. As free, integrated, and balanced human beings, we can steward the emergence of a soul-centric co-creative culture, one that empowers our uniqueness, honors the sacred and is deeply fulfilling."

—Katharine Roske
Co-author with Carolyn Anderson of
The Co-Creator's Handbook 2.0

"Dr. Freeman integrates a vast collection of insights to give us a path toward healing the multilayered fragments we all grapple with in this massive, out-of-control technological civilization. Hers is a truly integrative mind."

—Chellis Glendinning Ph.D, Psychologist and
author of *My Name Is Chellis and I'm in Recovery from Western Civilization* and other books

"There are many paths in life—some we stumble toward in blind hope of something changing, and some we walk with great intentions. So many have been on a lifelong journey toward wholeness and connecting longing for a deep inner connection with self and ultimately with deeper connections with each other. Joy Freeman's book 7 Keys to Connection is a gem. The book is counter shaming in its down to earth out of the box approach."

—Sheila Rubin, LMFT, RDT, BCT
Co-Creator Healing Shame Workshops

"It will never cease to amaze me how in sync my journey is with your book. I find myself turning to it when a crisis appears. Each time I am lead to the exact section I need in that moment and it is like every word on the page was written just for me and customized to meet my needs. Today I was lead to chapter 10 about taking risks and standing in my truth. This and the section on setting boundaries and being codependent were just what I needed to help me gain the strength to get genuinely excited about my new journey moving into the world on my own. That coupled with some of your personal stories has me in total awe of the synchronicity of your book and my life."

—C.B., counseling client

"Joy is a compassionate teacher with an ability to break things down into simplified and organized steps. She has a nonjudgmental loving heart with a discerning intelligent brain to help people access their full potential. Her way of expressing makes complex psychological concepts easy to understand. Having experienced her work with Internal Family Systems therapy, (that she writes extensively about in this book), along with her own intuitive guidance uncovered some powerful revelations about my challenges that were not accessible prior to our work. I recommend Joy in all of her expressive therapies and compassionate guidance roles and I especially recommend reading this book."

—L.M.K., Founder of Zen Health

"It is hard to express in words what I learned in this class with Joy. I can say this class has changed my life. I can now honor my truth and live in the realness of life. I have moved towards self-acceptance, inner peace and honoring my deepest truth more in 2 ½ months then I have in my whole life."

—Linley B., Student

"Thank you so much for this work. On the way home I started crying—I think it was because my inner self was so happy to have been seen and heard without judgment, unpracticed and unprepared—aha authentic! ….I am already drawing opportunities to speak my truth to me!….and would like to put myself in risk taking positions—like a new creative endeavor and speaking up on my feelings whenever possible!!!"

—Ann K., business owner

"I have been to many different kinds of therapy and never felt like I really got to the heart of the important issues, even after several visits and hundreds of dollars. I recently began work with Joy Freeman and had only three sessions with her. Not only did we get to the real issues in a deeper way than I ever thought possible, but I learned life-long skills to continue on my own. I feel that for the first time, I can see the light at the end of the tunnel. I see my life improving in real ways through the IFS and kind of creative work that Joy uses. The most hurtful wounds that have kept me from experiencing life to its fullest are the ones I have the power to let go of. I didn't realize this was possible until my sessions with Joy!"

—Eleanor Farjeon, Music Teacher/Flutist

"Experiencing work with Joy has uncovered such deep emotions that I can now get in touch with where my not so desirable habits have formed. Without judging myself I have found an answer to a more peaceful and rewarding life. By unblocking myself I have brought forth my creative voice and am achieving health and happiness. After each session with Joy I find out something more about myself. I implore you to let Joy help you. She is helping me."

—Anna S.

"This workshop has been the *most* transformational work I've ever done (and I've done lots of great stuff!) Somehow I've shifted at such a basic, fundamental level that my entire being has forever altered and opened up to love and life like never before."

—E.S.M., Assistant Project Director

For more testimonials go to www.drjoyfreeman.com

7 Keys to Connection

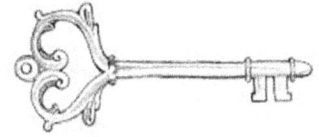

How to Move Beyond the Physical and Emotional Trauma of a Disconnected Culture

Joy Lynn Freeman D.C., Ph.D.c

Copyright © 2018 by Joy Lynn Freeman
Published by SoundStar Productions, Lake Worth, Fl, 33460
Cover Design: 99Designs – Irka Prima Sandana
Book Design: Medlar Publishing Solutions Pvt Ltd, India
Editor: Barbara Mc Nichol Editorial
Library of Congress Control Number: 2018902309
Publisher's Cataloging-In-Publication Data
(Prepared by The Donohue Group, Inc.)

    Names: Freeman, Joy Lynn.
    Title: 7 keys to connection : how to move beyond the physical and emotional trauma of a disconnected culture / Joy Lynn Freeman D.C., Ph.Dc.
    Other Titles: Seven keys to connection
    Description: Lake Worth, Fl : SoundStar Productions, [2018] | Includes bibliographical references.
    Identifiers: ISBN 978-0-9623861-7-6
    Subjects: LCSH: Self-acceptance. | Culture--Psychological aspects. | Generation Y--Psychology. | Interpersonal relations. | Depression, Mental. | Anxiety. | Compulsive behavior.
    Classification: LCC BF575.S37 F74 2018 | DDC 158.1--dc23

This book is designed to provide accurate and authoritative information in regard to the subject matter covered. Every effort has been made to ensure that it is correct and complete. However, neither the publisher nor the author are engaged in rendering personal professional advice or services via this book to the individual reader. This book is not intended as a substitute for advice from a trained counselor, therapist, or other similar professional. If you require such personal advice or other expert assistance, you should seek the services of a competent professional in the appropriate specialty, as can be found in the resources section of this book or by contacting the author for individual services via www.drjoyfreeman.com

Dedication

It saddens me to see so many of the Millennials suffering (and others as well) from depression, anxiety and all manner of addictive behaviors including substance abuse. This is happening in unprecedented numbers, as the world looks on in dismay, and most without a clue of why or what to do about it.

This book is dedicated to the many people in our disconnected culture, youth and otherwise, who live with daily feelings of aloneness, physical or emotional suffering and the many modes of attempts to escape this. I recognize the plight and confusion about how to deal with it. I honor the courage of those who choose to embark on the inner journey to move beyond it.

Acknowledgments

There have been many powerful teachers and mentors in my life to whom I want to give my deepest gratitude. Starting with Lisa DeLongchamps in the '70s, who taught us about mirrors, ownership and manifesting long before it showed up in any popular mainstream books. Gay and Kathlyn Hendricks whose brilliance regarding relationships and Body Centered Therapy first trained me in the 80s, in projections and somatic therapy, which is now one of the most viable forms of therapy for trauma. Irv Katz, master of Transformational Hypnotherapy, Gestalt, along with many other forms of therapy. He is chancellor of International University of Professional Studies IUPS, who supported my doctorate level work in the 1990s. Robert Frey, co-creator of Quantum Shift Retreats where together we offered powerful workshops using nature, deep process, ritual, and many forms of expressive arts. He was my beloved mentor in workshop facilitation who also helped me deepen my own Express your Soul's Voice Workshops. Bill Plotkin, whose wisdom in nature-based work, depth psychology, understandings of eco-psychology, and vision fasts have deeply affected me on many levels including my personal mode of earth-based spirituality. He and other individuals he has trained offer this work through his Animus Valley Institute. Rhiannon, whose unique improvisational singing work played a huge part in opening my singing voice, which has also become part of what I offer to others, not only to sing but to open their creativity in life.

In more recent years, my deepest gratitude to Richard Schwartz for his development of Internal Family Systems Therapy. This work has honed and improved my therapeutic work with individuals to such an amazing degree, as I know it has for many others, that I felt compelled to integrate it into my original 7 Keys. This was not an easy task, but it felt critical to do so, as its effect on transforming lives was beyond any other singular modality of therapy I have come across.

Most recently, I give gratitude to the work of Pat DeYoung who first opened my eyes to the concept of Shame that sits hidden beneath most all distortions of identity, along with Sheila Rubin and Bret Lyon whose Healing Shame Trainings and certification program has greatly expanded these understandings. The shame work has taken my own transformation and growth to yet another level. And lastly to Lawrence Heller the creator of NARM, Neuro Affective Relational Model, whose work brings great distinctions and specificities to help us understand what has gone wrong on the inter-and intra-psychic level from growing up as disconnected as we do in this culture.

I would also like to thank my mother Joy and my father Ben, who, though they did not have the understanding or perhaps the capabilities to attune and connect with me in a way that would have positively altered some aspects of the course of my life, they did give me grounding, safety, intelligence as parents, and encouragement to go for whatever path I might choose. Thank you, Joy and Ben, for though you are no longer with us, I experience your support now.

Contents

Introduction: Emotional Pain, Physical Conditions,
Addictions, and the 7 Keys xiii

Chapter 1: Roots of Addiction and Pain—Cultural
and Personal Trauma 1

Chapter 2: Soulcentric Developmental Wheel—
What are Your Missing Tasks?. 27

Chapter 3: Key 1 Feeling Your Feelings—
Demystifying Emotions 57

Chapter 4: Internal Family Systems (IFS)—Greater
Understanding of the Dynamics Within. 87

Chapter 5: Key 2 Developing the Witness—
Transforming the Inner Critic 109

Chapter 6: Key 3 What It Means to Love Ourselves—
How to Counter Shame. 121

Chapter 7: Key 4 The Art and Power of Surrender—
Integrating the Spiritual 141

Chapter 8: Key 5 Right Brain Integration—Soul Food 161

Chapter 9:	Key 6 Practices—Committing to Healthy Routines	175
Chapter 10:	Key 7 Foundation of Trust—The Ability to Take Risks	193
Chapter 11:	Key 7 Continued The Give Back—Worldly Soul Expression	213
Chapter 12:	Magic Happens—Where You Have Been and Where You are Headed	227
Chapter 13:	IFS Dialog Process—Moving from Egocentric to Soulcentric	235

Resources 265

About the Author 269

Introduction

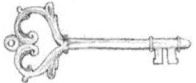

Emotional Pain, Physical Conditions, Addictions, and the 7 Keys

We live in a culture that fosters difficult emotional states, chronic physical conditions and many addictive behaviors. Most of us are products of an extremely linear, industrialized, and technological culture. This culture has disconnected humanity from its roots in Mother Earth and her rhythms. As humans, we've lost our authentic connection with nature, with ourselves, and with one another.

These "modern" cultural conditions have led to what I call The Great Disconnect—a black hole or negative void that contains one or more feelings of disconnection, discontent, hunger, hollow emptiness, and/or a pervasive sense that something is missing. Often, this negative void floats just below the surface in our lives yet we habitually push it away. We often try to cover it up, even in desperate ways. Some of us may not even realize it's there.

Yes, it is there.

The Great Disconnect exists for many who have been raised in abusive or neglected environments as well as for those who grew up in what was and is still considered "normal." This disconnect is present because of early trauma caused by dramatic, powerful events (called Shock Trauma). Yet it is also there from subtle, ongoing conditions that counter what's healthy and natural by being void of true, viscerally felt connection and safety (called Developmental Trauma). These can lead to feeling unloved, alone, afraid, depressed and more. It can be passed down through generations as well. This Disconnect stems not only from family issues or genetics but from religious and cultural issues as well. And for many, the Great Disconnect has become internalized as chronic illness, depression, substance addictions, anxiety, or just plain giving up.

Or you might see the opposite. The Great Disconnect drives people to a frenzy—an insane amount of busyness or the "never enough time" way that many people live. All to the fill the sense of *I'm not enough* that exists underneath our conscious awareness. When asked about it, they say, "But I *have to . . . there's just no other way.*" Perhaps this is true, but the inner urge that we have to do more, be better, or best, have more, or look a certain way for us to be of value, worthy or loveable is all built into our culture's values, attitudes, and beliefs. That we have to give more to the kids, have them be the smartest, and get into the best schools is driven by the same urge to fill an invisible and insatiable void.

We are all wired for love and belonging. But many things get in the way of our experiencing this on a viable level when we are young. Especially when we first show up on this earth. Often our early caretakers don't have the capacity, ability or willingness to love us, that is, to provide a safe bond of attuned connection to create what is called "a secure attachment". It then gets translated as I'm unlovable, I'm bad or I'm unworthy of any good. This has come to be known as feelings of Shame.

Many strategies develop to protect against feeling this, yet it continues to exist under the surface. There it can remain for a life time, greatly reducing the quality of life on many levels. These early feelings become compounded over time when care takers continue to speak, or act in shaming ways.

In the absence of connection, love or feelings of belonging you will always find suffering. It starts as a deeper hidden version but it eventually finds its way to the surface, be it physical conditions or pain, challenging emotional states, or all rolled up together as addictive behaviors.

Most of the Western world normalizes addictive behavior including ongoing states of depression and anxiety that underlie many addictions. Most of us repeat compulsive, impulsive, or excessive patterns in our thoughts, behaviors, and feelings, and are conditioned to say, "Oh, that's just life. It's how things are."

When thinking of addiction, images arise of homeless drunks or drug addicts strung out on the streets. In reality, most people engage in one form of addiction or another. And even if you're not actively addicted, odds are you're close to or tied in with someone who is.

Also, there is a similarity between addictions and chronic illness or physical pain, even that which arises from accidents. Even though they may not be something you can choose to stop as you might with addictive behaviors, they are all most often at the effect of deeper seated pain from a disconnect.[1]

Compulsive behavioral patterns and negative emotional states are virtually everywhere. They include workaholism or "do-aholism"; compulsive eating, anorexia, bulimia; anger and control issues;, abusive use of ordinary substances such as sugar, nicotine, and caffeine; giving or receiving physical, emotional, and/or psychological abuse; pervasive anxiety and unrelenting depression; obsessions with religion, news, television, or social media; excessive focus on exercise, weight, appearance, plastic surgery, fame or notoriety; overly engaged in hoarding material possessions, consumerism, gambling, internet pornography, sex, relationships, caretaking, power, or status; and very commonly physical conditions that defy explanation or medical treatment.

Many of these activities are either intrinsically innocent or healthy and even necessary! Food, for example, is necessary; so is exercise. Sex, love, and intimacy, emotions, productivity, and spiritual awareness are essential parts of daily living. So how do you know if you're engaging addictively?

---

[1] Learning to let go of seeing yourself as a victim of circumstances or others is something I wrote about in my previous book "Express Yourself: Discover Your Inner Truth, Creative Self and the Courage to Let It Out." Chapter 7, pp. 49–57.

Defining Addiction

An addictive behavior is something you cannot *not* do even when the effects of doing that activity produce negative results and/or pain in your life. All addictive behaviors are attempts to mask or diminish pain—whether we're fully conscious of this pain or it's held deeply inside. Repetitive emotional or physical pain is most often the effect of this buried pain attempting to express.

Yet almost always, attempts at hiding pain end up generating more pain. Here's the clue: If your relationships with food, sex, exercise, emotions, God, your partner and/or family members are healthy, you will feel good when and after you engage in those relationships most of the time. Your enjoyment will be real without any disconcerting (and sometimes tragic) after-effects or consequences.

Again, attempting to mask or diminish pain is the central common denominator in all addictive behavior. (And that pain is under most long term physical conditions as the ACE studies demonstrate, explained later in this chapter.) This attempt at masking then creates more pain, including exacerbating existing shame. The shame or guilt we feel for participating in what's harmful to self or others only drives us deeper into negative patterns and emotions. In turn, this increases the likelihood of repeating those patterns. When harmful patterns are perpetuated, we enter a vicious cycle that keeps us on a never-ending treadmill of shame, addiction, and perhaps recovery followed by relapse and more shame. Not being able to get over a physical condition or pain also creates a cycle of shame and negative emotions.

It Isn't Your Fault . . .

So I want to first state this truth: "It's not your fault!"

What?! That's right; addictions and chronic emotional and physical suffering is not your fault. At least in part.

You are an amazing, talented, unique human being with much to share. You have many natural gifts along with your beautiful and valuable qualities. *There is nothing intrinsically wrong with you.* That premise is reinforced throughout this book. Here, you'll learn how to transform your relationship with your emotions, thoughts and ideas, self-image, and people in your life. As you read it, you'll also learn to let go of self judgement as you realize how many aspects of yourself and your relationships with others got all messed up in the first place by conditions set up well beyond your control. You will also learn about shame, where the mere acknowledgement and understanding of it begins to lift it.

Know this: Many familial and cultural factors influenced how you got where you are. If you aren't aware of those factors or you don't have the tools to dismantle, overcome or move beyond them, how can you possibly hope for anything to be different?

. . . But It *Is* Your Responsibility

So, yes, it's not your fault you are caught in addiction or other ongoing negative physical or emotional states.

I said that.

What I *didn't* say, however, is that overcoming addition and repetitive negative states is *not* your responsibility. It absolutely *is* your responsibility.

You and only you are accountable for the quality of your life. If you feel unhappy with things as they are, only *you* can do the inner work necessary, and the outer work to improve your daily life and relationships. Only *you* can gain greater peace in your mind and vitality in your body, heart, and soul. If you want to change the quality of your life, *you* are the one who must do the work to make change possible. Helpers and support people yes! But it is you who does the real job.

Yes, I can lay out the 7 Keys to Connection on a table before you and give you step-by-step instructions. I can tell you exactly how to find the doors that are locked, and how to insert and turn the right keys until they click. But if you don't follow the maps to the doors or don't put the keys in the locks—if you don't turn the keys until the locks click and the doors swing open—then there's nothing anyone can do to help you.

So, while it's not your fault that you are where you're at right now, *you* are accountable for change. It's absolutely your responsibility to get yourself to someplace different. Much of the information in this book is mainly taught to therapists, and a special quality of therapist. The blessing is that with this book and your dedication you can do a lot on your own.

However, I cannot stress this enough: *You will need to apply yourself.* The 7 Keys process works with your active participation. You can work on your own or seek qualified help to help get started or at points along the way.

Will you grab this opportunity for change?

The Reward for Changing

Once you come to some important understandings, reconnect with the essence of who you really are and tap into your deeper truths, the mask of addictions, the shields of shame and the cloaks of depression or other debilitating emotions and physical conditions will loosen and fall away. From there, the power, exuberance, and motivation that lie beneath that blanket of pain or armor of addiction will come shining forth like a radiant sun. You'll feel joy, peace, vitality and a sense of purpose. Yes, this is possible.

With that "illumination" comes a new kind of yearning—a longing to be fully alive, to feel authentically free and do something that feels of purpose for you. Once you have a taste of how much more wonderful life feels without diverting, distracting, suppressing, and otherwise wasting your precious life force energy, you will step into a whole, new world.

You will realize the sources of your unproductive or self-harming patterns and extricate yourself from negative cycles of self-undoing. You will wake up to the challenges of the surrounding culture and learn to safely navigate in a society designed to addict you, repress you and keep you asleep. Your body and soul's natural inclinations to be healthy and alive will take the lead, walking you all the way home to your true Self.

Addiction in My Life

I called my main addictive pattern "do-aholism"—that is, I believed I always had to be doing something, and I could do it all at warp speed. In addition, my health was horrible. Starting in my early 20s, I felt tired, weak, and dizzy most of the time in addition to other physical symptoms. I also lived in an ongoing state of depression with simultaneous anxiety and feelings of insecurity. Despite all of this, I could function relatively well; people around me didn't know all this was going on for me.

Part of my motivation for what became years of study had been my own deeply held suffering, both physical and emotional. It fueled my search to turn this state of affairs around. I firmly believe that my situation stemmed from my parents' suffering. My mother was an alcoholic, a functioning one, but nevertheless an alcoholic. Alcoholism took her to an early grave. I did not take on her alcohol-drinking habit. However, my father was a workaholic, and I followed his path. I became a "do-aholic" with constant busyness even though my physical health did not support it.

My Own Quest

When I was relatively young, I set out on a quest for understanding what makes people healthy and happy, especially because my doctors had no idea how to help me. In my grade school years, my mother had wisely taken me for emotional help to a psychiatrist. Though he did help me deal with a bullying classmate, he did nothing to address my deeper issues. He was the same doctor who told my mother not to "open Pandora's box" on her issues. The resulting avoidance kept her addictions alive and ultimately contributed to her early death.

My path to health and recovery started in 1968 when I was 16 years old. Not much of a reader, I somehow got hold of a book called *How to Live to be 100 and Feel like a Million*. That was it. That led me on my passionate path to health.

My first foray focused on physical health. I became a chiropractor but eventually, my passion led me to explore cutting-edge work in the fields of psychology, psychotherapy, personal growth, and ultimately transpersonal psychology (a blend of spirituality and psychology) along with eco-psychology (how environment and culture affects us).

I eventually turned my attention toward the psycho-emotional basis of health rather than adhering to strictly physical aspects. Over a lifetime of self-motivated study in the field of psycho-immunology—the body-mind connection—I've come to understand much about the psycho-emotional basis of chronic suffering.

Prolonged psycho-emotional suffering—no matter how hidden it is from conscious awareness—can be truly insidious. It's often expressed as chronic illness, persistent pain, supposedly untreatable conditions, ongoing negative emotional states, or unhealthy patterns of behavior. This is where all manner of addictions or unhealthy, compulsive, and repetitive behaviors come in—whether substances are involved or not.

Although physical pain, emotional states and addictive behaviors present differently, their commonality is that many similar causal factors lie beneath the surface. As such, you can apply the 7 Keys to Connection—the core of this book—to difficult physical conditions, chronic negative emotional states as well as commonly recognized addictions.

For approximately 45 years, I have studied, used in my practice, and taught different modalities and points of view that ultimately created the health, contentment, and sense of peace and connection I experience today. Between these studies and working with people (both privately and in groups), I've observed common threads among people who are obvious addicts and those who suffer physical or emotional pain. I've also come to understand what's required to shift them at the core. From all of this, the 7 Keys to Connection were born.

I am now past the midpoint of my 60s. Without exaggeration, each year my health has gotten better, and I've gained freedom from many different physical pains to the point of being completely pain free for quite some time now. On some level, it feels like a miracle—but not an overnight miracle. That's because I've committed to this deeper path of transformation, including many life practices that have since been integrated into the 7 Keys. I know firsthand there's no pill that can "fix" everything quickly—no magic potion to take before bed so I'd wake up younger and healthier.

A Word About 12-Step Programs

If you're a recovering addict or thinking about entering a traditional 12-Step recovery program, I acknowledge it and see how the 7 Keys and the 12-Step programs can work together.

Definitely, 12-step-oriented groups have pulled many addicts out of deep water. While I feel sincere gratitude for founder Bill Wilson and all who further his work, in my opinion, 12-Step recovery programs don't provide enough for most people to go all the way to vital health. Why? Because they aren't designed to go into the depth of the core issues driving addiction. As a result, relapse rates among participants are high. The research on this varies so much that I cannot site a quote. Most just know this to be true. Though again it is way better than nothing for the percentage of people's lives that do change with it.

Yes, 12-Step programs address some causal factors so deep work isn't totally lacking. But yet deeper levels need to be excavated, which makes the 7 Keys process an excellent complement to 12-Step recovery programs. Because of this, I encourage those doing well with the program to continue while also applying the 7 Keys.

The 7 Keys work is based on the principle of having a Self, with a capital "S." I also refer to it as the Soul-Centered Self or just Soul Self. This Self is capable of wisely guiding your inner and outer lives. In the 7 Keys process, you'll find many tools and practices that build your relationship with that Self so you can travel together to higher ground.

To successfully build this relationship, though, you need to be ready for the journey, which may not be the case if you're in the early stages of sobriety. A 12-step program is perfect for early stage recovery because when one is deeply mired in any addictive pattern or substance, higher reasoning and connection with Self may not be available. You can get trapped in survival areas of the brain while the path to more evolved parts of the brain have just shut down. Various adaptive, egoic, or reactive states that have served you in the past may be in charge, inadvertently undermining what you heart truly desires.

Yes, 12-Step programs can get people out of the quicksand and moving toward higher ground. However, once you can stand on the ground provided by the 12-Step program, the 7 Keys process provides a solid path to "move beyond" toward a more centered, connected, self-trusting, and expressive life, full of vitality.

One final point. Most people in the 12-Step recovery movement say you never achieve full recovery from an addiction even when you are no longer using. With respect to all the wonderful work that has taken many far along the road to recovery, using the 7 Keys process, and if truly worked, you do have the potential to recover! You recover because the *true essence of you that's always present isn't addicted to anything.*

When a Person is Ready

I have co-created and facilitated a series of powerful retreats called Quantum Shift Retreats. In them, we integrated psycho-spiritual processes with nature, dancing, singing, and other transformational elements. In one powerful example, a participant woke up mid-retreat to a beautiful awareness. He excitedly announced that, though he'd been a functioning alcoholic for 27 years, he suddenly realized he no longer needed alcohol. I stayed in touch with him for many years. Even years later, he could still declare he never went back to his old addictions. With this work, we *do* believe in full recovery.

When a person is ready, the roots of addiction can be tilled, pulled, and transformed into fertilizer. Then whole new ways of being, thinking, and responding to life can be planted. Once the ground is properly weeded and prepared, then the new seeds can take hold. As one spiritual teacher said, "It's all grist for the mill."

Being ready requires a high degree of willingness along with desire, motivation, and higher functioning—that is, not being in the deep throws of a substance addiction—to be able to work these 7 Keys on one's own. Having a therapist or counselor to work with simultaneously is optimal. I suggest you at least have one support person, especially at the beginning. You'll find many therapists will endorse the processes described in this book and may be already working in this manner. (See the resources section at the end of the book for advanced modalities I recommend.)

What If You Don't See Yourself as an Addict?

What if you've never been addicted to a substance, never been in a program, and don't see yourself as an addict or living in a difficult emotional state?

The 7 Keys process assists fully functioning individuals who have less-than-debilitating or no obvious addictive patterns. Even if you don't see yourself as an addict, you can use the 7 Keys to liberate yourself from cultural and societal constraints that subconsciously stop you from fully expressing more of who you truly are. Turning the 7 Keys opens doors to new levels of contentment and aliveness. Most important, they lead to a release of creative energies, that include a sense of purpose.

I have taken an unpredictable, non-linear path of transformation in my life and made it doable, understandable, and organized—at least as organized as one's path to growth can be. I know the 7 Keys can work powerfully; they've worked with me, my clients, and my workshop participants. Individual aspects of these keys are found in other therapies and programs of personal transformation. However, you'll find all 7 Keys of Connection are uniquely presented together in this one book, along with many powerful, evidence-based methods of personal transformation integrated into them.

In some cases, this book might read like a text book to deeply "know thyself." It might not be as easy to read as some. However, please stick with it, because it's rich with insight into your inner life. In addition, many of the explanations and powerful processes you would have only received in a session with a therapist. And not all therapists work at this level. Like the best things in life, it requires commitment and devotion to raise your quality of life beyond what you have known or ever imagined possible.

Perhaps you are reading this book with a friend or relative in mind. That's great! Who knows what you might discover that leads *you* to a greater sense of connection and ease in your body and life.

At a cultural level, the 7 Keys process is an antidote for the Great Disconnect. Integrating these keys and their practices provide a remedy for the culture in which we live. Its tools and insights dismantle the programing that inadvertently has thrown us off course. They form a re-education and a re-membering for how to live in connection, harmony, and balance with ourselves, each other, and life. From this springs emotional and physical health as well as a deeper state of joy, peace, and vitality.

Overview of this Book and the 7 Keys
Chapter 1: The Roots of Addiction and Pain—
Cultural and Personal Trauma
The first chapter explores the Great Disconnect in more detail including cultural and familial trauma. It addresses the devastating effects of both these

two types of trauma, even that trauma we may not have acknowledged as such. This less understood but all too common form of early family trauma is now being recognized as Developmental Trauma and its deeper effects as Shame. Cultural trauma is examined through the lens of eco-psychology with quotes from powerful leaders in this field.

Chapter 2: Soulcentric Developmental Wheel— What are Your Missing Tasks?

This chapter takes an indigenous look at what are natural and normal stages of a human's development from birth to death along with organic "tasks" that should accompany each stage. Acknowledging the missing links helps us source some of our individual roots of pain or suffering as well as lift blame and shame that inhibits our development.

Chapter 3: Key 1 Feeling Your Feelings—Demystifying Emotions

Knowing what we truly want and what's right for us starts with being able to feel, honor, and express our emotions in a safe, healthy way. Both cultural and familial mandates about what we should and shouldn't be, do or feel has shut down our inner lines of communication. This key provides the first step to opening them. It also provides much information about emotions to counter the sense of their being a dark mystery. Chapter 3 also begins exploring "parts work" and introduces homework or Medicine Tasks.

Chapter 4: Internal Family Systems (IFS)— Greater Understanding of the Dynamics Within

This chapter outlines Internal Family Systems (IFS) concepts that are integrated into Keys 1 to 3, with a full self-guided process at the end in Chapter 13. IFS is an effective modality for understanding what might feel "crazy making" within us. It explains the many polarized viewpoints or beliefs and ways of being that can keep us locked in confusion and self-judgement. It also explains the dichotomy of why one part of us wants to be respected and honored yet another part will throw that desire out the window with self-defeating or addictive behaviors.

Chapter 5: Key 2 Developing the Witness—Transformation of the Inner Critic

Key 2 represents an important first step in transforming the negative voices within—those that judge, push, stop, shame us, cut off communication, or make us dependent on others at all costs. It helps us let go of judgment and blame, internally and toward others. Key 2 is a first step toward creating separation between you—the Self of you—and the many voices of those harsh, judgmental parts of you.

Chapter 6: Key 3 What It Means to Love Ourselves—How to Counter Shame

This key demystifies the nebulous term "Love Yourself." People often ask, "What does that mean? How do I go about doing that?" Chapter 6 offers down-to-earth understandings and practices for how to love yourself. It suggests tools to heal some of the disconnect within so ultimately the lost art of *connection* can be resurrected.

Chapter 7: Key 4 The Art and Power of Surrender—Integrating the Spiritual

Key 4 is the spiritual heart of the 7 Keys. Far from being a sign of weakness, surrender is an art form that takes inner strength yet occurs in a non-linear, even soft way. It involves letting go of control, being able to be comfortable in the unknown, and ultimately learning to trust life, Self, and Spirit. This allows life to flow as it is which brings peace of mind. Stress and struggle literally fall away. This chapter provides tools and practices to foster this.

Chapter 8: Key 5 Right Brain Integration—Soul Food

Key 5 is the fun, creative aspect of the Keys. Our overly linear culture wears on the body and psyche. Right brain activities—including time in nature, acts involving being in the moment, and doing creatively expressive activities—balance, soothe, and ease the journey. This is about participating at any level of skill. These activities feed and expand the presence of your Soul Self making them simultaneously fun and healing. Nature based cultures know of their powers and have integrated these *soulcraft* activities for centuries.

Chapter 9: Key 6 Practices—Committing to Healthy Routines
It is committing to a practice of our choosing (that can change over time) that sets the groundwork for deep transformative change. A practice can be regarding the body, mind, psyche, behavior, or a creative endeavor. They become an essential aspect of our personally designed healing path. This Chapter offers and explains a variety of options.

Chapter 10: Key 7 Foundation of Trust—The Ability to Take Risks
The previous 6 Keys help build a foundation of trust with Self and Spirit. This creates the strength and courage to take the risks necessary to create a life that fits the truth of who we are. Those risks include speaking our truth to someone, letting a person go, setting a boundary even if we fear loss, trying a creative endeavor, or going for a new livelihood that incorporates what we love and believe in. Moving towards a passion or a longing is an important step in moving beyond addictions. This chapter features many examples.

Chapter 11: Key 7 Continued The Give Back— Worldly Soul Expression
The road to recovery from addictive patterns and chronic physical or emotional health issues requires moving toward a fuller expression of who we have found ourselves to be. We might reach a point of deeply desiring and being ready to do what it takes to change jobs or careers, or simply provide a Give Back that feels good to the Soul Self. This chapter addresses what it takes to do this and how to avoid pitfalls that can get in the way.

Chapter 12: Magic Happens—Where You Have Been and Where You are Headed
This chapter brings it all full circle. It recaps the 7 Keys to Connection to reveal the magic that occurs within and in our outer world. It brings us to

where we started regarding the culture and how our deep changes and moving forward in life ultimately creates a positive outcome for the world at large.

Chapter 13: IFS Dialog Process—Moving from Egocentric to Soul-centric

This chapter features a step-by-step description of a full IFS transformational process with explanations along the way. This can be done alone, with a help person, or assisted by a professional versed in IFS work. Of course, the process varies from person to person given their individual aspects and circumstances. You'll find Chapter 13 provides an overall procedure to follow to assist you in transforming shame, blame and judgement of self or others, to compassion, acceptance, joy and connection.

A Guide to Your Inner World

The 7 Keys to Connection serves as a guide to your inner world, illuminating the patterns by which your Soul and the habits of your daily life are interwoven. You'll learn how to recognize, unweave, and reweave these patterns so you can have the most vital, beautiful life possible.

As you progress through the exercises in this book, you'll uncover and reveal your Soul-Centered Self from behind the layers of misunderstanding, fear, shame, numbing, secrets, and other shrouds of darkness. Once you get into deep communication with *you*, you'll move beyond the habit patterns and compulsions that no longer serve you. This book provides the tools, skills, insights, and understanding you need to make your journey successful.

Welcome to your path through the 7 Keys to Connection. May you find great benefit in this journey!

Joy Freeman

Chapter 1

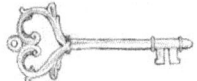

Roots of Addiction and Pain—Cultural and Personal Trauma

These are amazing times we live in. Westernized humanity has created a civilization that is at once miraculous and horrific. We are surrounded by advances in science and technology, but at the same time, we feel disconnected from ourselves, one another, and the earth.

In large part, we live in a society of the walking wounded, often disenfranchised or disassociated from what is true and real in life. We are challenged with numerous forms of emotional discord that arise spontaneously from this disconnection—from vague anxieties, boredom or depression to flagrant, even horrifying, forms of violence and abuse. We often normalize the effects of trauma, both in individual homes and globally. Many describe themselves as "not quite here" or just "numb."

In reality, this process of normalizing or minimizing our suffering is a failure of having empathy or compassion toward ourselves and one another. And it only furthers alienation. This culturally reinforced dissociation from our own vividly felt and fully lived experience is a significant aspect of the Great Disconnect.

The Great Disconnect

On an individual level, the Great Disconnect means feeling disconnected from our deeper selves, our emotions, and intuitions—our subtle senses. And with this a lack of inner peace or sense of purpose. It's also feeling disconnected from nature and what's harmonious to the soul. It's a loss of relationship with the heavens above and the earth below—missing a sense of the order of things, even feeling all alone in the world, floating, not linked to anything real.

What prevails is a lack of confidence or inability to trust that your core self is valued, worthy, or loved and that your simple beingness is enough. This creates difficulty in creating harmonious and authentic relations to others, be they family, friends or primary relationships. Overall, there's little or no deep sense of safety, intimacy or true belonging.

In my opinion, this Great Disconnect is at the root of the addictive and discontent culture in which we live.

We Can't Heal What We Refuse to See

The reinforcement of disconnection is so insidious and pervasive in our culture that its effects touch almost everyone to one degree or another. The Great Disconnect separates us from our core humanness. It spurs feelings of emptiness, confusion, hopelessness, isolation, and a host of other emotions such as sadness, anger, grief, shame, and guilt—whether we're clearly aware of them or they're buried beneath the surface in each individual's subconscious. These feelings—conscious and unconscious—instigate all manner of addictive or unhealthy behavior.

On top of this, societal programing supports avoidance behavior. This programming impresses on us the false idea that these "less than lovely" feelings are "not okay"; they signal weakness or illness. Instead of encouraging us to explore and process our deeper emotions, society conveys it's important to *avoid feeling anything unpleasant* at all costs.

Quite the contrary! These "judged" emotions are messengers from our inner Self. As part of our inner wisdom, they guide us to know what is true and accurate for us. The culture cuts us off from our inner wisdom by telling us our emotions and inner senses are not to be honored or given our attention.

We experience this message reinforced everywhere—In parenting with huge discrepancies between what is said and what is done; in TV shows and movies where people tell lies or stories rather than speak their truths; in how so many people around us operate from a "persona" or fakeness rather than coming from an authentic place; and how being authentic is not even something that very many people know how to be. Because without a deeper level of coming to "know thyself", authenticity is not even possible!

Gradually and to various degrees, we buy into this lie, that our inner feelings and truths are not valid or worthy, and this continues to perpetuate the Great Disconnect. This experience not only pervades the U.S., one of the planet's most abundant countries, it's growing to encompass countries around the globe, whether they're steeped in wealth or not. If you question this, look at how many people are using and/or overusing substances of any kind, live in chronic untreatable ill health, are incarcerated or are simply, deeply lonely.

Add to that those taking medical drugs for conditions such as depression and anxiety, attention disorder, sleep deprivation, and more. Totaling them, along with all the NPS usage—**Novel Psychoactive Substances, i.e., street drugs,** represents a huge percentage of the population around the world! This is true not only in most of the "civilized" western world but also in less developed countries. There are numerous surveys and studies on the net, though all differing slightly, that verify that all this drug usage, **medical or otherwise is becoming almost epidemic.**

The Great Disconnect touches multitudes because it's rooted in the fundamental values of Western "civilization," of which its effects can be devastating.

Negative Effects of the Great Disconnect

I recently read an online article in *The Guardian* that clearly expressed some of the negative effects of the Great Disconnect while emphasizing a need to assess our culture to correct the problem created. It noted suicide as a leading cause of death among young indigenous people worldwide. Imagine! The feelings of desperation that would lead these youth even beyond substance addictions to suicide.

Indigenous youth in particular feel the disparity from their connected roots to the current feelings of the Great Disconnect. For example, as cited in the same Guardian article, a 2016 news release by the Australian Bureau of Statistics, Aboriginal and Torres Strait Islander noted indigenous people die by suicide at a rate twice that of non-indigenous people. Westernized people have accommodated over the centuries, to our disconnected life styles. But these indigenous peoples, who not all that long ago lived closer to their natural rhythms, have more recently had their identities, practices, and values ripped away, leaving them more vulnerable.

According to the Guardian article, efforts to solve the problem using methods developed in non-indigenous communities have not reversed the trend. Indigenous communities have told the World Congress on Public Health that its typical treatments for drug and alcohol abuse (set up by the westernize agencies) has not been enough to reduce these global suicide rates. They feel strongly that strengthening indigenous culture, including its ways of connections to the earth and its rhythms, would help reduce these staggering suicide rates.[1]

Joe Williams, a famous Australian Soccer Player was very close to the hands of death by suicide due to the emotional pain of mental health issues. He states:

> The most significant part in my recovery has been the reconnection and reawakening in myself of my Aboriginal culture . . . For 60,000 years, our First Nations people respected, lived, loved and cared for each other and the land. My reconnection to those traditions through dance and culture clears my head, allows my spirit to be free. Dance provides connection to self, ancestors, others, land, spirit and our ancient songlines and lore. Through dance I am a much more settled and safe self. (More about the healing and reconnecting Soulcraft activities in Key 5 – Chapter 8.)

---

[1] https://www.theguardian.com/world/2017/apr/05/stronger-indigenous-culture-would-cut-suicide-rates-health-congress-told

... I believe there is something in this for all of us, no matter race or religion. Within this connection to (a more natural) culture I see a way to end the horrific suicide rate for not only our people, but all people. The answer is in connection. Whether you connect to the land, culture, family or friends (or self)—connection keeps us alive.[2]

Eco Psychology—Trauma and the Cultural Roots of Addictive Behavior

At the root of our oh-so-civilized addictive culture is trauma, with its associated emotional pain and where disconnect and suicide are the ultimate means of escape. Modern psychology wants to point to the emotional issues arising from improper parenting or challenging home life circumstances. We can't deny this is true and will be addressed later in this chapter and others in this book.

But the field of eco-psychology to which I wholeheartedly subscribe says it's also about the world around us, beyond even our families. It is societal, religious, and historic. It involves not only our personal experiences but the cultural programing that has been engrained and deepened over many generations.

We cannot deny the importance and relevance of the personal psycho-emotional issues, which most of this book will address. However, the growing field of eco-psychology puts a huge weight on environmental factors. Not so much about ecology, what you think of relative to recycling and what's good for the planet. But rather, it's about the entire field of existence a person grows up in—that is, the environmental culture. It asks these questions: What are the cultural beliefs and values? What does the culture hold sacred? What gives people their sense of value in their own eyes and those of others, including a higher power, whether it's called God or something else?

Eco-psychologists believe today's trauma-based addictive culture is rooted in the mass disconnect from what's natural, what's sacred, and what creates a deeper knowing and sense of connection with all of life. The Great Disconnect.

---

[2] https://www.theguardian.com/commentisfree/2017/apr/03/we-can-reduce-the-indigenous-suicide-rate-through-connection-to-culture

With that comes the deep-rooted pain that stems from unknowing shortfalls in child rearing of belittlement, neglect, abuse, or simply lack of attunement. All have their underpinnings in long-held cultural values and norms.

Fall Out of Balance

I regard the eco-psychology aspect of trauma as a multi-layered issue that started with our culture falling out of balance relative to yin and yang, masculine and feminine, head and heart, inherent knowledge versus what's controlled by church or state.

In *My Name is Chellis and I'm in Recovery from Western Civilization*,[3] Chellis Glendinning, Ph.D., explores our disconnection from the earth as the "original trauma" that has been added to and interwoven with subsequent traumas such as war, child abuse, degradation and abuse of woman, and genocide of indigenous peoples.[4] Many eco-psychologists believe this initial disconnect began 10,000 years ago with the domestication of plants and animals to meet our needs. Previous to this period, humans lived close to natural cycles and rhythms of the earth. I'm not advocating going back to primitive living or being hunter gatherers. Rather, I'm saying when we left behind these ways of being, we let go of important values intrinsic to creating a healthy, balanced life. If some degree of these earlier periods had remained, we'd have more health and balance, including many matriarchal values integrated into our current world.

Distinguishing Between Opposites

When I speak of matriarchy and patriarchy, yin and yang, or feminine and masculine, I'm not referring necessarily to men and women. Men can possess yin or feminine values and traits, just as women can possess the yang or masculine. In a healthy world, both genders would possess a good quantity of both qualities, with most men leaning a bit more toward the yang side and

---

[3] Chellis Glendinning Ph.D., *My Name is Chellis and I'm in Recovery from Western Civilization*, Shambhala, 1994.

[4] Editors: Theodore Roszak, Mary E. Gomes, and Allen D. Kanner, *Ecopsychology: Restoring the Earth, Healing The Mind*, Sierra Club Books, 1995, p. 41.

women the yin, rather than the far ends of each as happens today. Though, genders can be fluid, showing up in any number of combinations.

I also refer to this distinction as being left brain versus right brain, with "left brain" being more linear, structured, controlled than "right brain." The left brain values the material world and what can be seen or proven quantitatively. In this yang view, the world of mind and material rules. Also, it functions by control, and specifically control over others as it moves toward the more extreme left side.

By comparison, the yin is more nonlinear and creative. Thriving on connections, it values what can't be seen: emotions, intuitions, feelings, and surrender to the unknown. The trusting right-brain yin has faith in something bigger than the human self, even if logic can't prove it. Instead, proof comes in bodily sensations and subtle messages, which are valued and honored. Rather than being in control over others, the yin functions best in co-operation with them.

In general, you could say the yin world is of the earth—body, nature, and connection to those and others. Yet in its extreme right position, it can be ineffective and possess less-than-optimal qualities. If either of these aspects of yin or yang get too out of balance—too far to either extreme—then something important is missing. Moving away from the far ends of either one, closer towards center, changes the results in a positive way.

To summarize, our Western "civilized" culture has moved into a more extreme yang position over many centuries. What have we lost? The balance that more yin values could bring to us as individuals, cultural groups, and our earth itself. Many amazing and useful "things" have evolved out of the agricultural, then industrial, and now technological society, but we are hard pressed to fully enjoy them given all the psychological, emotional and physical maladies that currently exist.

Backing up this point of view, eco-psychologist Chellis Glendinning cites:

> This split between the wild and tame lies at the foundation of both the addictive personality and addictive aspects of technological society. Ultimately, such a split imprisons us in our human constructed reality and

causes all the unnecessary and troublesome dichotomies with which we grapple today—from male/female and mind/body, sex/spirit, to secular/sacred and technological/earth-based.

Nature-based people lived every day of their lives in the wilderness. We are only beginning to grasp how such a life served the inherent expectations of the human psyche for development to full maturation and health. In nature-based people who today maintain some vestiges of their relationship to Earth and their Earth based cultures, we can discern a decided sense of ease with daily life, a marked sense of Self and dignity, a wisdom that most of us can only admire from afar, and a lack of the addiction and abuse that have become systemic in the "civilized" world.

Technological society's dislocation from the only home we have ever known is a traumatic event that has occurred over generations, and that occurs again in each of our childhoods and in our daily lives. In the face of such a breach, symptoms of traumatic stress are no longer the rare event caused by a freak accident or battering weather, but the stuff of most every man and woman's daily life.

As human life comes to be structured increasingly by mechanistic means, the psyche restructures itself to survive. The technological construct erodes primary sources of satisfaction once found routinely in life in the wilds, such as physical nourishment, vital community, fresh foods, continuity between work and meaning, unhindered participation in life experiences, personal choices, community decisions and support, and spiritual connection with the natural world. These are needs we were born to have satisfied. In the absence of these, we will not be healthy. In their absence, bereft and in shock, the psyche finds some temporary satisfaction in pursuing secondary sources like drugs, violence, sex, material possessions, and machines (or a host of other addictions). While these stimulants may satisfy in the moment, they can never truly fulfill primary needs. And so the addictive process is born. We become obsessed with secondary sources as if our lives depended on them.

As the world has become less organic and more dependent on techno-fixes for problems created by earlier mechano-fixes, humans have substituted a new worldview for one once filled with clean rushing waters, coyotes, constellations of stars, tales of ancestors, and people working together in sacred purpose. But the ancestors from the Western world took on a crucial task of redefining their worldview in a state of psychic dislocation. And so they ended up projecting a world view that reflects rage, terror, and the dissociation of the traumatized state. They dreamed a world not of which humans are fully part but one that we can define, compartmentalize and control. They created linear perspective, the scientific-technological paradigm, and the mechanistic worldview.

Life on Earth encased in the product of such a construction is, to quote the Hopi, hopelessly koyaanisqatsi, or out of balance. As a psychologist, I believe that to address this imbalance at its roots will require more than public policy, regulation or legislation. It will require a collective psychological process to heal us technological peoples who, through a mechanized culture, have lost touch with our essential humanity.[5]

Riane Eisler is a systems scientist, writer, and social activist who has degrees in sociology and law. Described as a cultural historian and evolutionary theorist, she has popularized the notion of dominator culture and partnership (or a connecter) culture. Though she is not advocating moving back to a full matriarchy, the idea of a partnership culture would embrace the many values and ways of the Feminine (yin) from which we have strayed in both the industrial society and the technological society of today. She coined the term Dominator Culture to describe a system of dominance hierarchy ultimately backed up by fear or force (the extreme version of yang). A core component of this system of authoritarian rule (both family and state) is the subordination of women, which devalues feminine ways (yin).

In her book *The Chalice and the Blade: Our History, Our Future*, Eisler writes:

This shift to a dominator culture that started with mass agriculture (that is, growing more than was needed by the immediate community-ies), and the

---

[5] Chellis Glendinning, Ph.D., "Technology, Trauma and the Wild," *Ecopsychology: Restoring the Earth, Healing The Mind*, Sierra Club Books, 1995, pp. 52–54.

domestication of animals (domination of an aspect of the natural world), was further deepened as time went on by the church who sought to gain control and dominance of a large portion of the population at that time.

This growing population had been expressing feminine (yin) values in their deep devotion and connection to the magic and spiritual power of Jesus. There have since been many discovered writings that reflect Jesus's original messages that encouraged adherence to the natural values of the earth, body, and divine mother along with the divine father and other instruction in more matriarchal principles.

However most of these writings were stored away and the original teachings were integrated or altered in subsequent writings to reflect what was needed by the church, in connection with state, to gain the control that was desired.[6]

After this happened, those cultures still connected to the movements of the earth and stars began to be overtaken by church, state, and other yang-oriented powers. Prior to being taken over, life in these communities joyfully integrated free-form dance, music, song, and art as well as celebrations aligned with the seasons. While their earth-based celebrations ended up being eliminated, the religious holidays were set close to the existing times of solstice-based celebrations to line up with when these "heathens" were celebrating anyway.

This rolled into the period when the "witches" and/or those women of power called the "crones" were being burned at the stake. They understood much of the magic and nonlinear practices that Jesus had worked with. Most of these women used their knowledge of the unseen for positive purposes rather than the evil they were accused of. Thus, all things of the feminine that would make it hard for people to be controlled by church or state were being sublimated or forcefully eliminated.

Much has been documented historically on this subject and can easily be researched to verify its authenticity. I mention it to help explain how this

---

[6] Riane Eisler, *The Chalice & The Blade: Our History, Our Future*, HarperCollins NY, 1987, 1995.

history has led to the emotionally unbalanced, addictive and disconnected culture in which we now live.

Glendinning continues:

> As psychotherapist Terry Kellogg tells us, "addictive behavior is not natural to human species. It occurs because some untenable violation has happened to us."
>
> And indeed, we have undergone an untenable violation: a collective trauma that explains the insidious reality of addiction and abuse infusing our lives in mass technological society.
>
> The *Diagnostic and Statistical Manual of Mental Disorders* defines trauma as ". . . an event that is outside the range of human experience and that would be markedly distressing to almost anyone." The trauma endured by the technological people like ourselves is the systematic removal of our lives from the natural world: from the earthly textures, from the rhythms of sun and moon, from the bears and trees, from life force itself. This is also the systemic and systematic removal of our lives from the kinds of social and cultural experiences our ancestors assumed when they lived in rhythm with the natural world. (Author's note: This includes community music and art making, child rearing, rituals, life transition ceremonies, and so on.)
>
> It's interesting to note: Human beings have evolved over three million years and a hundred thousand generations. We are physically and psychologically built to thrive in intimacy with the earth. A mere three hundred generations ago or 0.003% of our time on earth, humans began the process of controlling the natural world through agriculture and animal domestication. After a more recent period of industrialization and now the technological age, our experience is indeed "outside the range of human experience" and by the evidence of the psychological distress, ecological destruction, and technological control, this way of life has been "markedly distressing" to almost everyone.[7]

---

[7] Editors: Theodore Roszak, Mary E. Gomes, and Allen D. Kanner, *Ecopsychology: Restoring the Earth, Healing The Mind*, Sierra Club Books, 1995, pp. 52–54.

Yes, and so much of what has arisen over the past .003% of our time on earth has also been seemingly wonderful and amazing yet, as Glendinning adds:

> . . . the very psychological qualities so earnestly sought in today's recovery, psychological and spiritual movements; the social equalities for which todays social justice movements struggle valiantly; and the ecological gains sought after by todays environmental movements, are the same qualities and conditions in which our species lived for more than 99.997% of its existence.[8]

In our culture, both men and women have been enculturated to value the male (yang) principles and diminish the feminine (yin)—even the women to whom it comes more naturally. Each of the 7 Keys encompasses a movement toward embracing, integrating, and revaluing those aspects of the yin and feminine that have been diminished, denigrated, or denied. Once this occurs as a cultural movement, society will be well on its way to a world of more inner peace, ecological balance, relational harmony, peace among cultures with differing beliefs and balance within ourselves and with each other.

Trauma at Home: Personal Roots of Addictive Behavior and Emotional Distress

One effect of this mass cultural trauma—being disconnected from the rhythms of earth, life, and community—is the personal trauma that occurs between mother and child or between family/caretakers and child. Out of the overall disconnect from the natural world comes a lack of ability for mothers to deeply connect with their newborn infants in ways that children would come to know fully of their magical essence, their value as human beings on this earth and to truly establish their presence here on earth. Where, as they grow up, they don't have to prove their value through accomplishment or adherence to family values. Where the essence of who they are is so valued, they have the freedom and psychological stability from which to stride forth being true to who they are, regardless if they fit into any norm or expectation.

---

[8] Ibid.

Dysregulation and Attachment Issues

Hence, with so many feeling out of connection, much has come to light through Affect Regulation and Attachment Theories, which helps explain the personal roots of emotional pain and addictive behaviors. This speaks to the lost ability for a mother to calmly look into the eyes of her child consistently enough to let that little being feel welcome and safe. It is also about the caregiver being unable to "be with" and respond to that child's emotions in ways that helps the child not be overwhelmed by them but rather to contain, accept, and integrate them. When caregivers can do these "regulated" things, this creates a healthy core connection. When they can't, "dysregulation"—disruption of the nervous system occurs called *hyper arousal* or *sympathetic dominance*, and usually continues for the remainder of a life. It is this ongoing state of hyper arousal that leads to so many emotional and physical health problems later in life, including addictions that attempt to mask the discomfort.

All of this lack of attunement in childhood and in particular infancy, along with neglect, stressful relationships between parents and more obvious physical forms of ongoing abuse or trauma are now being referred to as Developmental Trauma.

The following descriptions come from blog posts of psychotherapist Sebern Fisher:

> "Folks with difficult parents often grow up with a "fear-driven brain" as I did—and it's a huge relief to find out we're not freaks—we're a chunk of the mainstream. In fact, maybe 50% of Americans have some degree of this "attachment disorder" due to parents who were too scary to attach to. Of course it's not their fault either; odds are, our grandparents were too scary for our parents to attach to, and so on back, inter-generationally."[9]
>
> "Developmental trauma starts *in utero* when we don't have much more than a brain stem and goes on during the pre-conscious years. It can continue until 24 or 36 months depending on when the thinking brain (frontal cortex) comes on line. That's up to 45 months living in general anxiety

---

[9] Sebern F. Fisher, MA http://attachmentdisorderhealing.com/neurofeedback/

to non-stop terror—before age 3. A very long time to an infant. (and continues on after that)

Developmental Trauma occurs as a continual process, not discrete incidents, while a baby has not developed a thinking brain able to recall incidents. Frequently it occurs before there are any discrete incidents."[10]

When the mother does not take the time or have the patience to "attune" to the infant, or is not able to be with and respond to the infant's emotions in relatively short order, the results can end up being part of Developmental Trauma. (See the Still Face Experiment by Edward Tronick.[11])

To learn a lot more about the neuroscience of developmental trauma, affect regulation and attachment theories, I highly recommend looking up the works of the forerunners in these fields: Dr. Bessel van der Kolk, Dr. Allan Schore, and Dr. Daniel Siegel, and John Bowlby.[12]

Shame as Effect of Developmental Trauma

With this lack of secure and loving attachment, a deep level of shame occurs. Not so much the left brain cognitive type, as in "I feel badly I did something wrong", which is actually the experience of guilt. But rather a core shame reflecting a visceral feeling, usually unconscious, that says, "I am bad, defective, dirty, or unlovable." And this often starts at infancy (and even in the womb) and goes on through childhood. The parents of these children often have no concept that their inability or unwillingness to take the time

---

[10] http://attachmentdisorderhealing.com/developmental-trauma/

[11] https://youtu.be/apzXGEbZht0

[12] Dr. Bessel van der Kolk, a psychiatrist noted for his research in the area of post-traumatic stress since the 1970s. His work focuses on the interaction of attachment, neurobiology, and developmental aspects of trauma's effects on people. He identified and named Developmental Trauma. His book The Body Keeps the score, is a must read; Dr. Allan Schore, psychologist and researcher in the field of neuropsychology whose contributions have greatly affected trauma and attachment among other areas. He wrote many books on Affect regulation; Dr. Daniel Siegel, psychiatrist who wrote a number of important books on the developmental brain including *The Whole-Brain Child: 12 Revolutionary Strategies to Nurture Your Child's Developing Brain*; and John Bowlby psychiatrist leader and pioneer in Attachment Theory.

to connect and that many of their behaviors are shaming to their children. These parents are simply "dysregulated" themselves and hence unable to provide this all-important core sense of Self.

Patricia A. DeYoung explains this in her book *Understanding and Treating Chronic Shame*:

> Shame is an experience of one's felt sense of self disintegrating in relation to a dysregulating other. When we are at our most vulnerable (infant or child), our experience of being an integrated self depends on the emotional attunement or "regulation" we receive from those closest to us. A "dysregulating other" is someone close to us whose emotional responses leave us feeling fragmented instead. . . . A caregiver's affective attunement, or lack thereof, profoundly affects a child's chances for emotional well-being.
>
> . . . Then I become a self-disintegrating in relation to a dysregulating other. This is what happens . . . when the other's response fails to help me manage what I'm feeling. Instead of feeling connected to someone strong and calm, I feel alone. Instead of feeling contained, I feel out of control. Instead of feeling energetically focused, I feel overwhelmed. Instead of feeling that I'll be OK, I feel like I'm falling apart.[13]

Brene Brown, Ph.D. is a research professor at the University of Houston Graduate College of Social Work. She has led the research in shame for over 16 years and has integrated 200,000 pieces of data accumulated over 60 years. She states Shame is a Universal feeling that has been mostly unspoken about until very recently. And it is this very secrecy, silence and judgement that has had it growing so intensely over the years. Her definition: "Shame is the intensely painful feeling or experience of believing that we are flawed and therefore unworthy of love and belonging."[14]

---

[13] Patricia A. DeYoung, *Understanding and Treating Chronic Shame: A Relational/Neurobiological Approach*, Routledge, 2015, p. xiii, 21.

[14] Brene Brown, Ph.D: From Shame Shields: The Armor we Use to Protect Ourselves and Why it doesn't Serve Us, Pesi Pub & Media 2017 CE Course for therapists. Also: Women & Shame, 3C Press, Austin TX, 2004.

Sadly, this belief can become pervasive across the course of a life. Hence, a deep feeling of disconnection ensues, that is not correctable by any outer actions, other than bringing it out into the open with a truly safe and empathic other. However, it is also possible to transform by learning how to give love and acceptance to each and every previously unlovable or denied part of ourselves, along with other Keys addressed in this book. (More on shame in Key 3 Chapter 6 and how to transform it throughout.)

Internal Family Systems (IFS) theory indicates how our different adaptive and protective aspects "parts" of ourselves all serve to help us deal with, hide, or mask underlying feelings of disconnection and shame. We might see some of these parts as positive yet are obsessive in their attempts to make us do and look good, while some we may clearly not like as they lead us into negative behaviors or addictions, making us ineffective. Both create detrimental results in their overzealous efforts to help us in the only ways they know how. As a result, they keep us from being our most authentic, fulfilled, and connected selves. (More on this in future chapters.)

Add to all this, the yang medical world telling mothers (as happened in the '50s and '60s) that something better than breast feeding exists; that the child has no idea what it needs when it cries attempting to tell you it's needs; that you're better off to control its messages and get it on a schedule that you the adult determines is best, while the baby is allowed to scream until it breaks and complies. Yes, conformity starts being taught at an early age. Is it any wonder that many children develop what they now call Deviance Syndrome, or as adolescents go to extreme measures to break out of this compliance—even to the point of harming themselves.

Additionally, include in this picture any stress or disconnection between mother and father, which has become common in today's world. Then add the stress of only two people (and often only one) available as breadwinner and caretaker. In the past, a whole community or village took part in all the roles of raising children. All of these stresses play into a lack of "secure attachment" that research now tells us is so important for the development of resilience and well-being in children and throughout their lives.

When family stresses show up consistently—mixed with emotional and/or physical unavailability of one or both parents—this acts on young beings as a trauma, as does physical and/or sexual abuse. Watching one parent abuse the other physically or emotionally can form a trauma also. So too, direct verbal degradation or when a child has to assume a parentified role. Although most never think of their "normal" childhoods creating trauma, it has an official name in the psychology world—Developmental Trauma—while more obvious strong events are called Shock Trauma.

Of course, at young ages children cannot put their feelings into words or even thought, but on a deep subconscious level they know when something is inherently wrong! Daniel Siegel, M.D., in his book *Parenting from the Inside Out*, talks about implicit memory. He states:

> "Implicit memory results in the creation of particular circuits of the brain that are responsible for generating emotions, behavioral responses, perception, and probably encoding of bodily sensations. Implicit memory is a form of early nonverbal memory that is present at birth and continues throughout the life span.... (Some say it starts earlier while still in the womb.) . . . Through repeated experiences with our attachment figures, our mind creates models that affect our view of both others and ourselves. . . . The fascinating feature of implicit memory is that when it is being recalled it lacks an internal sensation that something is being "recalled" and the individual is not even aware that this internal experience is being generated from something from the past.". . . So all of these very early experiences involving senses, emotions and perceptions . . . "may influence our present experience (both perception and behavior) without our having any realization that we are being shaped by the past."[15]

More Than Addiction Results

Some form of trauma is at the root of all manner of long-term physical conditions as well. Eric Gentry, Ph.D., and Robert Rhoton, Psy.D., are both

---

[15] Daniel J. Siegel, M.D., and Mary Hartzell, M.Ed., Parenting from the Inside Out, Tarcher/Penguin, NY, 2013, pp. 11–12.

recognized leaders and trainers in the field of clinical traumatology and creators of the International Association of Trauma Professionals (IATP). In their Trauma Training Course, they speak of a study revealing the undeniable impact of all this childhood trauma on long-term physical conditions. They tell of the ACE "Adverse Childhood Experiences" study in which an ACE score is a tally of different types of abuse, neglect, and other hallmarks of a challenged childhood. According to a Kaiser Permanente Group study of 1995–1997 the rougher your childhood, the higher your ACE score is likely to be and the higher your risk for later health problems.

> In the early '90s, Kaiser Permanente Group in western California piloted a novel weight loss program. The science behind it and the results were good when people followed it, but they had trouble having people stay in the program or persist with the life style changes. They put the program together in the first place because they were trying to get chronic health issues under control, and they assumed weight was the issue. They developed a structured interview tool trying to understand the failure of this program. They had done many interviews but were not getting usable data. But one day the main interviewer, who was very tired and bored accidently blended a few questions together and asked the patient "how much did you weigh at your first sexual experience?" She burst into tears, said 40 pounds and began to tell a story of undisclosed incest in her family.
>
> This had them re-think their whole system of what they were really looking at. They began to ask themselves the question, are we dealing with adverse childhood experiences that are putting people on a pathway to chronic health issues? So they redesigned their study and even got help from the people at the CDC—Center for Disease Control, to do so. They then administered a new study integrating the ACE questionnaire to quantify the childhood adverse experience histories of 17,000 individuals.
>
> They found that the things that had happened to children before the age of 5 and 6 were having health impacts on people 50 to 60 years later. This was quite a novel idea at the time. But this was the first real evidence

that being in a state of Sympathetic dominance early in life and on a continual basis is very bad for your health.[16]

On Sympathetic Dominance

Our body's autonomic nervous system that governs unconscious activities of the body functions in two different ways: The Sympathetic nervous system prepares the body for intense physical activity and is referred to as the fight-or-flight response. The Parasympathetic nervous system has almost the exact opposite effect; it relaxes the body and inhibits or slows many high-energy functions. When in a state of stress, the body lives in what is called a Sympathetic State of Arousal—that is, increased tension throughout the musculature and hyperactivity of many of the body's core functions. Being in this state of hyper function for extended periods stresses the body and the psyche. Over time, living like this causes wear and tear on many organs and systems through altered functions. It can ultimately lead to all manner of physical illness. I suggest you research this further, as it explains what happens to our bodies and psyches after even subtle levels of ongoing trauma.

Here are highlights of the Kaiser Permanente Group study, as per Gentry and Rhoton:

> Part of what this study was looking at was this: Did the person prior to age 18 grow up in recurrent physical, emotion or sexual abuse, exploitation, emotional & physical neglect, divorce and separation; an alcohol or drug abuser in the home; was there an incarcerated or missing family member, someone who was chronically depressed, suicidal activity of any family member; had the mother (or father) been treated violently, and was there one or no parent? Each item was considered an Adverse Experience and was worth a point. Two of the strongest indicators/markers in this study as to whether someone would develop significant symptoms

---

[16] Eric Gentry, PhD, and Robert Rhoton, Psy.D., *The 10 Core Competencies of Trauma, PTSD, Grief & Loss*, PESI Publishing & Media, 2016.

later in life was 1) sexual abuse and 2) emotionally charged divorce or separation.

Outcome of the original study: 25% grew up with an alcohol or substance abuser; 25% had been beaten or abused as children. 66% had at least one of these adverse experiences and 1 in 6 people had 4 or more. What is most significant is that 90% of the chronic health clients that Kaiser Permanente had at the time of the study, had 4 or more of these in their histories. 4 or more is the point at which you are much more likely to have long-term health issues. However, in a lower economic bracket study they found it only took 3 or more.

Now the study has been administered to over 800,000 people over the years. It has also become clear from continued study that over 90% of people with mental health issues have had 3–4 or more as well. Whether dealing with addictions, anxiety, depression or chronic health issues, you cannot avoid looking at some form of trauma as underlying . . . and with that, dealing with a physiology that is in a chronically hyper aroused state . . . a central nervous system that is out of balance. Hence any treatment for addictions (or emotional distress) needs to address not only the psycho-emotional issues but include healthy practices that support physiological shifts as well.[17] (see Key 6 Chapter 9 for many options)

As stated on the CDC official web site, the ACE study can be distilled down to a visual pyramid that demonstrates how these Adverse Childhood Experiences strongly correlate to risk factors for disease, and reduced well-being throughout the progression of life. I highly recommend checking this out, if only for motivation to do the inner work and make important life changes.

Having experienced ACEs does not relegate us to a doomed life. Recent neuroscience research states that the brain can in fact create new connections

---

[17] Eric Gentry, PhD, and Robert Rhoton, Psy.D., *The 10 Core Competencies of Trauma, PTSD, Grief & Loss*, PESI Publishing & Media, 2016. https://www.cdc.gov/violenceprevention/acestudy/about.html

and even new neurons throughout out a person's life. So it is possible to change our neuro pathways and hence the effects of a challenged upbringing. I am writing about all of this to make clearer where the roots of much of our addictive behaviors and chronic emotional and physical health issues begin and to say again, that we are *not to blame*. However, it is our work to become more motivated to take actions to change our potential course.

Nature vs. Nurture: DNA and Epigenetics

People speak of hereditary influences for addictions, depression and more, often saying, "It's all in the family." But where the expression of such influences can be passed on in the genetic coding, it doesn't have to be played out. This is the premise of Epigenetics.

Much controversy exists over the nature vs. nurture issue—that is, nature is what you come in with (your genetic potentialities) while nurture is what goes on around you (whether at home or in your greater environment). The nurture side includes societal and religious values and is part of the study of epigenetics. Here's a basic explanation of this science.

Epigenetics controls genes: Certain circumstances in life can cause genes to be silenced or expressed over time. That is, they can be turned off (dormant) or turned on (active).

Anything can affect epigenetics: What you eat, where you live, who you interact with, how you are treated, when you sleep, how you exercise, what culture is around you. All of these can eventually cause chemical modifications around the genes that will turn those genes on or off over time.

Epigenetics are reversible: Research is demonstrating that, through the turning on of some dormant genes and off of others, *gene expressions can be changed!* Therefore, don't feel that just because a close relative had an unhealthy life expression, you're destined to have to repeat that negative path. Gene expression can be changed; so can brain pathways, as the science of neurobiology is also discovering. (Be sure to research this topic further online)

You might hear talk these days about the ability to "change one's DNA" as it relates to different forms of deep transformational work. I have witnessed many people's lives change dramatically to the point of moving beyond embedded issues on a core level. They are no longer in resistance to the ongoing downward pull toward these difficult emotional states and behaviors. For these individuals, their DNA or some root structures have shifted. That means again, even people who have familial tendencies toward these conditions can ultimately circumvent this propensity both for themselves and their children.

The work of change: The work that will affect your genes, DNA and neural pathways in general looks like this:

- discoveries made of deeper psycho-emotional issues that you might not currently be aware of
- Somatic (physical) experience of where and how these are held in the body
- cognitive understanding of the origins of and patterns arising from those issues
- greater awareness of protective strategies that ultimately limit you
- learning a different way to be with your inner self and emotions
- integrating many core life skills, tools, and practices designed for deep change.

It's possible to no longer be fighting with yourself but enjoy greater balance and harmony within and between different aspects or *parts* of yourself. Once dedicated to the work then the intensity that drives the core need and sources for the negative behaviors and emotions begins to fall away. In relation to addictions it goes from being an act of continued abstinence—a forever addict—to a deep psycho-emotional-spiritual shift.

Your Experience Growing Up

To begin the work, you will want to *stir the pot*. This means to ask yourself some questions, that you may or may not have thought about before, that can start to open the door to some underlying issues. It is helpful to write some of your answers down.

What do you know from when you were in the womb until you were a child? Was trauma happening to one parent or the other, or to you? Or was it a "normal" childhood in which your father was physically present in body but not "there" in any other way? Or maybe your mother was present but was over attentive, never letting you learn from your mistakes, always correcting you or "saving" you from potential harm? Or perhaps she was pre-occupied with all her responsibilities or had challenging relations with your father or another family member. Did this or something else prevent her from giving you the attention you needed, so in psychological jargon, you suffered from a *lack of attunement*. It is helpful to ask each of your parents separately what they knew about their situation or the other's, especially as it applies to time in the womb, your birth or early infancy.

Were your father and mother disconnected from each other except for providing you and your siblings with basic needs? Did one or the other designate you to be his or her savior, partner surrogate, apple of his or her eye, even the reason for living for one or both? This is called *emotional incest or abuse* because any of these roles carries too much responsibility for a child to take on. Or was one parent absent so you had to take care of other family members including the remaining parent? This behavior is especially harmful for anyone at a young age, and it's all too inappropriate for a child.

The Tragic Results of Trauma

The human psyche interprets situations such as these as "trauma," which means a portion of the brain experiences certain events as life threatening, especially true the younger the child. Then the feelings and emotions from these situations get locked inside because most parents were never taught or just weren't able to listen to and validate their children's emotions in a positive way. Often the events start at a pre-verbal time where later a speaking child doesn't even know why they feel the way they do or what they would need to say.

In addition, disabling life decisions—sometimes called contracts—are subconsciously made, due to these emotionally traumatic experiences. As a result, these decisions create blockages and patterns that later inhibit us from experiencing fulfilling, healthy, happy lives.

Another response to having our calls for connection or positive attention repeatedly ignored or met with something harsh instead, would be a part of us checks out or freezes energetically, (neurologically speaking, parts of the brain shut down). In indigenous teachings, this is called soul loss—that is, part of one's soul is lost in space and time. Most often that develops into "give up" and then later manifests as depression, turning to drugs or other debilitating behaviors or emotions.

Animals' Form of Trauma

In the growing field of trauma treatment, Steven Levine, a forerunner in this area, discovered that animals in the wild have a certain response to potentially life-threatening circumstances—the animal's form of trauma. Research found that the animal will fight, flee (run), or freeze (stop in its tracks) as a form of protective defense to potentially keep the animal alive. Interestingly, when they freeze, they shake for a bit—shake it off—after the threat is over.

In the human equivalent, because when we are too young to fight or run, we freeze, which often means certain parts of us emotionally shut down. Without someone to cry to, express to, or help us shake it off, the trauma dwells in the cellular memory of our being. This holding can remain throughout life and deeply affect choices, including addictive patterns. It also affects what we manifest, including repeating relationship patterns, varied success or failure in the world, and our capacity for physical and emotional health.

In addition to addictive behaviors, the unconscious suppression of these feelings or missing frozen parts often leads to widespread experience of depression. It can show up as anything from a low-level, ongoing kind to a full-blown, debilitating version. This low-level, ongoing depression—functional depression—had been one of my maladies in the past, as I noted in this book's Introduction. In the world of psychology, a common phrase is "It's not 'what are you depressed about?' but it's 'what are you depressing?'" In effect, it's asking, "What feelings are you holding down?"

The 7 Keys Provides Hope for Humanity

Despite what has been stated in this book thus far, I am far from pessimistic. In fact, I have a very strong sense of hope for humanity. The 7 Keys provides that way back to our human roots, our essential humanity of which Chellis Glendenning has written. It's how we find a true connection with ourselves, our Soul or Sacred Self—*and* a connection to Spirit. It supports us in more harmonious and fulfilling relationships with others. It also provides a way to our purpose, our *give back* to people, to community, to life.

> The 7 Keys work seeks to heal and transform our traumas and, with that, the core disconnect.

Adopting the 7 Keys of Connection will ultimately bring harmony to the system, both within ourselves and as reflected in outer living. It will also bring balance by counter balancing our linear, yang-oriented culture. How? By teaching us how to embrace and integrate feminine values into our everyday lives. Having left the original earth-based and yin-like values in the dust, we can now integrate the old with the new.

Shifts Occur, Addiction Falls Away

Once inner and outer shifts have occurred through regular practice of the 7 Keys, the desire for addictive or other negative behaviors tend to fall away of their own accord. At the very least, you'll move beyond the sense of emptiness, disconnection, psychological pain, and lack of meaning that drives addictions. As if by magic, this leaves us available for new choices, feelings, and ways to live life fully through new connections. We can finally experience real joy, vitality, and blessed freedom from the bondage of addiction and emotional suffering.

Despite our culture having us believe a cure is available with pills and quick fixes, the 7 Keys isn't an overnight remedy. You must apply yourself. You'd pick one aspect of the 7 Keys to start and commit to one practice at a time. Then by using the power of intention and willingness to do whatever it takes—and with deep earnest prayer to whomever you hold as a cohesive, positive force of the Universe, plus support from a peer and/or professionals, great progress will be made. I have seen it many times.

You're not bound to a life of your addictive behaviors or negative feelings, as many will imply you are. *It is possible to free oneself.* But just as water spirals in a whirlpool from the downward pull of gravity, so will your energies be pulled down if there's only inertia and nothing to counter its effect. That's why you must apply yourself with intention, particularly in the beginning, as you send a downward-spinning spiral upward!

One practice leads to another and another, thus creating a momentum. Some even feel joyful or fun while creating yet more uplifting energy. In time, you'll find you'll no longer be in a deep fight against your addictions or patterns of behavior. Rather, you're being organically lifted out of them.

> At some point in the 7 Keys process, you will have pulled out the roots of the weeds of old emotions, beliefs, and burdens. You have successfully transformed the parts of your inner being that held them. Perhaps you will have called back and re-integrated lost or frozen parts of Self. At that point, the seeds of new, healthy, soul-building practices will take hold. Allowing strong plants and beautiful flowers to bloom in the field that is your life.

Chapter 2

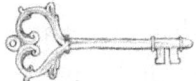

Soulcentric Developmental Wheel—What are Your Missing Tasks?

Assuming you have awareness of your own addictions and chronic emotional or physical states, I want to strongly emphasize this message: *Do not blame or negate yourself for these feelings or addictive behaviors.* Doing so only deepens the shame, self-judgment, or self-hatred that keeps it all locked in place. Remember that, whatever the state you're in or working to come out of, *it's not your fault!*

However, that doesn't mean you should lay blame on others or fail to admit some choices you've made could have been better. As I explained in Chapter 1, it can be helpful to release guilt and self-blame by understanding the existence of cultural patterns that have strayed far from what feels natural and right to one's soul. Plus, these cultural patterns have led to dysfunctional ways of being within families. Hence, it's understandable if you're among the huge percentage of everyday people with chronic physical conditions, negative emotions, or addictive behaviors and who might be at a loss to deal with something as insidious as a culture gone astray.

Along with cultural conditioning and its shortfalls to building authentic connections with others, ourselves, and life, specific missing links exist in the psychological development of our individual lives. So before discussing the 7 Keys for the healing of broken connections, let's delve into some of the roots of developmental breaks, from a Soul-centric orientation, that open the door for these challenging conditions, emotions and behaviors. Understanding them provides direction for transforming ourselves and how to be with our own offspring.

This chapter provides a roadmap based on the Soulcentric Developmental Wheel, which details what happens in a healthy culture or family during the childhood/adolescent development process and beyond. It discusses the different stages of a person's life and what, in the indigenous or natural way of thinking, are "tasks" that need to occur at each stage of development. Any shortfall in accomplishing each of these tasks lends itself to losing a link in creating stability and resiliency—also called developing a healthy ego.

Without the foundation of a healthy ego, one is not able to progress through the life stages that connects them to knowing themselves on the truest level, to connecting with their Soul Self and ultimately being able to experience the joy and fulfillment of bringing their Soul Gifts forth to share with the world. These missing links and wounded ego structures form part of the basis of falling prey to addictions and negative ways of thinking and feeling. It's time to understand some of what went wrong and put aside the need to blame and shame yourself or anyone else. Simply use this knowledge as motivation to work on correcting the missing links or doing the work to heal emotional wounding, as it's never too late.

However, the developer of this model notes that no task of any stage is ever fully completed. There are always unfinished aspects of the tasks of earlier (and current) stages. The question is about which tasks from earlier stages are *most unaddressed*.

Though there is a difference between addressing developmental deficits with their missing tasks and healing deep wounds from past emotional traumas. Many of the practices, processes and tools of the 7 keys can assist in both areas. Though the author of this model would like it understood that this work does not specifically deal with emotional trauma. However, as that is transformed via working with this book and optimally with a qualified professional as needed, it then becomes possible to integrate some of the

7 Keys work into the progression of the Soulcentric Wheel. Together they support you in ultimately experiencing the fulfillment of being in full connection to Soul, to life and your place in it.

Understanding the important tasks of each stage of this Soulcentric Developmental Wheel and making sure each task is accomplished—whether later in life or for one's own children—along with incorporating the practices in this chapter and those of the 7 Keys, will be important in moving you out of negative cycles of behavior and emotion to a Soul embodied purposeful life.

This Soulcentric Developmental Wheel was brought forth by Bill Plotkin, PhD, a depth psychologist, wilderness guide, and agent of cultural evolution. As founder of western Colorado's Animas Valley Institute in 1981, he has guided thousands of women and men through nature-based initiatory passages, including a contemporary, western adaptation of the pan-cultural vision quest. He calls these vision fasts or Animas quests.[1]

Here, I present an extremely simplified description of what Dr. Plotkin discusses in his book *Nature and the Human Soul: Cultivating Wholeness and Community in a Fragmented World*.[2] I strongly recommend reading this book as it contains so much more than I have barely begun to touch upon here. Also, please consider his first book *Soul Craft: Crossing into the Mysteries of Nature and Psyche*[3] and *Wild Mind: A field Guide to the Human Psyche*[4] for further discussion of a nature-based way of thinking and practicing as well as an ecological view point of depth psychology.

Speaking about the power and purpose of this model, Dr. Plotkin states:

(This wheel represents part of) a narrative of how we might grow whole, one life stage at a time, by embracing nature and soul as our wisest and

---

[1] For more on Bill Plotkin, Ph.D., vision fasts, his body of work, and much more: https://animas.org/

[2] Bill Plotkin, *Nature and the Human Soul: Cultivating Wholeness and Community in a Fragmented World*, New World Library, 2007.

[3] Bill Plotkin, *Soul Craft: Crossing into the Mysteries of Nature and Psyche*, New World Library, 2003.

[4] Bill Plotkin, *Wild Mind, A field Guide to the Human Psyche*, New World Library, 2013.

most trustworthy guides. This model for individual human development ultimately yields a strategy for cultural transformation, a way of progressing from our current *ego*-centric societies (materialistic, anthropocentric, competition based, class stratified, violence prone and unsustainable) to *soul*-centric ones (imaginative, *eco*-centric, cooperation based, just, compassionate and sustainable).

In contrast to those presented in most other developmental models, the stages of life portrayed here are essentially independent of chronological age, biological development, cognitive ability, and social role. Rather the progression from one stage to the next is spurred by the individual's progress with the specific psychological and spiritual tasks encountered at each stage.

This, then, is an ecopsychology of human maturation, a developmental psychology with a unique angle: it's portrayal not of typical or "average" human development but of exemplary development as it occurs in the healthiest contemporary people—and as *could* occur for everyone.[5]

This model explains how and why individuals can become weak enough to fall into addictive behaviors and debilitating states of mind and body as a lifelong pattern. It also creates a blueprint for how we can correct some of the missing pieces to strengthen ourselves at a core level. However, beyond cleaning up what was missing, the exciting part of this is to learn about the stages beyond childhood, beyond wounding and missing tasks, that can take us to being a contributing member of the connected whole of our world. That is, discovering on the deepest level, who we are and what our soul is calling us to do.

During the latter phases, we dive deep to experience Soul encounters and ultimately Soul Initiation:

During a soul encounter, you learn something about your destiny, which can be variously phrased as: why you were born, your mystical calling, what gift you're meant to bring to the world, your one true life, the larger story

---

[5] Bill Plotkin, *Nature and the Human Soul: Cultivating Wholeness and Community in a Fragmented World,* New World Library, 2007, p. 3.

you might live, your particular way of belonging to the Earth Community, the largest conversation you can have with the world, your unique psycho-ecological niche in the web of life, or your ultimate place.[6]

Soulcentric Developmental Wheel

To begin, let's look at the Wheel itself. Imagine a circle that you bisect from left to right and top to bottom creating four quarters. The point on the right side of the horizontal line is marked East, the bottom of the circle at the bottom of the vertical line through the center is South, and so on for the West and the North. There are two diagonal lines that bisect those sections, thus creating eight sections of a pie chart. We'll mainly discuss what transpires below the horizon line between the East and the West and the first phase above the horizon line.[7] (See chart below.)

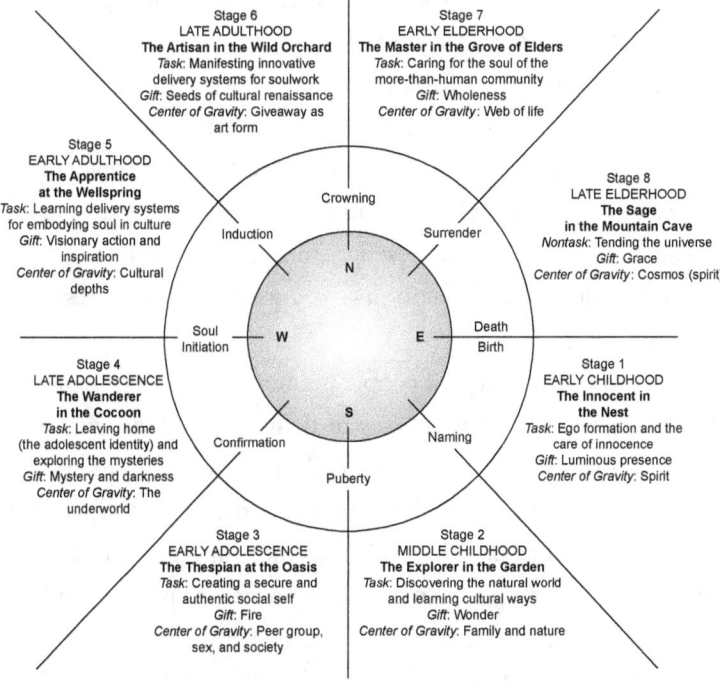

The Eight Soulcentric or Ecocentric Stages of Human Development

---

[6] Ibid, p. 267.
[7] Reprinted with permission from Bill Plotkin and New World Library, Novato, CA.

Though I have named an age at each stage, this age is a time when it would optimally occur and often does in healthy cultures. For each of the pie pieces representing stages of life, certain life "tasks" optimally need to occur. However as was explained in the quote above, through one's inner work and the maturation that ensues from that work, a task can be completed at any point in life.

Stage 1: The Innocent in the Nest—Early Childhood (Birth to Naming—age 4 to 5)

The East point on the horizon line is the point of birth (as well as the point of death). The first quadrant from the East horizon line to the next line is called the Nest. It represents the period of early childhood up to age four or five.

The First Task—Care of Innocence—mainly refers to the period of infancy. This task is a task of the parents or caretakers, while all other stages are about the individual's inner journey, with the caretakers playing a strong influencing part, while still in childhood.

In Stage 1, it's the task of the caretakers to see the magical nature, the innocence, and perfection of this little being no matter what outer attributes the child displays. This might mean calmly looking into the eyes of this little creature with love, reflecting back its purity, its close connection to life itself, and expressing gratitude for its presence. In modern psychology we call this act and other regular acts of attention—*attunement,* with the result of creating *secure attachment.*

Consider what percentage of people in our culture had this all-important first task fully met. Given the stresses of daily living or survival, unhealthy or difficult relations between parents, children born to mothers who were neither ready, willing, or able to be a parent, and a host of other challenges, how many are blessed to have had this extremely important task met?

Even in an ideal set-up of two parents who love each other, had their survival needs handled, and felt at peace within themselves, doctors still might have told mothers to feed baby with a bottle rather than directly connecting with the mother through breastfeeding. When a synthetic rubber nipple supplied with a liquid created by man or cow replaces flesh, skin, and heartbeat, something huge is missing.

The Second Task—**Ego Formation**—happens when the infant-becoming-child starts to become aware of himself or herself. These children can now tell stories using "I" in it. This awareness of themselves as separate beings marks this point of transition, a stage called Naming.

Stage 2: Explorer in the Garden—Middle Childhood (Naming (4–5) to Puberty (11–12))

The First Task—**Discovering the Enchantment of the Natural World**—features the outer wild world of nature: plants, trees, rivers, streams, animals, etc. This task is also about nature's inner world—human's nature as in their bodies, imagination, and emotions.

Consider how many children get outside to creatively play these days. With time spent on computers, phones, and other technical devices, how much connection to the outside natural world do they really get? Dual working parents or single parents tend to plop their kids in front of screens for hours. Even before technology became a staple in our lives, growing threats such as child abductions, bad influences related to drugs, and other safety concerns would keep children inside and under parents' watch.

In addition, given today's ubiquitous drive to "succeed," free time from school often gets structured in skill-building activities or trainings in areas of sports, arts, or academic excellence. Not that this is bad in and of itself but when is there time available for kids to access their innate creativity (other than in technological ways) or simply connect with nature?

When it comes to learning naturally about one's body, it seems to be one extreme or the other. It goes from a strong body shame perspective that's been pervasive in our culture—for example, reprimanding children for exploring their own bodies—to being exploited sexually at inappropriate ages. Also, the ideation of sexiness pervades our media, available for all to see. Its constant availability adds to the confusion children feel about their own perfectly healthy body curiosity. It also leads to inappropriate dressing and acting sexual at too young an age.

The Second Task—**learning cultural ways**—involves learning the cultural ways of the people around them and as a family member. You could say they're developing strategies for acceptance or, in some cases, childhood strategies for *survival*.

Wanting to fit into the family structure and the culture surrounding them is a perfectly natural and healthy urge. It's an important task of this age. However, shortfalls arise when the beliefs, habits, and behaviors of family members are unhealthy. They model behaviors that don't serve the individual.

An example is a funny yet sad viral video titled "Linda Honey, Listen to Me" in which three-year-old Mateo parrots (presumably) his father.[8] In this video, Mateo's mother tells him he cannot have cupcakes for dinner and reprimands him because he ate some anyway. Mateo says over and over "Linda, honey, you are not listening to me." He puts his hands on his hips, throws his head back, and closes his eyes, cutting off his mom time and again. He replicates everything down to the stance of his father saying things like "Linda, Honey, lookit, lookit, listen to me, listen to me." He responds to his mom's logic by defending himself and then again cuts her off verbally. "Linda honey, Linda honey, you are not listening to me, listen to me, listen to me."

Though we laugh at the absurdity of it, Mateo's young age demonstrates how early family culture programing can start. Whereas at three, it would be healthier to be developing his own ego structure rather than moving into the next phase of learning his family culture, which in this case doesn't look too great for any stage. Even in a healthy family, incorporating family culture is more natural after naming, rather than before when just beginning to develop their own ego, as is the case with Mateo at only three. Note how early unhealthy relating and communication styles can begin.

Humans learn the ways of their early caretaking culture. Those who have a loving, listening, honoring, supportive family structure will carry these attributes into the next stage. But if the natural tasks of this second stage have been negatively imprinted by our parents and/or the culture along with missing tasks before that, this lays the ground for what happens in the following Stage 3. In fact, it's where one usually sees addictions or other debilitating emotions and habits begin.

---

[8] https://www.youtube.com/watch?v=TP8RB7UZHKI

Note: The ages listed are based on what is natural. Given hormones in food and many other factors, puberty-like behaviors and body features can develop earlier than what's natural. This is especially true if children base their ability to fit in to their family culture based on that of an older sibling.

Stage 3: The Oasis: Social Individuation—Early Adolescence (Puberty to Confirmation)

Puberty normally takes place over four or five years between ages 11 and 15. The vertical line below the horizon represents the transition from childhood to adolescent and goes until the next 45-degree line, to the left side of this vertical. In this stage, the ego becomes rooted in society. Before, it was rooted in family. The end point or transition from this first phase of early adolescence to the next of late adolescence is called Confirmation.

The First Task—Create a Secure and Authentic Social Self—Fashioning a social presence that is both authentic (the nature task) and socially acceptable (the culture task). Optimally it generates adequate amounts of both social acceptance and self-approval. That means seeing oneself as a member of a community or peer group (cultural task) while maintaining a connection to the truth of who one is (the nature task). Stage 3 is meant to *create a secure social self while maintaining authenticity.*

In childhood, social acceptance is primarily seeing ourselves as a member of the family.

While in adolescence, the question becomes "How do I fit in with my peers?" Which at this stage, carries more importance than "How do I fit in with my family?" We tend to think this "fitting in with peers" is unhealthy when in fact it's quite natural. Yet with so many people missing important tasks that create a healthy ego, in addition to the emotional wounding of trauma, our culture encourages creating a *secure* social self at the expense of an *authentic* one. For these modern youth, an internal conflict is set up: acceptance versus authenticity. At some point, authenticity gets dropped off the task list and the sole focus becomes acceptance. The optimal question should be "How can I be accepted and still be real to who I am?"

In addition, rather than being motivated by what is true for a particular person, adaptive attitudes are adopted. In that case the question becomes "How do I be the best (that is, better than others or at least darn good), most beautiful, most rebellious, etc., so I can feel secure?" Later, if one never moves out of this, it might show up as going for being the most wealthy or having the most prestigious job. Thus, security and value become concerned about things outside of oneself that are impossible to control. Often, these identities (that which a person thinks their value is tied to) ends up creating feelings of disappointment, abandonment or failure. At the same time this exaggerates any feelings of "less than okay", "not enough" or "unlovable" already existing from missing tasks or wounding in their childhood.

At some point in the teen years (in a more natural cycle of things, but can happen at any age) youth start looking for more from life. The values of their parents or current culture at large may not fit for them. If no elders are around to help in this transition, they can make a mess of it. Teens get into drugs because, at some level, they know life has to be more than this—unless doing drugs is a mask to the underlying pain from missed tasks or a deeply wounded childhood. Then it can just be a downward spiral trap they can get caught in for years. But when that's not the case, on some level, they may think "I got good at this social game and peer acceptance, but it's not interesting enough. There's something else I'm not seeing or feeling, but I don't quite know what."

Teens usually respond to this stage by conforming or rebelling. If they don't go too far off the deep end in their rebelling (due to their self-esteem or early ego identity not being in place from too many missing tasks or wounds), it can be the healthier of the two choices. In fact, an aspect of it fits with what's natural for this stage. If a teen's rebellion is not just an expression of anger that comes from their deep woundedness, then he or she often becomes more open and ready for Soul connection sooner.

By comparison, the conformist is doing just that—fitting into what society sanctions. Conformists can fall into the trap of doing what is "right" and valued in the culture rather than following their true inner urgings, their soul callings. Due to the outer benefits they can get stuck there for a long time (possibly all of life) and always sense something's missing. They feel deep discontent or are just plain unhappy, and hence depression or other maladies set it. Though they may look good on the surface to the outer world, they commonly take on addictive behaviors that mask their inner sufferings.

When this tipping point happens in teen years, this is when the parent of a "good" kid becomes shocked that their shining star fell into drugs or depression. When that is not the case, they could stay stuck in the conformity aspect of early adolescence well into adulthood. Though there can be later life opportunities to break out of the trap of conformity and begin to look deeper.

***The Second Task*—Finding Out What Values, Desires, and Emotions are Authentically Mine**—leads to questions such as "What do I really feel (emotions)? What do I want that is true to my interests and passions (desires)? What do I love or find is important to me (values)?"

Sadly, in our culture, many never ask themselves these questions, thus remaining fixated in the adolescence phase their entire lives. Without life transition rituals and elders, the spontaneous transition into the Cocoon only occasionally occurs at an older age. Most tend to do what is culturally valued or what the family expected, as described above—the conformist. Or they become locked in counter roles of defiance, never to question or deeply explore the truth of who they are—the rebel.

What follows is what we might call a midlife crisis. It might look like this: once we have our "thing" together (what we believe will "do it" for us), after riding that wave for a bit, we feel we need more—more money, more career attainment, more beauty, better relationships—until we get it, and realize that won't fulfill us. Then our inner elder starts knocking on the door saying, "Come with me."

Here is a metaphor that explains it well: *You spent your whole life building your home, your life—two cars in the garage, a beautiful wife, two great kids, a great job with employees you rule—and you go to hang the last picture on the wall when there's a knock on the door (those feelings of discontent, of there's something more). It's your Soul calling. Then it all starts to break loose—affairs, unexpected behaviors, illness' and more.*

In an attempt to make this soul connection it often requires normal surface living stop. At any age an outer crisis may occur (losing a job, major health issue or accident for example), hitting bottom (from addictions perhaps) or simply experiencing a sudden onset of depression, confusion, or irrational behavior. This spur out of our "normal" everyday lives will often involve these traumas, illnesses, losses, or other circumstances forcing us to look deeply at our lives.

However, even though a person may experience a crisis that invites a connection with their Soul Self, many people return to "business as usual" later. They often don't take advantage of this opportunity. It's this constant state of going for social acceptance rather than authenticity or living an unquestioned life, mainly on the surface—a misalignment with Soul, that can cause one to shut down (depression, anxiety and more) or cover the inner conflict with an addictive behavior or substance.

When the natural tasks and issues of deep wounding are ignored, those addictions of behavior or emotions will commonly begin at this stage or the next and only deepen with time.

In some cases, a crisis does spur a deeper exploration. Once inner work begins to open the lid on old, withheld feelings and hopefully South work is done, (representing the life phase of the child) a person can get back in touch with the essential elements of who they are. Truthfully, we cannot find our full authenticity until we are more aware of our own feelings, desires, and values along with discovering and releasing buried emotions and beliefs. (We address this in Key 1 of the 7 Keys.)

Once we become aware of these, then other awareness', abilities, and practices are needed to bring forth a full transformation of these earlier issues (to be discussed in the other Keys). This level of work is best done before embarking on the deeper mystery aspects discussed in the next phase of the *Wanderer in the Cocoon* with its soul encounters and transition point at Soul Initiation.

If such crisis' have occurred for you, they are your later life opportunity to break out of the trap of conformity and begin to look deeper. The author of this model believes that for most in the Western world, this never or rarely happens. But if you are reading this book, perhaps this call and your willingness to follow it, whether associated with a crisis or not, has already begun.

Stage 4: The Wanderer in the Cocoon (the tomb for the adolescent and the womb for the adult)—Late Adolescence (Confirmation to Soul Initiation)

The straight vertical line that began Stage 3 of early adolescence is called Puberty; the 45-degree line that ends that stage and begins Stage 4, late adolescence is called Confirmation and goes until the horizontal line above it. (Soul Initiation) Confirmation is the passage from early adolescence to later stage adolescence.

The First Task—**Leaving Home** of the adolescent identity/personality—(culture task) is the call to relinquish adolescent identity and heed *the call to adventure*, to break from the known.

The Second Task—**Exploring the Mysteries** of nature and psyche—(nature task), is in preparation for *Soul Initiation*. These tasks may or may not involve leaving home physically, but they encompass the quest for true individuation—a search for our deepest truth and meaning, our life's purpose, our soul name. By the end of this stage, at Soul Initiation and moving into the next stage, we experience a metaphoric knowing that has us able to identify in general, our sacred work that captures our soul's essence. To know how it plays out exactly in our culture and time, is the work of the next phase, (Stage 5).

Wanderer

Confirmation (the beginning of this stage) notes a transition that moves us out of the first phase of adolescence, where we can say "I feel mostly good about myself most of the time. I know what is me and what are other parts of me or outer influences. I know who is being afraid or feels anger or jealousy, and I can be with that. I can also handle the 'stuff' of the world such as my finances. Overall, I am mostly true to me and still have friends."

If you are in this phase, you have probably broken off from the plan outlined for you by society, family, or cultural ideals in search of what feeds your soul and has meaning for you. You have some sense of your soul qualities and thus have broken free, out of what is usual and customary in your life. At this point you become the *wanderer*, looking for ways to learn new things and have new experiences that will help bring in, expand or make more clear your soul qualities and/or soul path. The work of the wanderer sets the foundation for your adulthood. (again, it can happen at any age, even what might typically be called adulthood numerically.) This path requires developing and practicing new skills to explore the realms of the soul. (Listed below)

It is important to understand that before you can deeply and fully embark on this stage, the bulk of your "south work" needs to be done or at least engaged in. South work is the work of addressing the issues of child hood and early adolescence. There can be some remaining elements, but the core healing of the deeper wounding or missing tasks needs to be completed before truly being able to go to this next level.

Much of the transformational processes and practices in the 7 Keys will move you through these earlier phases. This prepares you to be able to move into this Wanderer—Cocoon phase that will ultimately lead to Soul encounters and Soul Initiation. There are practices included in the 7 Keys, that support this phase. Some of these practices can be begun while still dealing with south work. There are others set out by Bill Plotkin for this phase listed below. To learn more about them it is best to read his books previously listed.

After completing most of your South work and having completed Stage 3—early adolescence, and once you have a secure and authentic social Self, you will be strong and clear enough for the deeper soul exploration of this phase. Up to this point, you may have figured out one social way to be in the world and once you have, you can now let much of that go.

For example, people in indigenous cultures do a walkabout, where they are taught in the ways of mystery by their elders, or they're taken up to the mountain for a transformational experience. The elder also teaches them Soulcraft skills (listed below) and about the shadow (unenlightened aspects of their being and any remaining childhood issues yet to be brought to light) as well as romance, sex, and so on. They're also required to experience an "ordeal" that will assist to foster their soul initiation. This all is about the call to leave the safety and security of what one might call home—that is, leave what is familiar. This place between the end of puberty—Confirmation and Soul Initiation is where we start differentiating life in relation to our soul rather than our outer societal norms and egocentric ways.

Into the Cocoon—the Mystery

Without the support of an elder and specific initiatory rites, where do we go when this inner-elder calls? The best way I can generalize it is to say, down and into the mysteries. An "ordeal" or crisis is often required to bring this work forth. Often what helps take us down is any of the five Ds—Divorce, Disease, Dissolution (of something important like a job), Drugs or unwavering Discontent. You could say they start a molting process, like the shedding from one caterpillar adolescent life to another. This can be the same period of crisis mentioned before, that can catapult us from the previous phase all the way into the deeper aspects of the mystery.

Here in these depths is where your ego perspectives are knocked sideways, where you are thrown into a different state of mind and see life through a different lens. This is often what it takes to officially leave home, to have the time and intention to genuinely look inside for deeper truths. Here we come to know the invisible aspects of ourselves—the Shadow. These are not only unconscious parts of ourselves, but those we would deny if we did not look open and honestly enough. Fear or challenging situations tend to bring up the Shadow.

Soul Initiation, the official end of this phase is at the horizon line at its most Western point. Hence the work occurring in this phase to bring you to this point, (and can continue on and off beyond this initial time), is called West work. Through this West work and "Soul Encounter" is when we open to what has the deepest purpose and meaning for us. Where in the previous stage, Oasis, it addresses feelings, values, and desires, the questions in the Cocoon stage that hold us are "What am I to do? What is my giveback? What are my natural gifts to share? How am I to belong? What is my heart song?"

These questions are not answered by decisions of our linier mind. Rather, they are discovered through our deeper experience, through soul encounter, through what occurs during this wanderer phase. It is about *discovering* what I was *born* to do. During this phase answers begin to come if only in a general sense.

Soul initiation, the passage that ends this stage happens when one has discovered the answer adequately.

> What occurs in the human Cocoon is similar in scope and profundity to what occurred in the first stage of life, the Nest. During that stage we made a great sea crossing from the pre-birth realm of spirit to the realm of human society and conscious self-awareness. Now we undergo a transmutation that is equally radical, mysterious, and momentous—we gradually make our way from a life centered in society and personality to a life centered in soul. From an individual whose goal is to improve his socioeconomic standing to one whose primary motivation is to discover his destiny and turn it into lived reality, a gift to others....
>
> The cocoon results in the disintegration of almost everything we know about the world and ourselves. The butterfly of course understands this... Inside the cocoon, you come to understand what the butterfly knows: you are preparing to die in order for something new to be born—and to take flight.[9]

When I first learned of this model I became excited saying, yes this is what happened to so many of us in the late 60s early 70s, as a cultural group. Consider how many young adults who'd grown up in the '50s with its staid values started taking hallucinogenic drugs in the late '60s and '70s. (Think of the movie *Pleasantville* set in the 1950s in which everything was black and white until the perspective changed and, with it, everything turned to color).

A mind shift doesn't have to come from drugs, but many people's perspectives changed dramatically after that. Those with enough early-met tasks

---

[9] Bill Plotkin, *Nature and the Human Soul: Cultivating Wholeness and Community in a Fragmented World,* New World Library, 2007, pp. 242, 243.

(even with some missing) did not fall prey to a life of drugs, but they did begin to look at life differently. Expansion occurred in the fields of natural health including many forms of yoga, psychology, deep healing work, and ecology. Also, technology blossomed exponentially after that. This came from those who broke out of the norm with its constricted way of thinking during that time. Bill Plotkin brought this to light so well in his book.

> For example, in the countercultural 1960s and 1970s, something extraordinary happened: much of an entire generation heard the call to adventure, said YES, and entered the Cocoon. The hippies recognized there had to be more to life than the American, or Western, dream. They employed a great variety of methods to lift the veil—psychedelics, music, dance, and Eastern spiritual practices—and most succeeded in one way or another. But with few elders and initiators to guide the way, and with the constant pressure from mainstream society to submit and conform, most were unable to effectively embody what they found in their wanderings. Relatively few reached the far shore of Soul Initiation and genuine adulthood."[10]

More was needed for many to take it into full soul initiation. Some did find their way there. Especially those who found the world of nature immersion, vision fast work and continued to employ on a regular basis what Bill Plotkin calls Soulcraft. What an excellent word, because you could say what you *craft* feeds your *Soul*. These activities include endeavors such as poetry, art, drumming, dance, music, or natural trance inducements of various forms. They pull us out of our linear brains and into a different more balanced and naturally open state of mind. (More detail on this in Key 5 – Chapter 8.) These are particularly supportive during Stage 4 and Stage 5 and become wonderful aspects of life at any stage. Though Bill offers more Soulcraft practices that have nothing to do with crafts or the arts as we think of them in normal culture.

---

[10] Ibid. p. 481.

Second Task—Into the Mysteries

Many sub-tasks occur in the process of preparing for the fuller relinquishing of adolescent identity as well as preparing for Soul Initiation.

> Where his first task is to leave his accustomed home, in the second he meanders toward a new abode and a second birth. He will find his new place—his soul-rooted way of belonging to the world—by exploring the mysteries of this own human consciousness and its relationship to the Earth and cosmos, which is to say the natural world.
>
> This second task has two components: (1) learning and employing techniques for soul encounter, practices that will help the Wanderer approach the soul and gather what he finds there, and (2) cultivating a soulful relationship to his life and to all life.[11]

Soul Encounter vs. Soul Initiation

The process of soul initiation (not capitalized) is what transpires over the time period that one is wandering, learning and practicing soulcraft skills, and experiencing various soul encounters. Soul encounters are experiences "of an image, symbol or story—something numinous or sacred at the very core of an individual's life, and which communicates something of the person's ultimate place in the world."[12] While Soul Initiation (capitalized) is the actual point of transition between the Phase of the Wanderer to the phase of the Apprentice. When in the Apprentice phase, Stage 5, the symbolic imagery of Soul Encounter, that is, the general sense and essence of one's soul gifts, takes on more specific meaning in the time and place of their culture.

Soul encounter is experienced in a number of ways; as a perception (visual, acoustic or kinesthetic)—your soul image; as a story you were born to live; or a magical meeting with an energetic being, or special place that communicates something of your destiny or some say Dharma, through

---

[11] Ibid. p. 266.
[12] Ibid. p. 267.

words, gesture or dream, and reveals something of your soul story and/or image.

> Woven in the fabric of your soul image is a mysterious symbol or theme that holds the secret of your life purpose. Through one or more soul encounters, you discover how that symbol or theme reveals the gift you were born to carry to others and how your soul powers are vehicles for doing so.
>
> Your soul story might be unveiled to you as a single revelatory experience—through a dream, a vision, a voice of the sacred or a sudden insight. On the other hand, the shape of your soul story might be only gradually revealed as you weave together the themes and symbols from the soul encounters you've had up to that point in your life.[13]

Soulcraft Skills

One thing about this period is that it cannot be rushed and takes as long as it takes. This patience and surrender to the entire wandering and soul encounter process is part of the initiatory work. However, additionally there are many skills and practices that support the learnings, growings and deepenings into the mysteries that ultimately reveal so much about the essence of who we are and what we have to bring forth. Though soul encounters can occur spontaneously without exercise of any skills, the following set of practices or "soulcraft skills" can be found in cultures across the globe and do encourage and support the experience of soul encounter.

> In nature-based cultures, there are a great variety of these soul-oriented practices, techniques, and ceremonies taught by initiation guides and elders to the Wanderer youth of their communities. These soul-encounter skills are essential at this time of life, every bit as important as the skills involved in hunting, horticulture, food preparation and shelter building.
>
> For Western teenagers too (those who have reached the Cocoon), developing soul-craft competence is more vital to their genuine personal

---

[13] Ibid. p. 268.

development than math, science, soccer and business know how. But in an ego centric society, exceedingly few youth, in their teens or twenties, ever gain proficiency in soulcraft skills.[14]

Moving into a different portion of the brain supports the process of soul encounter as we can access information other than what we experience in day-to-day life. Soulcraft practices can serve this function. Some of what is listed below are: "Body practices for altering consciousness: to perceive actualities and imagine possibilities that we might otherwise over look, and in doing so helping us weave the subtle and unseen forces of the world into form, making the unconscious conscious."[15]

The following is a list of Soulcraft practices set out by Dr. Plotkin that go well beyond creative or artistic endeavors. They're sometimes employed in the Oasis phase as prep but more typically employed during the Wanderer—Cocoon phase and often continue beyond. They all assist in honing skills of physical, psychological, social, and spiritual self-reliance and prepare the individual to open to and experience soul encounter and ultimately soul initiation. After which the individual moves into the next phase of honing their delivery systems for bringing their soul story, symbol or gift to their specific time and culture.

Soulcraft Processes
- Acquiring and developing a set of Soulcraft skills (see list below and Key 5 – Chapter 8)
- Volunteering—Giving of yourself in service within already established organizations. Or as some youth are doing these days creating their own ideas and organizations for service
- South work: Exploration to complete unfinished business from earlier stages

---

[14] Ibid. p. 272.
[15] Ibid. p. 273.

- Working with a Sacred Wound: a deep and meaningful wound that often carries the seeds of the gift you are to bring forth to the world
- Acquiring and developing the skills of Shadow work and Projection[16]
- Giving up addictions (both behavioral or any mind-altering substances that are taken more than occasionally)
- Learning to choose authenticity over acceptance and the ability to speak your truth
- Making peace with the past as preparation for leaving behind the life of the primary (early phase) ego.
- Learning the art of solitude or quiet and finding its gifts and beauty
- Discovering nature as a mirror and as a healer
- Letting yourself be deeply touched and affected by nature
- Learning the art of romance, relationship, and open honest communication
- Commencement of Mindfulness and/or Meditation practice
- Witnessing and, with it, expanding the presence of Soul Self (See Key 2 – Chapter 5)
(more details on much of this list will be expanded upon in the 7 Keys.)

Soulcraft Practices to support the above processes and encourage Soul encounter:

- Breathwork
- Ceremonial sweats and saunas
- Deep imagery journeys (especially those involving "power animals")
- Dreamwork
- Ecstatic trance dancing
- Fasting
- Journal work—writing to connect with one's own depths

---

[16] Note: *Express Yourself: Discover you Inner Truth, Creative Self and the Courage to Let It Out* by the author provides details in Chapter 7: Recognizing and Regaining the Power in Your Shadow Self.

- Self-generated ceremony—creating your own ceremonies to confirm or call in an important change. For more about this see below.[17]
- Soulful music, poetry or symbolic artwork (expressive, not for purpose of craft or show)
- The art of wandering in nature
- Trance drumming
- Underworld journeys facilitated by hallucinogenic substances in sacred ritualistic contexts with a qualified guide. (This is not for someone who has substance abuse issues, is active in a recovery process, or in need of a lot of South work healing.)

Stage 5: Soul Apprentice at the Wellspring (Soul-Rooted Individuation)—Early Adulthood (Soul Initiation to Induction)

Task—Learning to Embody Soul in culture—acquiring and implementing delivery systems for one's soul qualities.

As stated in the previous phase, when the images come through that reflect your deeper soul qualities *they can be the first profound glimpse of what you are here to do,* that not only gives your life purpose and meaning but that effects the whole. For now you are in a phase where the life of the collective maters as much to you as your individual existence. "You are now more an agent for the Mystery—for Soul and Spirit—than for your narrowly defined self."[18] In Dr. Plotkin's terminology, you move from Ego-centric to Eco-centric.

If we had a healthy childhood, we would have naturally moved out of egocentrism. But given the culture in which we live, which many feel is locked into an ego-centric adolescent phase, it can often take this long to get here to soul-centric/eco-centric. And quite often most never get here for all of life, unless there has been some outside support or strong inner calling.

When this glimpse comes through via soul encounters in images, stories or symbols it usually doesn't say it in cultural terms—that is, it doesn't

---

[17] http://www.schooloflostborders.org/content/self-generated-ceremony-meredith-little
[18] Ibid. p. 305.

state an exact job such as a chiropractor, a real estate agent, or a store owner. Rather, it speaks in soul quality terms—metaphors, poetry or symbols as discussed in the previous stage.

For Bill Plotkin his first image was that of a cocoon. He did not know exactly what this meant, but he did know cocoons to be a place of powerful transformation. Other than that he had no idea of what the image meant or how he might bring that forth to this world. Though he did have a general sense that creating conditions and settings for personal transformation was a core element of his calling. That particular soul encounter did not give him any specific details of what he now calls delivery systems. It did not say become a psychologist, a vision quest guide or even a writer. Yet over time and beyond Soul Initiation it evolved into his amazing and powerful nature, vision fast and depth work. This initial image of a cocoon with later symbols indicating he would weave cocoons of cultural transformation is what has transpired in a huge, beautiful and unexpected way.

For me, it was more of a story. What showed up was a vision of a pied piper leading people out of the ranks of normalcy into a sort of new brigade. This figure was playing a flute and dancing toward a positive beautiful place. People were dropping into this dancing line in large numbers. Not surprisingly, I use music, dance, drum and song as a huge part of the transformational work I have done, where everyone, at all levels gets to participate.

Interestingly in the last few years I re-entered an inward journey and revisited a wanderer phase. As Dr. Plotkin states:

> The Cocoon is by no means the only time when we wander psychospiritually.... In subsequent stages there'll be times (relatively brief) when we need to once again wander to reassess our lives—for instance when we near major transitions of Induction, Crowning and Surrender, and in times of spiritual crisis within each stage. Such times provoke a self-confrontation, a dying and a letting go, in preparation for a deeper understanding and embodiment in our lives.

Regardless of our age or developmental level, the Wanderer archetype operates with in us whenever we need greater depth or meaning or purpose in our lives. The wanderer within is always ready to search for soul and generate new ways of embodying the qualities of soul we have already uncovered."[19]

Out of this time of a later wandering for me, came greater stability within and a deeper commitment to focus and complete this book. And where a piece of my south work still plagued me in terms of my discomfort with standing before others, I accessed a deeper level of work in this realm. With that the willingness to do whatever it takes to bring this book to many others, including standing in front of people again.

To summarize a key aspect of this phase, Soul gives a metaphoric message of soul qualities prior, during and after Soul Initiation, and then Ego translates these soul qualities into soul work. It's the healthy ego's job to make a translation into the ways of the world that fit into our particular time and culture, or in Dr. Plotkins terms: its *delivery system*.

After learning to look to Soul, Self, Inner Guidance, the Mystery (however we name it) for directions rather than society, you'll find you are led more and more by soul than by ego. In addition, with focus on Soulcraft practices and what is contained in the 7 Keys, the presence and availability of Soul expands within us to take on a strong leadership role in our lives.

I tend to say that Ego becomes the servant of soul rather than ego leading the way. Ego then becomes rooted in soul. Although some schools of thought refer to ego in only a negative light or its adaptive states, in this model, the ego is a valuable part of ourselves when it's healthy and supportive of one's Soul Self. Dr. Plotkins model explains it beautifully:

> We descend into this world from spirit into a functional first, or primary ego in stages 1 through 3, an ego that is grounded primarily in human society. Then (optimally) our ego further matures as we align it with soul in stage 4, in time giving birth to a second-stage *soul-rooted* ego at Soul Initiation. Our

---

[19] Ibid. p. 298.

second-stage ego carries us through stage 7. At Surrender (passage to our last stage) we release our soul-rooted ego and achieve a third-stage *spirit-rooted* ego in stage 8. (that eventually takes us all the way home).[20]

Apprentice

This aspect involves acquiring the skills of your soul qualities, apprenticing yourself to those who excel at what your soul qualities are or what you're trying to bring forth. At this stage, you don't have to know exactly what it will look like when it comes out of you and into the world. Simply be an apprentice—study with or follow what feels good to your soul. This can occur in the context of school if that school offers aspects of your soul's calling. Or it might take a variety of forms. In this culture of synthesis with so much information available, it's not uncommon to work with a number of different trainings, teachers, or modalities. Or it can come from the course of jobs or experiences you're led to as you feel the call to explore.

All the while continuing to deepen your connection to Soul further, as you hone or develop new Soulcraft skills. Your ability to identify what you will do more specifically in worldly terms, will begin to emerge naturally over time.

To understand why Dr. Plotkin calls this stage Apprentice *at the Wellspring*, I suggest you read his book Nature and the Human Soul: Cultivating Wholeness and Community in a Fragmented World. From this you will also be able to receive the greater depth of his message.

Stage 6: The Artisan in the Wild Orchard—Late Adulthood (Induction to Crowning)
Task: Manifesting Innovative delivery systems for soul work.

After being a soul apprentice and studying with a master or masters to learn the ways of your soul gifts and accompanying delivery systems; and once you fully integrate the ways of these teachings; then you generate your own ways and expression of what you have learned.

---

[20] Ibid. p. 74.

> The Wellspring (Apprentice phase) ends when you've mastered one or more delivery systems for your soul image or story and you stop looking outside yourself for instruction or role models for embodying soul. You begin to fashion novel and creative forms that arise out of your own depths…. your soul rooted individuation has progressed to the point that, more often than not, you behave socially as the person you experience yourself to be privately.
>
> As a Soul Apprentice, you gradually understood your soul qualities in deeper ways, and you honed your skills at embodying those qualities through a particular craft.[21] (that you now bring forth in your own way).

You might already be putting your soul work forth in the world and yet be called by soul to let it all go as it may too closely represent the forms you originally learned. Only to bring forth something similar but in a whole new way, or else something completely different and unique to you.

> From time to time (you might) need to change the cultural context in which you embody soul, or you might need to learn an entirely new craft. Soul is the constant; its form and sphere of embodiment varies.[22]

I will warn you that this transition of Induction from the Apprentice to the Artisan, is not just an "oh boy I get to do my own thing." It can be filled with much difficulty, risk, fear or letting go. It is a time to step into the archetype associated with this stage—the Warrior.

> But this is not an occasion for ego inflation. As with all major life-stage transitions, this one entails as much dying as birthing, as much burden as blessing.…you're also being asked to step up to a position of greater responsibility, challenge and risk. Your student and apprentice days are

---

[21] Ibid. p. 353.
[22] Ibid. p. 353.

over. Now is the time to assume full obligations of cultural leadership, as well as the fulfillment and joy inherent in that status.[23]

If sharing these gifts is to be your livelihood, I encourage you to let yourself continue to do some survival work while you either apprentice or begin putting forth your soul work. Dr. Plotkin calls this your Survival Dance while working on your Soul Dance. Some jump fully into the soul dance idealistically, too fast, or too soon. Not only perhaps are they not ready on a worldly level but before doing enough of their South or West work. That's why they don't make it on a survival level. This can be re-wounding and cause them to step back too far and for too long out of fear. But do understand this, it's not necessary to do one's "soul work" as a livelihood. It can serve the same fulfilling role in one's life if done as a hobby or as pure service. (More about your Give Back—your Worldly Soul Expression in Key 7 part 2 – Chapter 11.)

I will be limited in what I say about this stage and the following stages, as the focus of this book is mostly on what gets us to this point of putting forth what is fully our soul expression, our gift from Mystery, our part in the Great Turning (a new way of being in our world), and that which gives a true feeling of purpose and connection. By the time we reach this marker of the Artisan we will have for the most part, moved beyond our child hood wounds, missing tasks and the effects of limiting emotions and addictive behaviors or substances. Also, at this point of being the creator of our own unique soul expression and the vehicles of delivery we have studied, we would also be feeling connected to ourselves, others, spirit and with a sense of belonging in this world.

Stage 7: The Master in the Grove of Elders—Early Elderhood (Crowning to Surrender)

Task: Caring for the Soul of the more-than-human Community.

This is the highest North point on the vertical line. It relates to having skill, leadership, and confidence in what you've come to learn and how you

---

[23] Ibid. p. 354.

have brought forth your gifts. The Master asks, "What can I do to bring my soul qualities forth to help the community?" Though on some level all healthy people are in service to their community in the ways inherent to their stage, beginning at the start of Stage 5 and, more generally, ever since childhood (in a healthy culture).

At this point, it's natural to be less concerned about survival and more about "how can I be of service?" They also teach the Apprentices as well as help the adolescents and children.

This period marks the early movement toward the end of *striving* and more to *being*. What happens regarding our soul gifts happen more as acts of Grace and less about doing. There is more focus on the web of the world.

Stage 8: The Sage in the Mountain Cave—Late Elderhood (Surrender to Death)

Task: None, but what happens (without deliberation) is tending the universe.

This is the 45-degree point that ends at the most East point on the horizontal line. This stage, up to the final point, which is death, is about sharing spirit-centered wisdom and preparing for death. It has focus on Spirit, transcendence, non-attachment and cultivating dis-identification with ego.

This is also a time where striving has more fully transitioned to being and where human compassion shows up more deeply than ever. Though do understand, old age and this stage are not synonymous. Very few in our egocentric culture actually reach this stage.

This stage requires giving up all attachment to ego and material things. If you have not forgiven or let go of resentments by now, (or items of hoarding) this is the time to work on it. Ego transcendence is the focus, so the Ego can become fully rooted in Spirit. Earlier stages address Soul embodiment, meaning how do I bring Soul into my body to express through and into my life. This stage lets go of all that. Rather, it's about uniting with that most spiritual essence in preparation for death.

Today, new age schools of thought and Eastern religion both teach Ego transcendence. However, when that's taken on at too early in life, it often expresses a desire to leave the planet. In some schools, it's referred to as Spirit Polarized. It can result from unaddressed woundedness where the person does not really want to be here, fully present on this earth. Hence, that person finds difficulty manifesting anything of substance, let alone his or her own soul work. Spiritual matters are used as an addiction to cover the pain of being here rather than going fully into it to heal it. However, when actually at this phase of life, any work to transcend the ego is the correct focus.

Again, if you want to dive more deeply into this work please consult Dr. Plotkin's book(s) previously mentioned.

Why the Soulcentric Wheel before the 7 Keys

I introduced the Soulcentric Wheel to help you understand our culture's departure from the natural cycle of life on our planet and a generalized model for a way back. This departure has been a source for so much inner turmoil, emptiness, and discontent.

I have also included it because I believe it explains what we might optimally experience in each stage of life, what maturing really means and to understand the passages we move through when we have faced and transformed our woundedness and childhood deficiencies. It demonstrates what is natural and normal in a healthy culture and in so doing hopefully motivating you to let go of some of the less than fulfilling societal programing.

I also hope that the positive potential of coming to know your Soul more deeply and ultimately your Soul Gifts, will provide inspiration to do the work of the 7 Keys to prepare you for such a journey.

Chapter 3

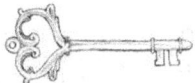

Key 1 Feeling Your Feelings— Demystifying Emotions

Key 1 relates to what's come to be known as emotional literacy. This means fully knowing what we feel, what our true desires are, and how to express them in safe, healthy ways. It's having access to our personal truth unhampered by others' views and opinions.

This is not talking about just surface-level wants and impulses that may be influenced by familial and societal expectations but to those coming from a deeper, more authentic level of knowing. It starts by becoming aware of and then honoring and valuing our emotions, intuitive hunches, bodily feelings, and subtle senses. Honoring these authentic feelings includes not judging them or the parts of ourselves that hold them.

Rather, achieving emotional literacy requires being willing to let yourself explore and feel (or at least acknowledge) buried hurts and encrusted emotions. This supports your current feelings and subtle intuitive senses to become fully available to you. When you pay attention and honor what they tell you—when you follow through on what's true for you—it opens the lines of communications within you. As a result, your internal guidance system becomes stronger regarding what you want to go toward and what you want to move away from.

Honoring Your Feelings

It's an upward spiraling process that continues to open over time. The more you listen and honor your feelings, the more clearly and surely you can hear them. The more you hear and then follow them, the more you're living in your truth. Personal coaches would say, "The closer you live to your values—what's most important to you—the happier and more at peace you are."

When not knowing (and thus not living in) one's truth, the further you are living from your values. That's when life feels off. Often you have no understanding of "why" and therefore no concept of "what" to do about it. Escaping into addictions might seem to be the only viable option.

If you say to yourself, "I never know what is the true Self of me speaking," likely these lines of communication have shut down. This is what happens after not listening for most of a lifetime. Hence, Key 1 is an important first step to opening these closed lines of communication. Sure, you may know when you are angry at someone or living in sadness or loneliness. But experiencing these feelings consistently indicates the tip of the iceberg and often results from being stuck in a maladapted part of oneself (a concept explained later). You may never know about the other emotions or vulnerabilities existing beneath!

Becoming aware of these first-level emotions isn't the same as fully living in one's truth. However, being open to these feelings—not judging them or the part of you that holds them—is a start in the right direction. Sometimes it takes working with a therapist or counselor to help unlock the closed door and release any backlog, to make the bridge between later life occurrences and earlier life experience. A professional can help you discover subconscious decisions, behavior patterns, and adaptations made as a result of those experiences and their associated emotions. However, if motivated, much can be done on your own with the information in the book.

Disconnection and Its Consequences

It is the connecting with, allowing space for, and having great empathy for all the pains and emotions of our "hurt child" parts that set in motion the healing and reconnecting process—as well as the road to recovery from addiction. As Patricia DeYoung states in her book on shame. "... shame can be seen as the disintegration of (our vulnerable) self, caused by faulty emotional connection with others ... a neurobiological state caused by profound interpersonal disconnection."[1]

DeYoung goes on to say:

> It's very difficult to change any addictive behavior through insight and force of will, for the addiction has become the fill-in for a deep desperate lack of something for which it can never substitute.
>
> Dr. Gabor Maté, a renowned addiction expert, maintains that this "something missing" is the experience of attunement—a specific quality of being-with required for the development of the brain's self-regulation circuits. "Attunement is literally, being 'in tune' with someone else's emotional states. It's not a question of parental love but of the parent's ability to be present emotionally in such a way that the infant or child feels understood, accepted, and mirrored."[2]
>
> Poorly attuned relationships leave a child with compromised abilities to regulate his own emotions and with a compromised sense of being a whole, vital and worthy self. Addictions "manage" emotions in ways that further undermine self.[3]
>
> We understand, however, that deep, pervasive shame (from that lack of connection) is the cause, not the result of the addiction, even though addiction increases the load of shame ... long-term disintegration of the (vulnerable) self becomes felt reality, along with the unremitting feelings of worthlessness and hopelessness ... the client will relapse to "fix" this intolerable situation.[4]

---

[1] Patricia A. DeYoung, *Understanding and Treating Chronic Shame: A Relational/Neurobiological Approach*, Routledge, 2015, pp. 64, 68.

[2] Dr. Gabor Maté, *In the Realm of the Hungary Ghosts: Close Encounters with Addiction*, Knopf, 2008, p. 238.

[3] Ibid. p. 247.

[4] Patricia A. DeYoung, *Understanding and Treating Chronic Shame: A Relational/Neurobiological Approach*, Routledge, 2015, p. 72.

It's quite a conundrum how disconnection and resultant addictive attempts to fix it has wreaked havoc on our otherwise miraculous modern lives. It's a sad state of affairs due to a lack of understanding and education. Typically, our culture doesn't teach parents how to make space for the emotions of their children, especially a number of years back. (Note: However, I do see it happening in some specialized schools and/or trainings such as Dr. Becky Bailey's Conscious Discipline.[5])

What does it mean to make space for emotions? Being willing to listen without judgment; empathizing with and thereby attuning to those emotions, whether a child's, another adult's or our own.

Key one is the first important step in healing our own core shame, not enough-ness, unworthiness, ongoing feelings of anger, resentment, anxiety or irritation, and feelings of aloneness or unlovability. It occurs by

- giving ourselves the gift of making space for our own emotions
- respecting and heeding messages within buried and current emotions
- giving conscious, safe expression to these emotions
- acknowledging our subtle senses

From here begins any recovery from addictive behaviors, or adverse feelings.

Not Feeling Safe or Supported

Are we constantly ignoring, denying, minimizing, or talking ourselves out of what we really feel? This furthers the disconnection within, being a lack of attunement with self, and causes us to lose the ability for trust—of ourselves, others and life. This begins when we are young, when we shut down emotionally to make a painful household bearable. Perhaps it wasn't safe to express what we felt. Or perhaps we didn't feel supported in expressing our emotions.

Maybe a stronger trauma occurred where a part of us checks out, freezes, and/or gives up. This shutdown can occur from intensely traumatic

---

[5] Becky A. Bailey, Ph.D., http://consciousdiscipline.com

experiences or long-term low-level ongoing pain. It could be something other than a disconnect felt from a parent's faulty ability to be present, connect, or attune. Perhaps at school, we may have felt forced to learn in a manner foreign to our natural learning style and made to feel stupid because of it. We might have dealt with other children's harsh behavior or simply faked the truth to maintain social acceptance.

Such adaptations of our behavior continue as we grow older. In the workplace, for example, we may compromise who we are to keep our jobs for perceived survival or continuing our material lifestyle. Alterations of our truths can expand into our relationships. We fear others' judgments or their reactions when we express what's true for us. With all of this, we become conditioned to closing the door on our true feelings.

And this continues in our daily lives. For example, if you feel angry or hurt due to a friend's or coworker's action or inaction, rather than tell the person what's really going on, you might tell yourself, it's no big deal. Perhaps something is constantly unfair or frustrates you. You might tell yourself to "live with it" for fear of upsetting the apple cart. Or you may tell yourself it's ridiculous to be upset about a particular occurrence. But what happens? You deny or diminish your true feelings when you do that. You may simply ignore your feelings. Or if you notice them, you might tell yourself all the reasons you shouldn't feel that way—and why you certainly shouldn't express them.

All this is called discounting your feelings—making them less than they are.

Alternatively, you may develop a pattern of spending much time in a default emotion such as anger. This covers other emotions—fear, sadness, hurt, grief—you aren't willing to acknowledge or feel. Or you might always be sad or depressed from being unaware of (thus unconsciously suppressing) anger or shame lurking beneath the surface.

What can you do? Every day, tell yourself its Ok to feel what you're feeling and that you want to know what the deeper layers of you are feeling. As the parts of you holding those feelings get that you really want to know, that you won't beat them up for those feelings, and will make a safe space for them, they start to reveal things to you.

Susan's Story

A woman named Susan came to me due to troubles in her relationship. Her boyfriend Mark consistently criticized her. He often spoke harshly to her and gave her little affection. Occasionally, he'd see other women, yet he expected her to keep house, make the meals, and bring in half the income.

Susan tolerated this for a long time because she was afraid Mark would leave her. Not surprisingly, she became increasingly depressed from denying her own feelings of frustration, hurt, and anger. When she could no longer ignore them, she came to me exhibiting many chronic physical conditions including great lethargy, headaches and back pain.

Susan presented a classic example of fear of abandonment, although in actuality, she had abandoned *herself* through years of denied and discounted feelings. In such circumstances, it's no wonder she didn't want to be left alone. She deeply believed no one would be there for her, not even herself, and that being alone would be far too scary.

Over time, Susan was able to nurture herself in multiple ways including honoring and expressing her feelings. As a result, she learned to take a stand on her own behalf. Susan grew to trust, love, and accept herself and, in doing that, had stopped abandoning herself. Her physical symptoms significantly improved or cleared up entirely.

In addition, she began to experience joy which had her not feel so threatened by the potential loss of her relationship. This brought a balance of power and, because of it, the relationship worked much better. She eventually left him to allow a more loving, honoring man into her life—as she had evolved to be herself.

Stop Discounting Feelings

Having strength and an inner relationship of trust develops from creating a safe, loving relationship within ourselves. Honoring and accepting your feelings is the essential first key in the process. However, to stop discounting your feelings, you must first become aware of when, where, and how you do it.

How many times have you looked back at a problematic circumstance and said, "I knew it; something told me not to do that," but you didn't pay attention to this inkling. How many times have you felt an emotion or reaction to someone's behavior but told yourself it wasn't right to feel that way. You rationalized your feeling by saying, "Those people meant well; they couldn't help it," or "That person has been so good to me, how can I be angry?" or "I'm a spiritual person; I should be bigger than this." Or the opposite, "I don't give a dam anyway; I hate that person." In that way, you're projecting blame rather than dropping into your vulnerable feelings underneath.

Typically, we turn to an endless repertoire of rationalizations to convince ourselves not to feel the way we do or justify an unkind emotion we're stuck in. Yes, at times, we know what we're feeling. However, quite often we have no conscious awareness of what we're feeling under the more habitual anger or sadness.

Not knowing what's going on under the surface is where addictions come in. When engaged in the addiction, we know we feel better in relation to the underlying angst. Whether it's substance abuse or a pattern of behavior, (as in not speaking your truth, caretaking others) those addictions take over as an ongoing aspect of life. However, the price for that short-term feel-good is much stronger negative feelings and circumstances in the long run. The addiction or pattern of distraction plays out as the ultimate distraction from deep emotional pain or unacceptable feelings.

Somatic Therapy Work

Somatic work is a recognized therapy modality for working with buried emotional issues. Though it has been around for more than four decades, it's now gaining credibility as one of the leading ways to work with developmental and shock trauma along with the withheld emotions and their associated life-constricting beliefs. It is very possible to work it with ourselves. I have done much healing work on my own using somatic work.

In its most simplistic description, somatic work involves putting our focus of attention into the physical sensations in our body. If asked what we sense in our bodies under normal circumstances, we might say, "Well, I don't feel anything." But if something is touching us emotionally and we sit still—no activities or addictive behaviors—and focus on the body, "scanning" it mentally, with particular attention on our torso, back, belly, mid abdomen, chest, neck, and shoulders, we can notice very subtle or even strong physical sensations. If they are to the point of ongoing pain then you can assume that some part of you is screaming for and in need of attention. When we ask on a metaphoric level, "What is this like?" we can receive a lot of clues about what's under the surface.

"Being With" Your Emotions

Say you put your focus on an area that shows up as a funny sensation in your belly. As you keep your attention there, the sensation becomes more specific. Ask yourself, for a metaphoric image or feeling sense on a material level of what this vague sensation is like. For example, maybe it's like a big ball of ropes knotted up or a fire burning inside. Perhaps an odd sensation near your heart feels like a big black void or a knife going from back to front. Or maybe you sense something around your throat that's squeezing it from the outside in. Or it seems something is stuck in there like a flat metal sheet cutting across, trying to separate your head from your body. The possibilities are endless. Allowing for an image or more specific sense is a way to allow the part holding the emotion to communicate. It begins to give you more connection with whatever part of you is associated with this feeling.

Sitting still and "being with" these feelings tells the part of you holding them that you're open to knowing what he or she is feeling and that you matter. Taking the time to focus attention and attune to yourself, gives this message of valuing, that you are important, lovable and good. Others who can reflect this back to you will come later. It starts with the Self of you to other hidden, shut down or unloved parts of you. Then these deeper parts of you will reveal more—more images, sensations, a memory, or even another emotion. In one sitting, you can keep "being with" these different feelings, layer by layer. Don't let any single emotion overtake you. Rather, witness each with openness and curiosity.

Perhaps you can't feel anything. If so, you can figure that the part is feeling numb. (Yes, numb is a feeling, so stay with it.) Notice if you try to run away from that with busy thoughts. If that happens, bring your attention back to the physical area and give your empathy to the part that feels numb. Tell it, "I am willing to have you show me more."

Eventually in this sitting or later, more will be revealed. But your simple willingness to "be with" the numbness sends a powerful message to your inner parts about your openness to its feelings. And these parts of yourself may have never felt that before, from you or anyone.

After a time of "being with" each layer of emotion, ask, "And what is under that?" It is common to experience a powerful and beautiful event when this "being with" pops through to a deep place of peace, joy, and love residing under it all. When that happens you're fully connecting with your Soul Self. You can let yourself experience the wonder of this for as long as you want. Then from this energy of true compassion and acceptance, you can return to each incident that showed up in this inquiry and bring forth a healing. That might call for saying things (using your imagination) that needed to be said to certain people or asking for mutual forgiveness. (You'll read more about this in the Full Dialog Process of Chapter 13.)

If a full pop-through experience does not occur it is fine. Just "being with" your feelings in your body still opens the door to what lies dormant beneath the surface. All this "being with" is in service of opening to the truth of who you are and what you feel. Ultimately, this, along with other tools and practices of the 7 Keys will move you toward a life that feels right for you. Feeling good by living true to your values of what is important or feels right is what helps addictions or repeating negative circumstances become a part of your past.

Your willingness to "be with" your feelings is the first step to creating a true "connection" to your inner self. However, it comes with first letting yourself feel the pain inside for a while. If that pain is too much to deal with alone, work with professionals who can support you in this. They should be versed in a form of somatic work, such as Hakomi, Somatic Experiencing, Body Psychotherapy, NeuroAffective Relational Model (NARM), Expressive

Arts Therapies, or Internal Family Systems (IFS) therapy. Typically, these therapies go deeper than what's considered normal talk therapy. (As part of the IFS Dialog Process, Chapter 13 goes into more detail about somatic work before engaging in the dialog.) When researching a therapist, ask if they are trauma or shame informed or integrate any of the somatic therapies. At the end of this book you will find a resource list of different modalities to consider. Most have web sites with lists of their trained practitioners.

Steps to Turning Patterns of Pain Around

Here's a summary of the steps required:

1) Access your willingness to do what it takes to bring about the healing/transformation of your deepest emotions.
2) Develop your witness or (a more popular term is) *mindfulness*, to be conscious of when certain emotions or patterns of behavior are running. Identify what triggers them.
3) Stop and "be with" those feelings without judging them or the parts that carry them. You'll be able to feel them *in your body*, what we call somatic work.
4) Practice expressing your emotions in healthy ways. (Along with expressing verbally to others in non-violent ways, read Chapter 9 of my book *Express Yourself* for many other options for how to safely release the energy on and express your emotions.[6])
5) Befriend those parts of you that hold those feelings as well as those parts that protect you from the pain they carry. (Befriending means learning more about those parts, appreciating each part for what it experienced or for the job it was attempting to do via a pattern of behavior.) From its perspective, the part believed it was being helpful. Know that all parts have valuable aspects to them, even if it seems they only caused you problems.

---

[6] Joy Lynn Freeman, *Express Yourself: Discover you Inner Truth, Creative Self and the Courage to Let It Out*. Soundstar Productions, 1999, p. 6–77.

6) Retrieve a part if it's frozen in space and time. (In neurobiological terms, it means opening new brain pathways.)
7) Release the burdens the parts carry—their past traumatic experience; emotions such as deep-seated guilt, shame, anger or grief; decisions or unconscious contracts made; or firmly held negative beliefs.
8) Integrate the best of those parts by reminding them and focusing on their useful and positive qualities, resources and attributes. This is a key step to transform them from undermining to being supportive. (More details of this specific process will be brought forth in the Full Dialog Process in Chapter 13.)

The 7 Keys, with their tools, practices, and valuable information play into these steps of turning patterns of pain around and can transform the roots of addiction. They also contain the elements of a positive life-long path.

What We Resist Persists

As stated earlier, we often avoid feelings that we judge to be less desirable or socially unacceptable, including anger, hurt, sadness, or fear. Unfortunately, this tactic doesn't work because what we resist, persists—that is, what we try to block from our experience gets intensified.

For example, a man named Richard was often plagued by jealousy. He regularly fantasized that his girlfriend would leave him for another man. Each day, he'd wake with feelings of anxiety related to these fears. Although he realized they were irrational, the more he despised such feelings and tried to ignore them, the more intense they became. He used avoidance tactics such as eating a lot, keeping super busy, or demanding his girlfriend ease his fears with constant physical closeness. He ended up pushing her away since she withdrew from this clutching, thereby creating the very situation he feared.

The more we focus on that which we fear, the more we manifest it. Expressed another way, we say "where the thought goes, energy flows." Then we empower with negative emotion what we fear or frequently complain about, thus becoming a self-fulfilling prophecy.

The other side of the equation is denial or an unwillingness to "be with" an emotion. My mother frequently said, "Just rise above it." In essence, she was telling me to ignore any uncomfortable feelings. However, this philosophy didn't work well for her. She died an early death from the effects of her addictions—due to her attempt to ignore and rise above it all. And though she was wise enough to see a psychiatrist, he unfortunately told her she was "coping" the best of anyone he'd ever met. He suggested that working with her deepest feelings would be like opening Pandora's box, so he recommended against it! Looking back, it was *not* opening that box and working with its contents that made her unable to move beyond her addictions. She ultimately died at a relatively young age.

Of course, I imagine he said that because he had no real tools for how to work with what would be found. Perhaps he felt the contents of the box would scare him. But today, therapists have powerful tools and techniques for working with the emotional effect of trauma or anything else that might arise.

Many of us feel impassioned to help people wake up to their fullest, most expressive and joyful selves. We have taken it upon ourselves to learn how to work with these powerful processes—not only for others but for moving beyond limitations in our own lives. Impassioned healers range from medically trained therapists (psychiatrists) to psychologists and psychotherapists, to peer counselors, to unlicensed healers who have searched much of their lives for these healing tools.

This book emphasizes what you can do *for* yourself and even *by* yourself. However, when dealing with unconscious, deep-seated feelings and beliefs (some call these Burdens), as I have stated, it's often best to work with professionals trained in this area. It's like having someone hold your hand as you go down the stairs to the deeper, darker places you can't reach on your own. Because you're breaking old habit patterns of emotion, thought and behavior, having an experienced professional to check in with and support you can be wise. This is true especially if you're engaging in destructive addictive behaviors or had a childhood that you can say felt strongly traumatic.

The Cost of Holding Back

There can be other consequences of denying uncomfortable feelings. When we hold back feelings that we label (even subconsciously) as undesirable, we also hold back the full expression of feelings we consider desirable. We can compare our entire range of feelings to a big pot of soup—they're all in there. While we're holding down anger, we can't express true joy—and that includes any anger we're not fully aware of. Although we can pretend to be having a good time, we cannot express a pure state of happiness without first lifting the lid on the other feelings as well. In fact, we waste vital energy keeping a lid on these painful or uncomfortable feelings. This most often results in depression, fatigue, and numerous health problems. Depression is a repressed emotion, a blockage in energy flow. As therapists say, "It's not what you are depressed about; it is what are you depressing."

Conversely, when we let ourselves feel our feelings and emotions, we come to a place of compassion and acceptance for the parts of ourselves that have held them. This allows the blocked energy to move, and ultimately contributes to feelings of vitality and aliveness. This also helps build a relationship of trust between our Self and our inner parts. So again, this important first Key of allowing and accepting all feelings, including the painful or uncomfortable ones that we may have judged as unacceptable, opens the door to this trust.

Communicating with Our Inner Being

Our inner being communicates to us in two ways: (1) through subtle feelings and senses including intuition and (2) through the physical senses of the body, which as described in somatic work, is part of the process of feeling emotions. Body messages can be subtle and gentle or strong and painful, depending on our ability to listen. After years of paying little attention, lines of communication diminish. Our inner being gives up and shuts down. We might experience this as depression and/or fatigue. Or it might be forced to scream at us so we *will* pay attention, usually through strong body messages of pain, illness, accidents, or a serious physical or emotional breakdown.

For example, when the inner being wants to say, "I want a break; I want to play; I want to rest," we can refuse to listen. However, if the desire is strong enough, the inner being may cause us to get sick or have an accident, forcing us to stop pushing ourselves. Or if we feel sick to our stomachs about how someone is treating us, we may experience a stomach ache or intestinal condition such as Crohn's Disease or irritable bowl.

Commonly, people re-experience early childhood pain via a toxic relationship. When they don't seek help or do the work to discover and heal the triggering aspects as well as the inability to leave the relationship, this might throw them into substance addictions.

> As we become adept at listening to and honoring our inner messages, our inner being can communicate in gentler, subtler ways.

In addition, when emotions are not allowed expression at the time they're experienced, they become locked in the body—that is, stored in the cellular memory of various organs and tissues. Not only is the energy of such emotion stored energetically, but a chemical reaction occurs in the body. Just as endorphins are released with positive feelings, other potentially debilitating hormones are released with negative emotions. When these hormones accumulate, they can become toxic.

Many of these are hormones that suppress our immune function, which affects our ability to fight illness.

Emotion is Energy in Motion

Speaking about emotions also speaks about energy. The word "emotion" can be understood as "e-motion"—energy in motion. The emotional body is the more energetic component of us compared with the physical body. When the emotional body is allowed to express freely without judgment, it's vibrating fully. Conversely, the vibration slows down when we can't be who we are or can't express ourselves. This occurs, for example, when we discount our feelings, engage in self-pity, judgment, guilt, blame, or generally resist any emotion. Over a long enough period, we feel sluggish, depressed, and dispassionate.

Emotions that fully vibrate are referred to as wave energy. Allowing it to flow fully means letting ourselves experience an emotion without resistance. It moves through us like a wave. When we practice allowing emotions to move through us rather than denying them, they naturally dissipate in a shorter time than they would otherwise. We can help that wave movement with body-centered practices that involve moving, breathing, or sounding. (This is described in Chapter 9 "Moving Emotional Energy" in *Express Yourself*.[7])

I like the distinction Dr. William Glasser, author of *Control Theory*,[8] makes between what he refers to as "pure feelings" and "long-term feeling behaviors." Pure feelings occur in a relatively brief period when an experience triggers an immediate response or when emotional healing work allows buried feelings to surface. When the feelings have been truly felt without resistance or judgment, they naturally dissipate. We see it in children who move from tears to laughter in minutes when there's no adult constriction around those tears.

However, when emotions emerge, the more common reaction is to contract within ourselves and resist them. We also tend to tell ourselves stories that have us wallowing in self-pity. Or we make the other person wrong, or we think like a victim about how people did us wrong. These escalate or prolong the feelings.

When we do this, we delay their natural flow and exhibit what Dr. Glasser calls "long-term feeling behaviors" in which you choose to continue experiencing the feeling. Because the initial feeling just happened, we believe its continuation is also just happening and that we have no choice in the matter. Not so. It's resisting the situation and the feelings about it that perpetuates it, and can lead to the long-term feeling behavior of various addictions.

Flow Like a Wave

The trick is to allow the existence of the emotion—as mentioned earlier, to "be with" the feeling without judgment about it or a lot of story about having

---

[7] Joy Lynn Freeman, *Express Yourself: Discover you Inner Truth, Creative Self and the Courage to Let It Out.* Soundstar Productions, 1999.

[8] William Glasser, *Control Theory: A New Explanation of How We Control Our Lives*, Harper & Row, 1985.

been wronged or what you fear is going to happen to you. Keep breathing with deeper fuller breaths. Every time the story comes to mind, rope in those thoughts and examine where the feeling sensation exists in your body. Tell yourself, "It's okay to feel this feeling" or "I'm safe to feel this feeling" while you're breathing deeply. You can say a prayer and ask for help. Allow it to pass rather than tighten up and resist it. Another practice called Emotional Freedom Technique—EFT or Tapping, includes statements of self-forgiveness as you tap certain acupuncture points while feeling the uncomfortable emotion.[9]

Perhaps you're receiving some benefit from being in this emotional state. Maybe you're getting attention, being taken care of, or not having to take responsibility. For these reasons, the emotion continues, leaving you unhappy and ineffective. Learn to let your feelings flow through you like a wave until they come to a natural completion, then consciously and constructively release the energy. This is a powerful practice you can incorporate into your life every day.

Yin vs. Yang Energy

Emotions are one of the nonlinear, less-structured aspects of us associated with the right brain or feminine aspect of being—not feminine in terms of gender but in terms of yin and yang principles, which both genders possess (as discussed in Chapter 1). Magnetic yin energy "comes in" while radiant yang energy "goes out."

In addition, yin goes *down* toward the earth. Being fully present in our bodies and feeling fully present on this earth through emotions is a yin quality. Yang goes *up* and is more centered on the mind and/or spirit.

We need both yin and yang, it only becomes a problem when we live in one side to the exclusion of the other. Response to different forms of trauma—be it intense traumatic events or the Complex Trauma aka Developmental Trauma of abandonment, neglect, lack of tangible connection, age inappropriate responsibility, and more—often has one living mostly on the

---

[9] https://www.thetappingsolution.com/what-is-eft-tapping

extreme yang side. Some call it "living in your head," which is living in a mental state and avoiding habitation of one's body and the lack of emotions that goes with that. It often shows up as a state of constant busyness or super competency—what I call do-aholism.

When people have engaged in healing trauma and thus have re-inhabited their bodies in a way that brings them down to earth, and have reintegrated aspects of themselves that have shut down, then their bodies begin to vibrate more fully. Said another way, when the emotions have had the right to exist and express in a space of non-judgment and are held with compassion by your inner Self (perhaps with the support of another caring human being), the life force wakes up and increases. That's why exhausted or depressed people regain their energy after doing the work. I know this from personal experience. Today, I have a tremendous amount of energy and health because of doing this kind of work.

Vibrational Frequency
When your emotional body is fully vibrating, your yin energy is available to you. Yin energy is magnetic, which gives it the ability to magnetize people, places, and things. In other words, as you allow emotional aspects to be fully expressed in healthy ways without judgment, the vibrational frequency accelerates. You are then better able to be sensitive to, and thus distinguish what is right and true for you, as well as better able to attract that to you—for example, work that feels right to you or positive relationships that support you. In a similar way, when situations or people *not* right for you show up, this greater sensitivity helps you in avoiding those.

Sometimes the response to trauma can be the opposite of the far extreme yang "in-the-head" response just discussed. Rather, they can be toward the far extreme yin side. That shows up as being in an emotional state often with an inability to focus, function, or accomplish tasks. It can even have you in constant overwhelm or chaos.

Whether it plays out more yin or yang, you can get stuck in one emotion or another; usually anger—outgoing yang, or sadness—inward yin. That blocks what wants to be felt and expressed waiting beneath. When one is often angry, it is usually sadness, grief, or a sense of helplessness that isn't being accessed. And if someone gets stuck in sadness, it is often anger that lies beneath waiting to be found. Under both of them will frequently be the deeper core shame related to early lack of connection or attunement and with it the sense of unworthiness, unlovability and not enough-ness.

To clarify, if we spend much of our time in one emotion, it doesn't mean we have the clear ability to feel our feelings. Rather, it means we're stuck in one emotion; we're resisting other feelings that lay beneath, that want to be known, felt, and accepted. Living in one of these emotional extremes creates a flood of that emotion, which is detrimental to the system. It certainly doesn't support the positive sensitivity of a fully vibrating emotional body.

It's likely that what we call into our lives from the vibration of one main emotion will match that emotion in vibrational frequency. Hence, you might ask, "Why do I always experience these challenging kinds of relationships or situations no matter what I do or how much I want them to change?" But when we do the work to find, feel, and transform what is buried in the unconscious and lying await beneath the surface, those circumstances will change along with it.

Taking training in anger management can be good. However, when a deep trigger occurs, no amount of management can stop a highly charged reaction. Just as the core sources of addiction require a deeper level of healing, so do these intensely emotional responses to others and life circumstances.

Highly charged emotions of anger or sadness, along with depression, go hand and hand with addictions. Whether they're substances or detrimental patterns of behavior, they require a deeper level of transformation not typically found in normal recovery programs or even some modes of therapy within recovery centers. But even when effective therapy is accessed, the additional elements and practices associated with the 7 Keys, when truly integrated into one's life, has the capacity to bring forth a more permanent state of recovery.

Emotions Lock Beliefs in Place

Emotions affect our belief systems. As long as we resist our feelings, we are trapped by the beliefs *and* behaviors formed as a result of these. *It is the emotional experience that locks our beliefs in place.*

For example, our beliefs about life, people in general, men, women, or money are fixed by the emotions we felt when we repeatedly saw or experienced something happen. That includes when we heard phrases said or beliefs implied repeatedly, or when traumatic events occurred. As noted, we call these Burdens. We make mental or subconscious decisions (some call this "contracts") because of these emotional experiences that can affect our entire lives. We can attempt to transform these beliefs through mental exercises, but if the emotional core remains untapped, we'll be plagued by the effects of these Burdens.

One can also be affected by generational or cultural burdens such as occurs in all forms of persecution. We call these Legacy Burdens. Current research demonstrates these burdens are transferred cellularly through the DNA. They're also passed through the words, actions, and attitudes of parents and one's dominate culture. Often, they take three generations for their strength to "mellow out."

What can you do? You may have already done work to change a situation in your life but still find yourself repeating the same pattern. Thus, working to change the beliefs alone—through affirmations, hypnosis, or other mind-oriented techniques—often prove to be only partially effective. Although such techniques may change beliefs that have not been locked in by strong emotions, altering the beliefs that developed when emotions were involved, called core beliefs, requires getting to the root, or core emotion associated with them. Examples of core beliefs are "I'm not good enough," "I'm not worthy," "I'm not lovable," "I do not deserve to be here," "I do not want to be here," "I am bad," "I'm defective," "I have to prove myself to be of value," or "I do not deserve to receive abundance or anything good."

Yes, it takes more than being aware of this intellectually. It requires *feeling* it on an emotional level, even if just briefly, at the same time something occurs to release or transform it. Again, the assistance of professionals might be critical, and somatic work can help transform beliefs that are rooted in your being through an emotional experience.

"Nice Guy" Story

In my practice, I worked with a man who had a pattern of behavior I'd call "nice guy." He had a habit of relationships with controlling women. Any type of controlling behavior would greatly upset him, as he said, "It really pushes my buttons." In talking about his mother with me, he said how wonderfully generous she'd been with her time and energy. But when I asked him to elaborate, it became apparent she was overbearing and controlling in her care of him. While growing up, he had difficulty learning from his own mistakes; she was always correcting him and making sure that he did things "right." Not only did he harbor anger and resentment about this at a level he was completely unaware of, but it created a core belief about being incapable—which explains his attraction to capable and yet seemingly controlling women.

Slowly, he began to access the deep anger he felt regarding his mother's overbearing behavior. This was difficult because he felt guilty when he experienced anything other than loving and grateful toward the woman who had "sacrificed" so much for him. He was convinced he couldn't possibly be harboring feelings of anger toward his mother.

However, as he surrendered to his emotional body's feelings rather than his logical mind, he tapped a volcano of emotion. The degree to which he ultimately released his anger paralleled the intensity with which he'd resisted his feelings.

After this releasing, it became evident he'd tapped into an empowered part of himself. His voice lowered from its high-pitched, disembodied tonal quality. He carried this empowerment into his life and later was able to firmly but gently speak his truth to his girlfriend. He set boundaries for himself, including with his mother, and functioned in a more passionate and powerful way than ever before.

Unfortunately, you can be totally unconscious of deep emotions from your past and their associated limiting beliefs. Your mental defense systems hide them. Sometimes these are stored as a result of "implicit" memory from pre verbal times. Rather than the things you had the capacity to remember with "explicit" memory. For example, you may think your relationship with a parent is fine, yet simultaneously a deeper part of you feels angry or resentful. Although you may be able to say, "They just are who they are, they don't upset me anymore," the emotional withholds and scars of the past remain if you don't seek them out and work with them.

Even when their young lives seemed relatively normal, most people raised in this modern culture have repressed emotional experiences. Notice the nature of your current daily life. If you're not passionately engaged in your work, fulfilled and satisfied in your relationships, or experiencing a general sense of peace, contentment, and joy, chances are you have stored material to work with.

By allowing yourself to feel, know, and accept all aspects of your being, these emotions and the beliefs associated with them will begin to surface. But don't force them. Instead, completely surrender to them and accept what you feel day to day. As a result, your inner being will gradually feel safe enough to reveal what suppressed beliefs and emotions reside inside.

Note: To do the work on your own, you'll find The Parts work sections helpful, you can do the Medicine Tasks at the end of each Chapter or you can go through the full Dialog Process in Chapter 13. However, nothing can replace the safety and specificity of working with someone trained to assist you in this process.

The Power in Parts Work

We call working with and understanding the motivations, feelings, and beliefs of different aspects of our inner life Parts Work.

The most potent version of Parts Work that integrates the psycho-emotional and somatic with the non-denominational spiritual—in 12 Steps, "the God of your understanding" is Internal Family Systems (IFS). This fast-growing modality of transformation has proven to be comprehensive and effective when any form of trauma has occurred. It serves to help heal traumatic pain from our growing-up years, whether caused through direct incidents, abandonment, disconnection, or misappropriated roles. The different forms of trauma, Developmental or Shock Trauma, can greatly affect a child's life into adulthood until the work is done to bring it to the surface and transform it.

IFS, explained in more detail in Chapter 4, works with the dynamic that exists between different parts within us. Like our outer family, we think of it as the family of characters within us. Each character has different motivations, behaviors, beliefs, attitudes, and directives. We often feel pulled in different directions, depending on which part is running the show at a particular time. These parts are often at odds with each other. Many people experience hope, relief, compassion for oneself, and an understanding of their addictions or behaviors simply by learning about how the parts work together and against each other.

The ultimate goal of the work, though, is to be led by Self—the part that's directly connected to our higher self—rather than our various parts. This can bring forth the unified, centered, creative, compassionate, healthy, and joyful you. This is the truth of who you are under it all.

How the Parts Model Works

How many times have you been faced with a life choice but couldn't take action because one part of you felt moved to do one thing while a feeling (usually a sense of guilt or form of "should or should not") demanded another way and left you unable to move in any direction? You may have been saying, "One part of me wants this, but another part says something else." This sense of conflicting parts, voices, or energies within us can keep us locked up and blocked from creating a life that matches the truth of who we are. Sometimes four or more different voices or energetics operate at the same time, adding confusion.

Most people have heard the term "the still small voice." The voice of the Soul Self (aka the Self) is indeed a gentle voice. It will not push its way to the surface over the big, loud voices of shoulds, guilts, and other critical styles of the protective or defensive parts within. Over time and with practice, your Soul Self can become the leader. The other parts will begin to trust its wisdom and ability to take care of them in a balanced way rather than the extreme ways and roles of the parts.

The Soul Self comes naturally from a place of compassion, acceptance, patience, curiosity, and clarity along with other positive qualities. When the other parts learn to trust and surrender to its leadership, life takes on greater balance, peace, health, and accuracy relative to who you really are. (You'll learn the specifics on these parts, their types, and relationships to each other in Chapter 4.)

Re-establishing Trust with Self

To develop a relationship of trust with our true Self, one of the first steps is applying Key 1 in our lives to find, feel and express our truths. When we come to trust our inner Self fully, all the other parts of ourselves willingly integrate and support our truths with the aim of creating a healthy and authentic life. Developing this trust within us—that is, where all parts of ourselves let go of their overbearing control and come to trust Self—is a step-by-step process. Just as it takes a lot of love for an abused child or a beaten dog to trust someone without flinching, so it is with our inner being. It's possible we've spent years telling our selves what we should or shouldn't feel or do and experiencing this battle between the parts points of view. Often, we put everyone else ahead of us, and discounted or denied different emotions. So understandably, re-establishing a relationship of trust with Self can take time, focus, and work. All the other Keys support this process of gaining trust as well.

Establishing increased levels of trust begins with opening the lines of communication between our true Self and other parts of our selves. As this inner trust develops, simultaneously so does our trust in what I call the Benevolent Forces of the Universe (or in 12-Step language, "the God of our understanding").

The Inner Child and Other Names for It

We hear talk about the inner child—that aspect of our inner being that has desires, feelings, and emotions, and often is completely vulnerable. Not all aspects of the inner being are of the child. Some, for example, are protective or controlling parts. However, the inner child is directly related to the emotional body and often holds the frozen energy of past traumatic incidents or ongoing conditions. We can cite different names for this aspect of our inner being: the *wounded or unhappy child*, the *vulnerable* one, or the *exile* as it's called in IFS. (It's named exile because it is the part that's been exiled and walled off by other parts that don't want it exposed.)

It has also been called the *adaptive* child because he or she has adapted to circumstances in a variety of ways. That might include taking on specific personalities and ways of being, unsupportive beliefs, making certain decisions about life and others, or just checking out and shutting down. In the shamanic or indigenous viewpoint, this checking out—freezing in space and time—is called soul loss. The Parts Work is effectively a western version of Soul Retrieval—bringing that lost aspect of soul (the part) back to life.

Defensive devices of the protective parts of a child helped him or her survive unpleasant or very difficult situations. But these no longer serve the adult and in fact cause other limitations or problems in current life. However, it is possible as an adult to transform and give new roles to these protective parts and to have inner child aspects transformed from a wounded child into a nurtured child.

The health and happiness of the inner child/vulnerable parts determines their capacity for playfulness, spontaneity, and creativity with a general feeling of aliveness, health, and joy. In addition, our inner child directly links to our intuition. Thus, as we open the channels to a happier, nurtured inner child, we simultaneously open the way to *our* greatest vitality, joy, and creative self. This can simultaneously open us to our spiritual Self.

Medicine Tasks as Homework

I call doing the 7 Keys homework "Medicine Tasks." This comes from my orientation toward indigenous cultures where elders give Medicine Tasks to older adolescents at the age their soul initiation process begins. These tasks are designed to help the youth grow out of their ego-centric ways as a natural phase of separating from their families and moving out into the world. However, as they move beyond adolescence and into adulthood, it's necessary to be guided by their soul rather than their ego. In a natural culture, this transition is usually ushered in by an elder. Here and now this work supports you in accessing your own inner elder. After doing this work, a healthy ego needed for fully functioning on this planet is regained. A healthy ego is one that has grown to be able to trust and can surrender to the leadership of Self/Spirit.

Access Willingness First

When you work with Medicine Tasks, you want to first access your willingness to embark on this journey and put forth the effort needed to do the work. If you are still deeply engrossed in "using" (especially if using substances), you would receive support in going through abstinence and/or detoxing first. This could involve going to a detox or rehab center or at least joining a group to help you quit. The support of the others in the group combined with the spiritual component is necessary, especially in the beginning when it takes a lot of effort to abstain. Think of it as taking a wheel that's rolling downhill in one direction. How do you get it to stop *first* before you can do the work to get it spinning in the other direction? It might seem like a lot of energy is required, but once the wheel gets going in the new direction, the amount of effort levels out and the work garners its own momentum.

With a group, whether a 12-Step group, workshops or future 7 Keys groups, you have the Soul Selves of others helping to keep your own Self present. The part of you that's attached to the addiction or detrimental behavior as a coping strategy is usually in charge. It could even be a maladaptive part is "blended" with you, which means the addiction, beliefs, attitudes or actions have overtaken you, completely covering the presence of the Self. While in this state, it's not possible to be aware of the wisdom, peace, and centeredness of the Self.

Being in a group that includes others who have moved beyond this fully blended state and are becoming more Self led, can support you. It is time to access more of your own Self. Your Self gains from the support of the others in the room to expand its presence in your life. Today, with a website called The Rooms, you can find and access a group that works for you online. Some of these Rooms groups are quite progressive, where they don't even look like normal 12-Step programs because they also relate to relationship issues and subjects beyond chemical dependencies.

Once you have accessed your deep openness and willingness to do whatever it takes, you'll be ready for some more active steps, and the questions that follow will help. You may have already done important initial steps in a 12-Step recovery program—an excellent place to start. Or perhaps you have read other books or taken some growth oriented workshops. Within the 7 Keys are related steps as well as many additional tools, practices, and processes that flush out a deeper core of causes for addictive or other negative behaviors or experiences in your life.

Ultimately, once you're past the initial stages of recovery, the 7 Keys plus the Parts Work will help you experience less interference from your adaptive parts as well as an expanded presence of your Soul-Centered Self (explained in Chapter 4).

If you aren't inclined to join a 12-Step program or workshop, this work can exist on its own. However, in the beginning, you may want the support of a therapist well versed in the work of recovery and/or IFS.

☼ Medicine Tasks ☼

1) Access your willingness to engage in this journey.
On paper, answer the following questions:

- Am I willing to feel what wants to be felt, see what wants to be seen, or know what my Soul Self or any other parts of me wants me to know to live the life that is my authentic life to live—the life that fits who I truly am?

- Am I willing to do whatever it takes, even if it means being uncomfortable for a while, dwelling in an unknown space or feel emotions I've been unaware of or not felt for some time?
- Am I willing to take time and put forth energy to build a loving, healthy relationship with parts of myself and with my Self?

I realize that you might not be able to access your full willingness. Remember, people are generally more motivated by *moving away from pain* than they are *moving toward pleasure*. Your protector parts—both those that manage you in ways accepted by the world but most often to an extreme—that no longer serves you will tell you why you should NOT be willing. If that happens, let your mind focus on *what you would have to continue to live with* if you didn't do the work necessary to change. This will help give you extra strength and motivation to override your protector's resistances. Exercise 2 is not meant to depress you; rather, it's essential to access your *true willingness* before the work begins. To that end, you want to understand the actual price of not doing the work (or doing it with half a heart).

2) *Find and maintain your motivation regarding your willingness to do the work.*

To help you stand up to the parts of you that might get in your way, answer the following questions:

- If I do not find the willingness to do what it takes to make the internal shifts necessary to bring about real-life change, what will continue to happen? What life circumstances will continue to exist?
- If they continue for another year, what will my life look like? What will I miss out on?
- If they continue for the next 5, 10, or 20 years, what will be other repercussions?
- If I have children, how will not shifting affect them or other people close to me?

3) *Free write your answer to these questions:*

- Do I allow myself the space and time to feel what I might happen to be feeling in the course of a day?
- Do I honor what those feelings are trying to tell me?
- Is there an emotion I'm carrying from the past that my busyness, co-dependence, or other addictions keep me from feeling?
- What did I get as a child that I should not have (e.g., abuse, hearing father abuse mother or vice versa, too much responsibility at a young age, denigration and criticism, neglect, physical abuse, etc.)?
- What did I not get that I should have gotten? (e.g., attunement as an infant—calm, smiling, with loving eye connection, nurturance, support for who I am, safety, play time, creative freedom and expression, kindness, healthy parenting, loving connection with family, etc.)
- If I have not yet explored my past, am I willing to face my buried feelings and perhaps find assistance in doing so?

After thinking about these questions:

4) *Take action that will better connect me to my feelings, open lines of communication with my inner aspects, and/or enhance my relationship of trust with Self.*

- Do free writing in the morning before starting your day or at night before bed. This means just start writing about anything that transpired that day or is going on in your life. No censoring, even if some part of you wants to curse or make judgements—be the compassionate all accepting observer to what other parts of you may want to be saying. Ask questions of whomever seems to show up in the writing, to have the expressing part go deeper. Though it might all start out very light—just write anything that comes through. You will often be surprised of what wants to be said.

- Make more space and time for sitting quietly or walking in nature where you give feelings the space to arise and be felt, even if you're unclear what they mean.
- Do the somatic process described in this chapter and in more depth as described in the dialog process in Chapter 13.
- Talk to a trusted friend about feelings that are trying to come through. Work with a therapist to begin flushing them out.

If you're not ready to choose or commit to an action step, don't be discouraged. As you read on you will learn about more steps that you *will* want to take. Work at your own pace. You can put your toe in the water or take an all-out plunge.

Whatever you are ready for, I welcome you down this path.

Chapter 4

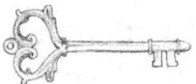

Internal Family Systems (IFS)—Greater Understanding of the Dynamics Within

Key 1 introduced the psycho-emotional-spiritual modality called Internal Family Systems, or IFS, developed by Dr. Richard Schwartz. To fully understand Keys 1 to 3, it's important to further explain this work. Having grown and enhanced over three decades, it is now considered an evidence-based therapeutic modality. This means it has proven itself as a viable and successful treatment modality for trauma, depression, addictions and much more.

NREPP is the National Registry for Evidence-based Programs and Practices, a national repository that is maintained by the U.S. government's Substance Abuse and Mental Health Services Administration (SAMHSA). Interventions listed in NREPP, now including IFS, have been subject to independent, rigorous scrutiny and are deemed to show significant impact on individual outcomes relating to mental health.[1]

---

[1] https://selfleadership.org

Understanding what goes on within us often brings a sense of peace as well as a good start for the transformation process. In addition, when the left brain is engaged (what helps us understand things from a linear and logical fashion—the why and how), we're willing to "let go" into the less-than-logical intuitive feelings and experiences necessary for true transformation.

How to Work with IFS and the 7 Keys

In Chapter 13, you will find a full IFS Dialog Process with explanations and exercises you can do yourself. If you find it challenging to work the process on your own, have a friend talk you through it or find a counselor or therapist who works with this deeply transformational modality. Still, you can do a lot on your own with the 7 Keys and the exercises in this book. Whether working alone or with a counselor, the intention is to ultimately teach you to do the work yourself. This helps you take on Self Leadership and run your own show. I also refer to the Self as the Soul-Centered Self or Soul Self. All of these terms represent this essential part of ourselves.

For me, the Soul is our earthly connection to Spirit or the God of our understanding—a higher energy moving through us as humans on this earth. We can also call this higher energy the Benevolent Forces of the Universe because of its positive unifying force for good. Others might refer to this as God (Judeo-Christian) or Spirit (Native American) and countless other names.

Self Leadership Defined

With Self Leadership, the family of internal energies—the parts within us—can be led by our Soul Self rather than our big bully parts, got-it-all-together parts, our vulnerable parts, or our parts responsible for addictions. Jungian analyst Bill Plotkin, PhD, calls it becoming Soul-centric rather than ego-centric.

In a Soul-centric approach, the ego exists to serve one's soul rather than the maladaptive parts of ego running the show. When that happens, your healthy ego is operating in the way it was meant to—helping you bring forth your soul gifts to serve others and the earth while completing the circle of "give back" as seen in indigenous cultures. These gifts can be things you manifest in the outer world or simply "being" a loving, kind or caring individual extending your energies to others.

Interestingly, the dynamic among your internal parts often takes on similar dynamics as a personal family, hence the name Internal Family Systems. Dr. Schwartz, IFS's founder, was originally a family systems therapist who noticed the systems in outer families, their cultures, and religions correlated with the "parts within" that his clients kept speaking about.

In the early days, most therapists didn't recognize the validity of the "parts within," but over time, Dr. Schwartz could no longer deny their existence. He brought an enhanced form to the process to make it the sophisticated work it has become today. (Though it requires years for therapists to master IFS, you'll glean enough of the work through this book to make positive strides on your own.)

Assisting Parts to Step Back and Trust

This IFS model is based on the premise that we all are whole and centered at our core. We bring forth this healthy core by assisting other parts to step back and trust our Soul-Centered Self. In general, this trust is established when all parts feel "heard" in their totality and have been accepted and appreciated for what they've attempted to do to be supportive earlier in life and now, even though it usually becomes detrimental as life goes on. We ultimately come to a place of full understanding and compassion for each and every part no matter the difficulty a part may have caused us or how much one part angers or judges another.

We might start out wanting some of our parts to just go away. But this only keeps their negative stance and influence in our lives locked in place. It is the full welcoming with its understanding and compassion that will shift the energies. Once these parts have been fully received, as described above and in the Full Dialog Process, and we have made friends with them to the point of understanding their actions and motivations along with their fears and insecurities, it's possible to transform them and use their positive traits in supportive ways. These trouble-causing parts are trapped in the past; they don't even know that it's safe or even possible to stop doing what's no longer effective. Our conscious mind might know this, but the parts do not until we've worked with them.

And as mentioned earlier, many parts come about from circumstances that are in your implicit memory (pre-conscious awareness) while some happened from things you can remember (explicit memory).

Witnessing (explained in Key 2) comes first followed by dialoging that helps us separate our core Soul-Centered Self from other parts. We learn to sense what part is leading the show in any moment. The more the parts can be distinguished and held as separate, the less potential for our Soul Self to be overtaken by any of these other misguided parts.

Again, think of these parts like any family or group of people. Once all members feel heard and accepted for where they're coming from and why they do what they do (whether all parties agree with it or not), a sense of peace and greater relaxation ensues. That peace signals a trust in the Self as a capable leader. Then we can move forward as a cohesive unit, even with differing parts intact. Over time, they become transformed to be supportive in ways that are guided by the Self.

The Voice of the Soul Self

The gentle voice of the Soul Self usually comes through in dreams, synchronicities, symbols, feelings, subtle knowings, or intuitive sensibilities rather than words. It won't push its way over the bigger, louder voices and styles of the demands from our protector parts—what IFS has named the managers and firefighters (described later in this chapter). Rather, it's the noticing or witnessing that makes space for the Self to come through. IFS calls it a *process of emergence* of what's already there rather than a creation of what is not.

Over time and with practice, our Soul Self becomes the leader as the other parts begin to trust its guidance and care. The Self's leadership comes naturally from a place of compassion, acceptance, patience, curiosity, and other positive qualities. When our parts surrender to it, life takes on more balance, peace, and accuracy about who we really are.

Internal Family Systems (IFS)—Greater Understanding of the Dynamics Within

IFS categorizes parts into these types of players:

1) The Protectors
   - Managers
   - The Firefighters
2) The Exiles
3) The Self

The Managers

The parts called the managers tend to be controlling or critical in style. They also have many other maladaptive or extreme roles they take on, including these common ones:

- being a perfectionist with unrealistic standards (with you never able to live up to them)
- critically judging self and others
- constantly evaluating ourselves and comparing to others
- feeling envious or jealous of others
- continually worrying
- coming from give up or passivity due to fear of failure
- playing it safe and not allowing risk-taking
- being invisible by not expressing oneself
- attempting to control others, situations, or life
- trying to be the biggest or best
- over pleasing (pleasing is deemed more important than truth-telling)
- appearing to have it all together, excessively upright or model citizen
- being a "knower" over expressing one's knowledge—(to reinforce one's sense of value)
- working hard to gain acknowledgement by others, for validation and/or keep afloat
- excessive caretaking (even when it's detrimental to oneself)
- denying that anything is off or needs looking at

Though there are many styles, the essence of theses role is to *keep everything under control,* which includes:

- appearing you have it together (to yourself and especially to others)
- obtain validation, especially when covering feelings of worthlessness or unlovability
- maintaining the status quo (to prevent change which would have you feel out of control)
- avoiding being too big or visible or appearing too small or weak

These all have the job of keeping the exiles—the parts within us that harbor unacceptable or painful emotions—from escaping their hiding place. Managers exile these parts to the dungeons of our psyches as a protective measure, so no one will see them and judge, ridicule, or hurt them. Ironically, often it's other parts within us that do the worst ridiculing.

Remember, in one's younger years, these protector parts could have meant survival, but in most adults, they equate to losing vital aspects of oneself. This makes it impossible to express all of who we are and thus reduces our ability to live a joyful, healthy, fulfilling life.

Questions About Your Childhood

To help find the style of the managers in your life, look at what's *not* working and think back to your early childhood. For example, if you were a victim of abuse or harsh treatment, then a part of you might have taken the role of *perpetrator* of that abuse. Or perhaps you maintained the role of *quiet victim* because other forms of self-protection would have been impossible or dangerous due to your young age and need to survive. Maybe there was little structure for safety in your home because of alcoholism or other addictions.

You can discover a lot by answering these questions related to your childhood:

- Did you develop a manager who would make sure you never veered far from the straight and narrow, leaving little room for creativity or personal expression in exchange for a sense of safety?

- Did a part of you become a "control freak" to ensure everything stays under control and organized as you attempt to feel that everything is okay?
- Did you have a parent who was so harshly strict that your managers came in to make sure you'd never be that rigid yourself? As a result, you may have rebelled against anything that looked slightly like structure or authority.
- Did you become super critical to ensure you were looking and being "good" so you'd receive approval from those around you?
- Did it appear you grew up in a "normal" home, but your parents weren't around or were preoccupied, so you found ways to be okay with your aloneness? Perhaps you push away intimacy to more closely resemble this lack of connection.

You get the idea. It takes deep, honest soul searching to tap into the patterns from your developmental years and recognize the managers you drew in to keep you feeling safe, perhaps invisible, approved of, seen or loved.

At first glance, what transpired in childhood may not seem all that traumatic, but you might have experienced a form of neglect, unavailability, emotional abuse, abandonment, or lack of any real attunement or connection, what therapists call Developmental Trauma. Because this trauma commonly exists in our culture, a great many people resort to various addictive behaviors as a result.

Though these managers may have unique characteristics and different values, most of them perform these three common functions:

- to make you look good in the eyes of others and itself (the manager) based on its values
- to live up to some outside standard
- to prevent triggering (that is—feeling painful emotions held by the exiles)

If you recall, the exiles are wounded aspects that carry your intense, buried emotions. The protectors—both the managers and the firefighters—

do *not* want the exiles triggered. They aim to control both your internal and external world to prevent buried feelings from rising to the surface and allowing the vulnerability of the exiles to come forth.

> ### Styles of Behavior
>
> These managers commonly do their protecting through shaming, blaming, and criticizing. As noted, there are many styles of behaviors managers take on when attempting to control your life (explained in Key 2 – Chapter 5), and some are listed here. Which of these have relevance in your life? What behaviors would you add?
>
> | | | |
> |---|---|---|
> | Sentry | Judger | Drama queen or king |
> | Critic | Victim | Perpetual victim |
> | Analyzer | Perfectionist | Patient (or the sick one) |
> | Pessimist | Super cool guy | Knower (has all the |
> | Caretaker | Oh so sexy gal | knowledge or the |
> | Censor | Super competent | "always right" one) |
> | Worrier | Independent | |
> | Complainer | Rebel | |

These managers carry huge burdens of responsibility that are often unnecessary. Your work is to identify those burdens, beliefs, or fears and then get these hard-working parts to understand their extreme roles are no longer valid. You want them to be transformed by trusting the Self and creating new game plans on how to better support you.

The Firefighters

This category of parts is extremely important regarding all manner of addictions, be they substance oriented or habitual patterns that limit you.

As stated, the managers work overtime to keep your system under their control. They ensure you look good, act right, attract kudos, or at least avoid ridicule. They attempt to keep you safe from perceived perpetrators or having others abandon you. They also help you live up to expectations, maintain your material-world comforts and lifestyle, and, at a minimum, ensure your basic survival.

> ### Stuck Energies
> Understand that your manager's strategies may have served you in your younger years. But today, living with these stuck energies isn't healthy. You are older, and you have a wise Self within you. Yet even though circumstances have changed, these stuck energies continue to act in the same old ways that are mainly detrimental.
>
> Once you've identified your stuck energies, it's time to tap into their original purpose. You'll discover what they're striving to protect you from or attempting to obtain. Your Soul Self has great compassion for all of this. And as you make those connections, you begin the transformation process.

Despite one's best efforts, though, you can't always maintain the huge burdens of responsibility dictated by the managers. Having done their best to keep it all under control, they just can't hold down the pain any longer. So what happens when the exile is deeply triggered by a person or circumstances and can't live up to the manager's dictates? What happens when shame, inadequacies, weaknesses, or helplessness erupt? You experience an explosion of emotion from the exiles. They'll either surface as an ongoing leak that feels like anxiety, tension, or depression, or they'll burst out uncontrollably.

Ta daaa—enter the firefighters for emergency masking.

The firefighters' job is to douse this fire, distracting or dissociating your system from the pain. Your responses can be frantic, reactive, or impulsive—called *hyper arousal* in the therapy world. Or they could go in the other direction, turning inward and disappearing into depression or other forms of shut down. That's called *hypo arousal.*

Addictions Enter the Picture

This is when addictions walk into the picture in the form of substances, caretaking or enabling, and/or any other distractions. Addictions can keep you absorbed in a seemingly joyful high or so dulled out that you're not available to feel what's happening inside. Perhaps that sounds like a good idea—to not feel the underlying pain—except for this factor. When you keep down your vulnerable feelings—exiling the exiles—your potential for joy, vitality, and fully giving your gifts to the world is held down with them.

Addictions have varying degrees of negative effects on our lives. Some are socially sanctioned and considered a normal part of life (e.g., food, exercise, internet, etc), making it hard to be aware when its use turns into an addictive pattern. It takes honest self-examination to know if ongoing behaviors have rolled over to firefighters' strategies to avoid or mask underlying feelings. Addictive behaviors might include:

- Overusing substances (zoning out on alcohol, pot, or hard drugs)
- Shopping or overspending
- Experiencing illnesses or accidents frequently
- Surfing the internet incessantly
- Engaging in porn or gambling
- Binging and/or purging
- Eating compulsively or excessively not eating
- Bursting out in anger or instigating fighting
- Self harming (cutting)
- Hoarding
- Thinking about suicide and fantasizing its benefits (suicidal ideation)
- Caretaking/enabling
- Becoming OCD
- Using sarcasm or complaint
- Abusing others physically, emotionally or sexually
- Obsessing about sex
- Cutting off relationships
- Living in isolation
- Seeking thrills (as in extreme sports)
- Being incessantly busy (workaholism or do-aholism)

All of these reduce or cover deep feelings of emotional pain such as guilt, shame, loneliness, and feeling "not enough." Firefighters attempt to help, delivering some form of pleasure or diversion, but that can cause one's life force to go sideways. Energies get wasted to such a degree, it's impossible to accomplish the goals or desires that provide a more deeply fulfilling purpose in life. We all possess unique gifts that engaging in will bring fulfillment and joy. But these controlling parts will not let us acknowledge they exist or will distract us enough to keep us from using them. Yet more reason to expose, befriend and transform these extreme parts of ourselves.

The Managers and Firefighters—Commonalities and Differences

Both the managers and the firefighters share the job of containing the exiles, thus protecting them and the entire system from their feelings. However, the firefighters go about it in polar opposite ways. While the managers often strive toward an unrealistic standard to look acceptable to the outer world, the firefighter could care less and can end up rebelling against the manager. Its addictions, distractions, disassociations, and unorthodox behaviors act out against the intensity of these rules, demands, and expectations. Its main goal? To "get the hell out of here" so any emotional pain is numbed or at least dulled. In response to that, the managers judge, shame, and blame the firefighters for their behaviors, creating a vicious circle. *Managers control; firefighters release.*

Actions of the firefighters tend to have an element of pleasure (for the moment) and create a sense of expansion. By comparison, the managers have a contracting or constricting energy. In fact, the managers are often ashamed of the firefighters' actions and try to hide them.

These two different categories of parts can trigger each other toward extremes. On the one hand, you might be upright, always striving to have it all together—as a business owner, a super parent, a highly competent worker, or someone who takes care of everyone else's needs. On the other hand, you might be fighting an inward battle with addictions or self-destructive behaviors. The interplay of these opposites keeps you locked in a steady state of polarization. In this way, the parts can't change independently of each other. The solution? Both need to be heard and then go through the IFS process.

Many people often think they don't carry the emotions of anger, rage, sadness, or deep grief because both the managers and firefighters have done a great job of keeping these exiles quiet. They've been masking, repressing, or hiding the core pain. For untold years, the managers have been trying to prevent what might trigger the exiles, while firefighters react with addictions of substances or behaviors *after* the exile has been triggered. At that point, it's too late to contain the flames.

Both the managers and firefighters do not trust the Soul-Centered Self. Believing they're the only ones able to run the show, they don't let the Self lead. They also fear the Self getting close to the exiles. A key goal of this work is getting these protectors to relax and back down from their hyper-vigilant defensive positions. They come to trust the Self when they feel heard, understood, and appreciated for the positive aspects of their roles. This is true, even if another part is angry at them for the results of their actions and directives. Feeling safe enough to let the Self in involves asking what these protectors are afraid of, then addressing each of those fears and ultimately getting permission to move in closer to the exiles. That's IFS's approach. (This is discussed further in the full Dialog Process of Chapter 13.)

Inner Child Work

Over the last 20 or so years, inner child work has become a powerful addition to the personal growth movement. Missing from it, though, is working with the managers and the firefighters, especially before going straight to deal with the exiles. Many times, the protectors either put up a block to prevent access to the frozen energies of that child (the exile), or they return later to sabotage the progress made after the exile has expressed. This can happen even when a "safe" party such as a therapist or counselor intervenes and helps the exile in feeling and expressing their deepest truths. Then a protector might end up punishing the exile for having expressed too much, which only more deeply locks it back in.

Before I learned these advancements and distinctions about first getting the managers and firefighters on board, as a therapist I had occasionally seen this backlash. Using my somatic therapy training, I gained the ability to go directly to those deep feelings, often very quickly. When clients walked out of the session, they felt relatively strong, centered, and ready to move forward. But if we hadn't worked with these protectors, sometimes the manager or firefighter would resurface and with an intensity. That could undermine our progress and throw clients back into their old, bad patterns. The managers and the firefighters both need to understand the value of letting the Self get close to the exiles. Then those protectors are able to let the exile feel and express. They come to trust the Self and that its new way of protection will be okay. Just as in any family, complete communications with feeling fully heard and understood carries considerable value.

The Exiles

In IFS language, exiles are those vulnerable parts within you. They have core memories (both implicit and explicit) of experiences, beliefs, and life decisions, and they've become frozen in space and time due to either major traumatic events (Shock Trauma) or ongoing lower-level trauma (Complex or Developmental Trauma) as explained earlier.

These exiles carry with them strong emotions, be it loneliness, hopelessness, intense fear, sadness, grief, anger, rage, and/or often unjustified guilt or shame. The managers and the firefighters want to keep the system—that is, your internal world—from feeling these emotions. Why? For many reasons: because it's painful or deeply uncomfortable to feel them; because feeling them might throw off the current status quo; or because at one point they could have been so overwhelming or unsafe to feel them that it would have meant death.

One child can have a number of different aspects that take on different energetic configurations. In one example, there might be a child who was deeply hurt and felt helpless to ever get love because one parent was unavailable, perhaps due to his or her addictions, unavailability, or disappearance. Once that aspect or part is noticed, the client might name it Sad Janey or Unloved Nicole or whatever fits.

Perhaps that child had a parent who was sexually abusive. As a result, another part of that child is simultaneously angry. Maybe this happened so young when the child's protective disassociation at the time was so complete that she grew up rarely feeling anger. But through the trust gained of the Self and the managers and firefighters backing off, this anger could finally be expressed. Simple words such as "I'm angry" can start the flow. This aspect might be given the name Angry Alice or, if fear was the predominant feeling, Little Scared One.

If you have no consciousness of how your exiles might feel, you're not alone. When any form of trauma has been involved, the threatened part of the child dissociates, checks out, or becomes frozen in space and time. That's why this work is so important.

The Neuroscience of Trauma

In neurobiological terms we say a part of the brain has *gone off line*. Recent studies of the neuroscience of trauma have demonstrated that part of the brain shuts down with trauma. In fact, researchers have found ways to view the trauma area in the brain on an MRI. It can show where certain parts of the brain that should light up with activity do not. In effect, those parts have gone numb, inactive. Literally, something has shut down and become "frozen."

Yes, neuroscience also shows it's possible to be re-awakened or "thawed." It's possible to create new brain pathways from the fear/survival areas of the brain to areas of higher reasoning, peacefulness, and the ability to trust and feel calm.

Loss and Retrieval

By studying shamanism, I learned that shamans call this loss of energetic aspects of oneself "soul loss." Doing the 7 Keys work and especially the Dialog Process is a form of "soul retrieval." Shamanic soul retrieval requires an outside person who goes to the part itself and encourages it to return. In our 21st century form of it, individuals themselves take an active role in the "retrieval" of the part, though a practitioner usually supports and guides the process.

How does it become possible to bring the lost part back from hiding and being exiled? It happens when both it and its protecting parts feel safe enough with your Soul-Centered Self and have begun to trust in Self's ability to take a leadership role. The exile often times expresses a timidity at first to come out of hiding, but if enough compassionate loving kindness has been shown to the exile from Self and other parts that might have been abusive to it, then it's almost always willing.

If that seems like a foreign concept, don't worry. If only hearing about the value in that doesn't trigger possibilities for you, then the fuller Dialog Process will. (See Chapter 13.) As part of this process, after the retrieval comes the opportunity for our parts to let go of, *unburden,* the emotions, mistaken beliefs, sense of responsibility, and decisions of the past—whether held consciously or not.

You might have more than one exiled part requiring this retrieval/unburdening process. Even the managers sometimes carry burdens from witnessing a child's experience. But once you learn the process, you can go back and work with other specific parts as they come up.

> You'll discover much acceptance and compassion in this process of dialoging and unburdening, of which your Soul-Centered Self is naturally capable. In general, the managers carry burdens of responsibility while the exiles carry burdens of shame, despair, neediness, fear, helplessness, and hopelessness. When any of these get too intensely triggered (or you never stopped being in those feelings since childhood), the firefighters rise to the occasion. At that point the whole internal system is rendered vulnerable. This is how addictions and negative behaviors start at what seems like a very young age.

The parts take on these maladaptive roles not only from life's challenges but from family genetics. If a family line issue exists, this explains some of the belief systems we might have taken on that don't make sense, seem extreme, or have no relevance today. These *legacy burdens* are now being brought to reality through genetic research.

Doing the work requires allowing our intuition to prevail. Images, thoughts and feelings will arise with both messages and answers to specific questions addressed of the parts. Even if we have no apparent conscious memory of something, you can trust what arises when it tends to just feel "right." Also, certain metaphoric images seem to just magically fit into place and ultimately help it all make total sense. A logic that comes from a place other than the linier story telling mind.

Need for Redemption

The exiles carry an incessant need for redemption, which means we might spend our entire lives trying to get a mother-like figure to love us or a father-like figure to acknowledge us. We might make frequent attempts at healing a mother or father figure (via a partner who represents them) from their addiction or patterns so they can be available to love us.

This need for redemption exists especially when the core part is still frozen in space and time—as if getting this redemption would make it finally safe to return. But of course, until the part has truly transformed, redemption rarely occurs. Yet it's possible if you have a conscious partner who's willing to work with you doing Imago Relationship Therapy[2], or other powerful interpersonal forms of therapy.

Remember, though, it's mainly you—your Soul Self—who can love this frozen part back to life, rather than constantly trying to find the love you desire outside of yourself. Later, after this level of healing work, it's possible for another person to reflect that self-love back to you. With love coming in from an outer source, this brings the healing full circle. In my awareness, it's rare that a person with an exile carrying intense feelings of being unlovable can call in a truly compassionate person to love them. When and if they do, they tend not to be able to receive it, then push that person out, one way or another.

Do you see a parallel here to inner child work, with the exile being the wounded child? Without the joy of the inner child (the exile and what it's feeling), substantially moving forward in life is difficult. Some of my clients who had no success with various forms of therapy apply this transformational parts work and then say things like "I feel part of life again." *Once checked-out parts become fully present, then the work can work!*

The tools, understandings, and practices remaining within the 7 Keys can deeply enhance one's strengths, abilities, and sense of purpose. We need the creativity, curiosity, joyful aliveness, and natural propensities of a child to be fully present and feel healthy, happy, and alive. We also need it fully present to bring our natural gifts into the world. This ultimate expression or "give back" of what's meaningful to us is exactly what creates the feeling of fulfillment.

---

[2] http:/imagorelationships.org & Harville, Hendrix, *Getting the Love You Want*, Holt and Co, LLC, 1988, 2008. (20th—Anniversary edition).

The Soul Self—Your Essential Core

The Self, Soul Self, or Soul-Centered Self is both connected to a higher power of your understanding and has that energy within it and you. You could say it's your essential core Self with the capacity to guide your whole internal system and lead your life.

In their natural states (rather than the extreme roles they take on), these parts have qualities that assist the Self. They're resources to be accessed as you move through life. They support the Self in its expression on this earth in a way that feels right and natural to the whole being. The Self has no power to fully express through you that isn't granted by the parts, but the parts cannot function at their best without leadership by the Self.

The work you're embarking on opens the lines of communication with and between all parts of you. It also involves creating a safe space within you for the parts to come forth. That means accessing your Soul-Centered Self that has the capacity to accept insecurities, painful feelings, and weaknesses. The Self can also accept and find value in the original intentions of the parts that have otherwise been critical, pushy, demanding, suppressive, or distracting. As stated, when the parts feel heard and accepted by the Self, then they come out of their polarized positions against other parts. They move out of their extreme roles, step back enough to allow safe access to the exiles, and then become supportive resources for the work, expression, and intentions of the Soul Self.

The general qualities of the Soul-Centered Self are:

- Calmness—even in the midst of stress or challenge
- Curiosity—as related to others' (and our own) behaviors rather than blame, judgment, criticism, or claiming victimhood
- Compassion—seeing beneath surface expression of others (as well as ourselves) and feeling into and/or understanding the pain or fear that lies beneath
- Confidence—having the ability to be self-assured, even during non-acceptance by others for a choice or action made, for making a mistake or not accomplishing what you're going for or not living up to an outside standard.

- Courage—speaking your truth, especially if it goes against the norm or a valued person's opinions. It's also the ability to take risks to go for new things, standup for injustices, and be in the unknown. It's a willingness to experience your own vulnerabilities and feelings as well as share awareness and remorse for behaviors of your extreme parts especially when others are affected (as occurs in the 12-Step program in making amends).
- Clarity—being able to see the truth behind your and others' actions and stay connected to that rather than react from a part. It is also knowing your truth and what your heart really wants.
- Connectedness—having the ability to feel safe to be yourself and connect with others authentically, consciously, and healthfully. It's also the ability to feel connected to life, nature or Spirit, a sense of a higher power.
- Creativity—enjoying the freedom to express your creativity without the burden of self judgment or shame for imperfections or inexperience.

With this work, you aim to have the parts (when in their extreme roles) step back and allow Soul Self to lead the way. That's when these qualities naturally emerge without effort. Rather than trying to infuse certain characteristics and qualities against the resistance of the parts, this *process of emergence* supports the parts in ways that invite them to happily step back. That way, their own useful qualities and those of Self naturally come forth.

This is a core difference from other models of therapy or recovery calling for intense discipline. In the beginning, a greater conscious awareness maybe required. However, once a level of trust and positive experience is gained, the parts do not resist. In fact, all start to move forward together as a peaceful, integrated, family unit.

About the Homework—Medicine Tasks

After you do the Accessing a Willingness Exercise in Chapter 3 for Key 1, create a list of what you believe are the different voices or parts within you. Pay special attention to those that cause you distress or seem to undermine what your heart really wants.

When doing this, it's helpful to give each one a distinguishing name related to how each one feels or acts. When you trust your intuition to come up with a good name to use, you'll know because it just feels "right." This name helps bring clarity to the energy that's been running you. For instance, you might use names such as the Pusher or the Boss. If there's a gender feel to it, you might give it a prefix such as Mr., Ms., or Miss—e.g., Ms. Perfect or its opposite, Mr. Rebel. It could be Mr. Not Okay to be Lazy or Ms. Avoid Stillness at All Costs. It's up to you!

After putting much feeling into it, one client said, "There's a part that feels rebellious—Mr. Rebel." This part came up when he realized he had a highly moral "upright" part emerging from his church's and family's belief about homosexuals, which he was. It came clear that this rebel part was his sex-addiction firefighter polarizing against this overly moral and upright part.

It doesn't matter if you're male or female, the energy you identify might have a different gender than yours. Often, the part takes on the gender of the main person or group of people it learned its style from. Examples: Mr. Got it All Together, Ms. Look Great All the Time, Mr. Never Drop the Ball, Miss Hot Stuff, Ms. Save the World, and so on. These are typically manager parts.

Some of my clients like to use alliterative names. Examples: Over-Giving Gary (a codependent part), Ms. Sandra Smirnoff (an alcoholic firefighter part), No Way José (a part that pushes out anyone who might be interested). Or the name might reflect both what it does and the feeling associated with it. Example: The Squelcher (a part that stops all attempts at expression, creativity, or emergence into the world).

Exiles might have names such as Scared One, Little _____ (your childhood name or nickname), Susie Q, Lonely One, Angry Girl, Hater, Miss No Hope, or whatever the prevailing feeling might be. However, it's possible you're not in touch with what the exile is feeling, especially if the managers have been doing their jobs well. (Key 3 – Chapter 6 about Self Love and Compassion discusses exiles in detail.) The Full Dialog Process at the end of the book addresses processes and communications to help you find what your exiled parts are feeling.

It's usually best to start with the managers because without their permission, it can be difficult to access the exiles (though they usually give permission at some point in the process). Remember, if you go straight to exiles and dig too deeply into their feelings without the manager's permission, you can experience a backlash. Later, the manager and/or the firefighter could fight hard to keep any exposure to an exile from happening again.

So start by noticing and working with a manager or a firefighter. When they can trust and allow the Self to lead, it feels safer for the exiles to come forth and be worked with.

☼ Medicine Tasks ☼

Naming Parts
In this process you will start to feel into the "color" or style of your managers and firefighters. Give a name to the part that best describes the energy that it carries. (as described in more detail above).

Though we are starting with the protectors, if exiles should come up, notice those feelings and the nature or quality of the part that is feeling that emotion. You can give it a name at this time as well. If the feeling starts to become very strong, tell this exile it is not Ok to overwhelm you and that we will be back to work with it after we have worked with some managers or firefighters. It will then be safer to do so. (You'll work with the exiles more in Key 3 – Chapter 6 and in the IFS Dialog Process.)

1) Managers

- Make a list of your managers. What are each one's different strategies for making sure you look good, appear together to yourself and/or the outer world, attempt to control what feels scary or uncontrollable, or a particular standard it wants you to live up to? What natural abilities do you focus on to an extreme? How do you consistently pressure or berate yourself?

- After writing down the way a manger operates, feel into its qualities and or motivations and come up with a name that most accurately captures its energy. Examples: Mr. Police (intensely protects by pushing the opposite sex out), Ms. Whip You into Shape (a motivator that uses a whip to get you to get things done or to exercise, etc.), Mary of the Moral (constant reminder of what good girls do and don't do), and so on. (Perhaps re-read, About the Homework, above.)

2) *Firefighters*

- Make a list of your firefighters. What are your different strategies for making sure your emotions stay under wraps, or for coping when something extra triggers you? How do you unwind from outer pressures and/or those from within led by your managers—that is, pressure to succeed, constant thoughts and worry about money, how you believe you should be, what you're too much or not enough of, what you're doing or not doing that you should be? And the list goes on. How do you escape this barrage?
- After writing down the way a firefighter operates, feel into its qualities and/or motivations to come up with a name that accurately captures its energy. Examples: Ms. Shopper, Mr. Wild Man (who likes to tie one on), Miss Sweety Pie (a sugar-aholic), Driven Danny (a workaholic), and so on.

Some of these parts with their behaviors can act as either managers or firefighters. You might notice a greater sense of desperation and intensity when a certain behavior falls in the firefighter category. However, it's not critical to know which one; they are both a form of protector.

Key 2 Medicine Tasks talks about what to do next with your awareness of these parts.

Chapter 5

Key 2 Developing the Witness— Transforming the Inner Critic

Key 2 addresses the first phase of transforming the inner critic and other negative voices of the managers. The managers use many styles of operating but most fall into three general categories:

- Looking good to the world
- Codependency
- Words and tones

Looking good to the world: This type of manager includes those who push us to succeed in ways that look good to the world, or they bring extra attention via our physicality, image, accomplishment, and/or material possessions. Most have standards we can't live up to, causing us internal stress or struggle. Many like to show off these outer items because they believe that's what gives them value. Therefore, they attract people to them who also value those things rather than the authentic person they are. This can show up as superficial relationships and result in pain and abandonment.

Co-dependency: Some managers cause us to put attention on caretaking others, avoiding others' reactions, or attempting to control others and circumstances. This approach can cost dearly in time, energy, money, and missed opportunities. It can also create chaos.

The drive to be a caretaker is often an addiction in itself; it's a person's attempt to give others what he or she craves—someone's care, attention, and love. When the intense focus of attention comes from this place, it almost always creates drama and negative retaliation from the person receiving it. This approach can show up from both managers or firefighters. Either way, we can tell when it goes beyond being a kind, giving person in a healthy sense. It's wreaking havoc!

Use of words and tones: These managers project shame, blame, criticism, and judgment on ourselves and others. Let's call this type of manager the Inner Critic, though it uses different styles to convey its negative attitude and mode of motivation. It can show up as recounting mistakes, comparing, complaining, and a host of other "styles" of expression.

The first type of manager—looking good to the world—often enlists the manager's third strategy of criticism, blaming, and self-judgment when not living up to the standards the manager or another part has set. And even when the standards are not high, the general state of "not enoughness" leads to similar self-talk and outer speak. This shames the individual to whom it's projected (be it oneself or another). Often the person feeling this way within, is speaking it aloud toward others. If you think that name calling or meanness of any kind toward others has no effect on the person expressing, think again.

The saying goes, "If you always do what you've always done, you will always get what you always got." The judging manager/protector doesn't want you taking chances. It would rather have you be safe and miserable or at least unfulfilled than take a risk of any kind. But risk-taking is required to feel vital, alive, and on purpose—that is, to create anything new and more wonderful. Yes, as one of your protectors, it has had a positive intent in mind but one that no longer works. Though as part of the transformation process, do your best to not judge this judger.

> **Harming Yourself**
>
> Did you know that when you judge someone else, your psyche takes it as judging yourself! The subconscious does not differentiate between negative accusations of others from those toward ourselves. Complaining falls into this category as well. So even if you think you're only judging, complaining, or criticizing things or people outside of you, you are still deeply harming yourself.
>
> If you knock yourself down every time you do not live up to some outside standards of beauty, actions, or roles (for example, mothering, supporting your family, being a woman or a man, etc.), you will never be able to step out of your current box and do anything differently than you already know or do. That includes when you make mistakes or when the harsh judger wants you to be "perfect" at whatever you do.

At this point most of us know on an outer level that these tactics are no longer needed for our protection, but these locked in protectors and exiles don't know that yet and will continue to operate this way until they get it. The witnessing or noticing the tactics and intentions of these parts is one of the first steps in the process of having them let go of their former ways.

Developing the Witness to Bring Forth the Soul Self

Short of doing the full transformational process, noticing and then softening our Inner Critic lets us move out of a life that doesn't fully work. When our vulnerable parts are not met with blame, shame, and judgmental voices, a relationship of safety and trust can slowly develop. This ultimately takes us to the state of mind of being open to try new things. We can step out in new ways and make changes necessary to have our life "meet" who we truly are. This raises our vibration, which ultimately increases our vitality, joy, and health.

Developing the Witness—noticing the parts and how they operate—starts the process. It separates, strengthens, and makes space for the centered, wise, spiritually connected aspect of ourselves to emerge—the Self. It knows what's good for us and can take the lead rather than allowing the negative, fearful, controlling, limiting, or demanding parts of ourselves have control.

Allowing yourself to touch these less-than-lovely places and then hold them with compassion opens the lines of communication and makes space for transforming the energies of the protectors. Ultimately, you aim to replace the critical voices with an internal voice that is nurturing, loving, and accepting. In effect, you're re-parenting yourself by creating new tracks of experience in your consciousness. (More about how to do this in Key 3 – Chapter 6.)

The Shadow

Yes, these controlling but formerly protecting parts did a great job keeping us safe. They were allies in the only ways they knew how for the hardships of infant, childhood and adolescent survival. In not knowing any other ways they unknowingly hampered our efforts at individuation and shoved our most radiant selves into the shadow!

Whether it's discovering old, withheld feelings from the past—an aspect of Key 1—or Developing the Witness that allows you to clearly see the extent of your protector's actions and critical voice—Key 2—you ultimately want to be able to transform them. Both of these involve becoming aware of what you're not readily aware of and might not like to see or feel. Hence, they are part of what's called the Shadow.

Embedded in the difficult aspects of the Shadow are also our gifts as well as our positive energies and qualities—along with other aspects that make life worth living. Delving into the Shadow might not seem like a walk in the park, but it's well worth the effort. Given some momentum, the process gets easier and actually enjoyable over time.

> Dr. Bill Plotkin calls these demanding yet protective parts, our Loyal Soldiers. He describes it this way:
>
> > The Loyal Soldier—a courageous, wise, and stubborn sub-personality that formed during our childhood and created a variety of strategies to help us survive the realities (often dysfunctional) of our families and culture. It keeps us 'safe' by making us small or limited, or by further traumatizing us.

It is this intrapsychic element that shovels chunks of our wholeness into our Shadow so that we will appear acceptable or invisible to the powers that be.[1]

> ## The Loyal Soldiers of World War II
> Some Japanese civilians sailing around the South Pacific seas found Japanese soldiers stranded on a remote Pacific island 20 years after the war had ended. Still in a warring stance, these protecting soldiers didn't know the war had ended. They had faithfully kept their post fortified and defended for two full decades!
>
> Those who arrived told the soldiers, "Thank you for your loyalty, but the war is over." However, no matter how many times the soldiers heard it—"the war is over"—they couldn't let go of their belief that they needed to stay and protect the island. Even after the civilians got them to see the truth, they still didn't fully let down. They were finally rehabilitated once they were honored with a full fanfare and then given other jobs to do. This transformed them into contributing modern-day members of their culture at that time.

What happened with the Loyal Soldiers of WWII explains the function and ultimate transformation of our own protectors. From a psychology viewpoint, our protector parts have performed its function loyally for so many years and believes a war is still on. These protector/loyal soldiers still hold that it must keep us from expressing or being ourselves to protect us from ridicule or harm. Their job had also been to have us feel accepted by our caretakers and later by the world around us, with the intention that we'd never have to feel the intense pain of disappointment, fear or loneliness again.

To this same end they also have us believe that "I don't matter" and "no one will love me," along with other beliefs of unworthiness, that imply, "I am nothing or bad, and nothing is ever enough" or other variations. These all fit into what is now being called Shame or Identity Distortions.

---

[1] For more on Bill Plotkin, Ph.D., vision fasts, his body of work, and much more: https://animas.org/

In the same way that the actual soldiers were rehabilitated by being heard and given new jobs, a similar process occurs within to transform our own inner Loyal Soldiers.

(See the IFS Dialog Process in Chapter 13 for detail about transforming these loyal soldiers or protectors—the managers and firefighters.)

Transforming the Inner Critic and the Role of Gratitude

In transforming one's harsh, limiting inner and outer dialog into an empowering expression, we can turn to gratitude. It's high on the list for what will cure negativity in one's life, even if we have to make ourselves express gratitude when we only feel like grumbling. With nurturing self talk (discussed more in Key 3), this can turn us and our circumstances around if we stick with it consistently enough.

Gratitude played a big role in my life in addition to integrating the works of Esther Hicks (Abraham) and applying improv theater's YES/AND technique. Let me explain.

Esther Hicks's work brought forth this powerful yet simple thought: When we put regular attention, constant thought, or frequent verbal expression on what we *don't* want that is currently happening, (as Hicks calls it "reporting current reality"), this practice establishes our future reality. It anchors in that reality, which is why similar challenges get re-created in the future.

I understand the need to express our frustrations or unhappy aspects of something, or say we believe we've been a victim of something or someone. Acknowledging our feelings around not-so-lovely happenings when they first occur or telling the story, gets it off our chests. This initial expression helps relieve the internal pressure of frustration, anger, or sadness we feel—a part of Key 1. But ruminating about it or repeatedly telling everyone we know about it (especially from a victim or "poor me" stance) only ensures that similar problems will reoccur.

At the time, I was dealing with some circumstances I didn't like, which I'd been complaining to friends about—"reporting" as Hicks calls it. Up to that point, a lot had already changed for the better for me. But in certain unrelenting circumstances, I still felt stuck. I had gotten to the point of no longer speaking judgmentally to myself about me or my actions, foibles, or mistakes—or if did, I'd quickly shift it. Yet even though I'd made strides to not be a complainer, when I felt slighted, wronged, or deeply challenged, I still wanted to talk about it honestly and often. That's why I'd find myself repeating my "current reality" with its challenges over and over. It seemed normal and not all that negative. After all, I was just expressing my current life story, right? Yet, I was missing something important.

> **Where the Mind Goes, Energy Flows**
> How can we expect things to improve if we constantly repeat and affirm what we don't want! Reporting our story to all our friends doesn't help anything because "where the mind goes, energy flows," thus creating more of what you don't want. This is more than a saying—it's extremely true!

YES/AND Technique

When I really understood what Hicks was saying, it changed my whole orientation and my life took an overall turn for the positive. I started paying attention to how often I thought about or told any of my life stories in the form of complaining. That's when I made a commitment to tell my negative stories less often—a time or two would be enough. Then I came up with a way to make a statement that integrated my former urge to express my current reality even with something negative in it, along with a positive statement of how I was holding it to be. It came out of the YES/AND exercise we did in theater improv classes.

In this exercise, one person starts by making up a scene or storyline. Then someone goes up and, working off that starting scene, improvises something starting with YES/AND that tacks onto the first story. If a participant by habit accidentally jumped in and started with NO/BUT, you could just watch the scenario die—that is, the energy stopped flowing and creativity left the moment. Both people involved could hardly think of what to do or say next. This was a very graphic demonstration of what resistance to what is and negativity can do.

By comparison, a simple YES allowed the scenario idea to live. And adding an AND let us seamlessly take the scene forward in a positive, creative way. (This mirrors the philosophy in the martial art of aikido—that is, take the negative attack, go with it, then turn it around. Presto, we are now in a powerful position relative to our opponent.)

I think of the NO/BUT as being similar to moaning about a circumstance. We're saying, "NO/BUT I don't want this." Its holding a negative stance on it." Though this negativity can be turned around.

It occurred to me to use the YES/AND technique whenever I heard myself reporting a negative current reality story. I consciously let go of my resistance to the situation, which made space for it to exist—the YES part—then I'd say AND followed by something positive. For example, "This (situation) is happening AND (a positive possibility related to the issue) is coming my way soon." That affirming, positive outcome is something I want to see happen.

In a real-life story, I had a property in Costa Rica that I had renovated to be a retreat center but had left it in the hands of the wrong people. They left the property without telling me. I got a call from someone telling me that robbers with a truck had been destroying the property for days and were carting away major parts of the buildings piece by piece; doors, windows, water pumps, appliances, etc. Next to go was the roof material.

It had become uninhabitable. I stood to lose everything because in that country if native squatters come and camp there for a relatively short period of time, they get title to the property! With my new commitment in place, when I told the story I told it briefly and added AND I know some miracles are on their way. It is too big and long a story to tell you here. I can only say that many amazing miracles happened in terms of the recovery of this property, when my financial status at the time indicated it would be impossible. I have stuck to the YES/AND technique ever since and even enhanced it.

I can make the affirmation part stronger by stating it in the present tense. Rather than saying "This (result) is coming soon," I'd say, "This (result) is here." For example, my car broke down and needs $600 worth of work AND $600 or more is miraculously appearing, or, is here now!.

To this YES/AND affirmation, I also shifted it to be an expression of gratitude. I make a current statement and then add, "AND I am grateful for . . ." I look to find something in that situation or perhaps something unrelated I can feel thankful for. For example, "A drunk driver just drove into the side of my house AND I am grateful I have insurance AND that I have a house to be run into even if I didn't have insurance."

Sometimes the add on part of YES/AND ends up affirming what I'm creating. Other times, it's something I'm grateful for within the circumstance, or just in life in general and sometimes it's both! For example, "My child just got a D in a class AND I'm grateful she is healthy, happy and now is more committed than ever to her school work." "My partner fell off the wagon again AND I'm grateful he's even more motivated to work on his life with focus and intention and that I am so healthy." (Note: The more you focus on your own or others' relapses or mistakes, the more likely you'll get more of that. The more you do the turnarounds and focus on where you or they are heading, there are fewer reasons to relapse, especially with oneself.)

Using this simple yet powerful technique can turn your negative energy around. It constitutes another way to be forgiving and loving toward yourself regarding what you do or perceive is being done to you. You can also use it when you're complaining about others. Finding the YES/AND with another's frustrating behaviors reads as self-love to your psyche while it also helps your relationship with that person.

This may sound like a boring old "think positive" message. However, amazing miracles await when you relentlessly witness this repetition of negative stories (or obsessing to yourself) and commit to this turnaround. Normal positive thinking doesn't work for some because, typically, they don't see for themselves how often or all the different ways they tell themselves or express negative statements. This is why witnessing is an important step.

What I have expressed in Key 2 so far leads to new habits of communicating with yourself and others. However, many of your parts already noted might resist these new practices. You might find it effective to skip to Chapter 13 and work the IFS Dialog Process while you're still reading the Keys. The 7 Keys offer many practices and ways to speak, or be that can replace old habits with new life-altering patterns. From these new patterns of behavior, changes within the brain are created. And this can be taken to a deeper level. The IFS work can make deep transformational shifts that support you in making desired behavior changes, including the underlying need for substance abuse or other addictive behaviors.

Miraculous!

The possibilities of what to be grateful for within a situation are always present. And the possibilities for gratitude are greater than you might imagine, so look for them. This one practice has changed things dramatically for my inner relationship.

From actively engaging regularly in this YES/AND and Gratitude practice, in a short time I tired of hearing myself telling negative stories. I simply lost interest. As a result, when a negative subject I had formerly been repeating came up again, I'd either say nothing or shift over to what I was in the process of creating for myself. Oh, how my stressed feelings decreased and feelings of flow increased! My energy, happiness, and peace of mind shifted and so did the circumstances. Miraculous!!!

☀ Medicine Tasks ☀

1) Developing the Witness

After naming some of your troublesome parts (Chapter 4), the next task involves paying attention to when the parts are in action or ruling our thoughts. When this takeover feels strong and all-consuming, we call it blending. Often, that blending with a part is constant, especially when it consistently tells us negative things about ourselves or when it instills fear, shame, or blame.

Paying attention to when our parts are ruling our thoughts I have been referring to as Developing the Witness. This means noticing, paying attention, and tracking (as one teacher called it). In indigenous training, this tracking or paying attention to small details of animal tracks, excrements, behaviors, and so on fosters ultimate awareness and understanding of the animal being tracked. This supports the tracker being in control of what happens with this animal rather than being its victim—an apropos metaphor for the Witnessing practice.

For humans, tracking or witnessing means accessing a valid awareness of our actions, thoughts, and words. After we've accessed a willingness and named the parts based on their behaviors or feelings (Key 1), we simply notice what's happening. We'd say something like "Oh I see the pusher is taking over," or "I feel the pull and drive of my firefighter (your addiction) happening."

A big aspect of Witnessing—and different than what you may have previously done when noticing a pull into an addictive habit—is to both notice it and not judge it. Often the manager judges the firefighter part, so this takes double noticing to recognize. For example, "I notice Mr. Moral (the manager) shaming me for having considered the pulls or even engaging in the pulls of Sir Sex Crazy (the firefighter)."

Before we can bring the Self more actively into our lives, at first, we might find it difficult to do anything other than notice. And it's necessary to notice the judging part as well as the part pulling on us. Again, we don't want to judge the judger! We might still be engaging in what ever the parts MO (modus operandi) is, but just to notice-witness without judging is a first most important step.

Witnessing step: Witnessing serves to drive a wedge between the Self and the protector parts, be they managers or firefighters. The more you notice them without judgment, the blending weakens, the parts take a step back, and the Self has more space to step forward. It can become more alive and present in your life.

Your homework is to notice (without judgment) when any of your parts are expressing their particular form of behavior. Do your best not to judge the behaviors nor the parts carrying the feelings and beliefs (the exiles) that motivate protectors to take on these behaviors. If you can't help judging (which indicates you are blending with a part), then notice what's happening. Perhaps there's one part doing the undesired behavior and another part (or two or three) that judges these behaviors. Later comes the step of befriending the part and asking it to step back. (explained in the IFS dialog, Chapter 13) But for now, it's enough to witness this interplay of parts.

Writing step: At the end of the day, write down all the different parts you've witnessed. This includes the thoughts you heard inside, the words you said outside, or certain behaviors that transpired from a protector part. If you noticed the emotions of an exile, record that as well.

Know that neither the part doing the behavior nor the part judging it is *you*. Neither one is the True You, which you'll come to experience over time. Your goal is for your Soul Centered-Self to take a stronger role in guiding your life, and Witnessing is part of the process. Going forward, be patient without judging and do what you can at your own pace. Deeper changes will emerge, sometimes quickly and sometimes over time.

2) *Unblending the Parts*

Naming and Witnessing are the first steps in the IFS process because they begin to separate—unblend, the True You from your parts. The more unblending occurs, the more you "get" that these parts are adapted aspects of you with certain behaviors they believe they need to do. As a result, you'll create more space for the Self to emerge. (You'll learn more about this concept in the Full Dialog Process.) Always remember, your parts are not the True You!

Chapter 6

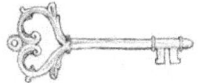

Key 3 What It Means to Love Ourselves—How to Counter Shame

Learning how to make Loving Ourselves more than a nice idea, relationship experts Drs. John and Julie Gottman talk and write about the Four Horsemen of the Apocalypse regarding Relationships.[1] These relate to four core ways of behaving that kills relationships. From the degree these four behaviors exist within a relationship, divorces or breakups can be predicted with 90% accuracy.

In the same light, if these attitudes and behaviors exist within oneself, there's a strong likelihood of self-hatred with its deep shame, anger, depression, addiction, and/or illness.

The Four Horsemen of the Apocalypse regarding Relationships are:

1) Criticism: I spoke about this in relation to ourselves in Key 2.
2) Contempt: Expressions of superiority (i.e., implying the "other" is inferior); using sarcasm, cynicism; name calling (including psychological

---

[1] Drs. John and Julie Schwartz Gottman https://www.gottman.com/blog/the-four-horsemen-recognizing-criticism-contempt-defensiveness-and-stonewalling/ 7 Principals for Making Marriage Work, Random House.

assessments), eyeball rolling, sneering; using mockery, anger, hostile words/voice tones.

With the relationship within, contempt refers to one part treating another part in this intense, demeaning manner, often consistently. It can include flipping to the opposite position from superiority to "poor me."

3) Defensiveness: Self-protection through righteous indignation; playing the victim, blaming underhandedly, being passive aggressiveness (i.e., other than straight-out ways of showing anger while believing you don't have or express anger).

With the relationship within, defensiveness plays out as self-talk (and outer talk) about how people or situations have "done you wrong." Anger exists below the surface, often covered by a fake niceness or a sense of spiritual superiority. This internal anger slips out to others and/or turns into illness due to the negativity within. It goes underground.

4) Stonewalling: One partner withdraws from the conversation, shuts down, goes within, or walks away, often in response to the other's expression of criticism and contempt (Horsemen 1 and 2).

With the relationship within, communication has just shut down to the point that people don't know what they feel, need, or want. They express themselves minimally, and they usually feel depressed with no idea why. It's a state of give up. These who shut down within themselves often end up on meds that don't work or develop a form of addiction. It's also the freeze state that occurs in association with shame that occurs as a result of Developmental Trauma, previously discussed.

Corrective Behaviors

With a strong dedication to making changes, these behaviors can be turned around. However, sometimes this negativity is so deeply embedded, it's advised to work with a therapist, especially at first, to get out of the quicksand of self-loathing or "shame identification." Its flip side is "pride identification" in which people do their best to appear together, wonderful, beautiful, smart, successful, and so on—all while hiding core feelings of inadequacy.

In addition to getting professional help, you can do much to reverse shame or pride identification on your own. You can turn around these behaviors and heal through a process called Actively Loving Ourselves.

How does this chapter help you Actively Love Yourself?

- It speaks to you in detail about shame and how to start melting the inner freeze state associated with it.
- It provides tools and activities related to these Four Horsemen behaviors responsible for the demise of both external and internal relationships.
- It spells out several practices for Actively Loving Yourself in the Medicine Tasks section.

In addition, the full IFS Dialog process in Chapter 13 gives details on how to offer compassion and love to each of the previously unacceptable "parts" of yourself.

Shame and How to Transform It

The feelings of shame—believing (even if only on a subconscious level) you are bad, defective, unlovable, dirty, and so on—are initiated in a number of different ways. Experts are expanding our understanding of shame, with three of them cited here: Patricia A. DeYoung, MSW, PhD, Sheila Rubin, LMFT, and Brett Lyon, PhD.

Patricia A. DeYoung: Dr. DeYoung explains shame as a disintegration or fragmenting of Self in relation to an unregulated other—that is, someone incapable of connecting and attuning, especially at the time of infancy. Referring to psychologist Richard Geist, De Young states, ". . . what shamed clients missed is the dance of mutual emotional engagement between child and parent that creates a lively, whole, secure self. Shamed clients never had a chance at this sustained connection. The absence of mutual connection was where their chronic shame started, and that absence continues."[2]

---

[2] Patricia A. DeYoung, MSW, PhD, *Understanding and Treating Chronic Shame: A Relational/Neurobiological Approach*, Routledge, 2015, p. 118.

The word shame has another different meaning that relates to feeling badly about an action or behavior you have engaged in. This is guilt. The type of shame I am talking about here is a core shame that is not necessarily related to behavior. When we do not experience "attunement" with a healthy present caretaker, we end up feeling defective, like a no self. An important aspect of us has not been fully brought in. If you recall from the Developmental Wheel of Chapter 2, the first task is the parents job—to bring forth the presence and innocence of the magical child. Without that something is missing regardless of how well you "do" in the world. Whether it is something clearly traumatic or simply from a lack of attunement and connection as a child, core feelings of shame and not being enough can set in.

Brett Lyon, PhD, speaks about how shame can develop from being different. If you're different from others and hide your differences to fit in with others, shame is born. You're no longer able to be yourself in society. Even without meaning to, parents can shame their children by insisting they hide their differences, either because they are embarrassed about them, fear them, or want to help their child to better navigate in a complex social world. They say or imply, "Don't let anyone know. Don't let anyone see what makes you different." These words (or indications) can only lead the child to one conclusion: "There's something wrong with me. If I'm truly myself, I will harm others or they will harm me. I need to hide."[3]

Shame can also come from direct and obvious traumas. Dr. Lyon explains how this happens on a physiological level. To paraphrase: When stress is great, the sympathetic nervous system automatically goes to a fight-or-flight response. This is built into our body's system. It can happen in response to an external threat or the perception of threat. Either fighting or fleeing can resolve the stress. If neither is possible or successful, the sympathetic arousal can get so extreme that it becomes too much for the body to handle.

---

[3] Bret Lyon, Ph.D. http://www.healingshame.com/articles/Melting_the_Shame_Freeze_in_Disneys_Frozen.pdf.

At this point, a failsafe survival mechanism kicks in. The parasympathetic system spikes. The parasympathetic aspect of the nervous system is that which counters the sympathetic. Sympathetic—amps it up in prep to fight or flee, parasympathetic, slows it down. But in intense situations the parasympathetic can come in so strongly that it overwhelms the sympathetic arousal and sends the person into a state of freeze. This can be full collapse, dissociation, or a partial freeze such as an inability to think clearly, access words or emotions, or move parts of the body. This might last a short time—such as a possum freezing and becoming reanimated after the predator leaves—or continue indefinitely.[4]

When the sympathetic system hits this overwhelm place, the parasympathetic system can shut down the entire system. This freeze state is what happens in all forms of trauma and then the shame response often results. As Dr. Lyons wrote:

> Sylvan Tomkins, the great emotions theorist, saw shame as a binding emotion. Its very nature is to bind with other emotions. It is designed that way for a reason: To keep us from acting. Every emotion has an action tendency. The tendency of anger is to lash out, the tendency of grief is to cry and seek comfort, the tendency of fear is to run away. The tendency of shame is to freeze, hide, disappear. Shame has been called "the master emotion" because it can serve as a control on all of the others. Shame binds with other emotions to lower their affect and prevent a discharge in action. In this way, it keeps us safe and helps us to learn and obey social rules. Unfortunately, shame is so powerful that a little goes a long way. The healthy tendency to stop, pay attention to others and reassess can quickly morph into a freeze state, covering up all other emotions.[5]

Dr. Lyons defines shame as being a combination of an emotion and a freeze state.[6] The good news about this is when the emotions bound to the

---

[4] Bret Lyon, PhD, http://www.healingshame.com/articles/Anatomy_of_a_Freeze.pdf.
[5] Bret Lyon, PhD, http://www.healingshame.com/articles/Unbinding_Shame.pdf
[6] Bret Lyon, PhD, definitions, http://www.healingshame.com/resources.html

freeze are brought up to receive "light and air," shame can be transformed such that a person can lead a much more successful life.

Dr. DeYoung writes in *Understanding and Treating Chronic Shame* that a common response to shame is to hide, which is the most toxic of responses. By comparison, the least automatic—exposing the source of the shame—is the most healing. The presence of a "compassionate other" helps to allow in that light of day. Dr. DeYoung says others will only help if you know they won't further shame or blame you as you expose these pains.[7]

That "compassionate other" can start out by being the Self aspect of ourselves. With enough self-honoring and expressing through writing, self-talk, and more attention regarding our emotions, pains, and difficult stories, others will appear who can receive them. It's this unbinding of the emotion with the freeze that can free the shame state to be transformed.

Stresses around failure, inability to perform well, or destructive activities (like addictions) are all things that distract us from the deeper feelings. These painful held feelings include absence of connectedness, longing to be known and loved, and wanting oneself to "matter." There are feelings of deep grief for having never experienced this. It is the ability to deeply feel and express this grief that can unbind it from the shame.[8]

Dr. DeYoung adds, "People who suffer from chronic shame are likely to carry around a sense of emotional impoverishment, of somehow never enough. Some spend their adult lives acquiring material goods and satisfactions to make up for what's missing."[9] However, owning an emotional need associated with many insatiable elements can bring up more shame about that need.

It is helpful to know that ". . . shame is probably the most painful emotion human beings can feel, and that not only does it feel excruciating, it's so disconnecting and isolating that it can go on for a very long time without anyone noticing, except the person feeling the shame. So hearing that shame is an experience very common to humanity can help relieve the

---

[7] Patricia A. DeYoung, *Understanding and Treating Chronic Shame: A Relational/Neurobiological Approach*, Routledge, 2015, p. 116.

[8] Ibid. p. 117–118.

[9] Patricia A. DeYoung, *Understanding and Treating Chronic Shame: A Relational/Neurobiological Approach*, Routledge, 2015, p. 126.

loneliness of shamed clients and ease the humiliation they feel about feeling shame."[10]

Shaming can happen from within when you feel your actions go against a learned moral or norm. Shame can also set in from parents shaming their children with demeaning, harsh words or tones. Also from their judgements about actions or ways of being.

With so many different ways that shame can be instilled, it's no wonder the depression, anxiety and addictions that develop as a result is so rampant in our culture. Dr Sheila Rubin states:

> There is shame when a person feels a break interpersonally (between individuals). And there is further, profound shame when a person feels a break inside himself or herself. It is the feeling of shame that somehow clients leave out of sessions unless the therapist knows to look for it and brings it up. And it is this very mysterious feeling that can keep people stuck in depression for so long, and not finish their therapy. I believe that shame is seldom addressed in therapy. Unhealed shame can keep a person in a depressive state for years, or keep them living only partly the life they could be living.
>
> Shame is at the core of the inner critic, perfectionism, depression, and low self-esteem. It is something that may be overlooked if we are not looking for it.[11]

A powerful healing starts with ourselves—the accepting love and openhearted reception to all that we feel, including our deep hurts and wounds—makes this connection within. It begins to reconnect the intrapersonal (within ourselves) break. This is where the IFS Parts work can be so profound. In her book, Dr. De Young suggests IFS as a great technique to use when working with shame.[12]

---

[10] Ibid. p. 124.

[11] Sheila Rubin, LMFT, RDT, BCT, The Use of the Creative Therapies In Treating Depression, Ed-Stephanie Brooke and Charles Meyers, 2015, Charles Thomas Publishers, her Chapter Almost Magic: Working with the Shame Under the Depression, p. 231.

[12] Patricia A. DeYoung, *Understanding and Treating Chronic Shame: A Relational/Neurobiological Approach*, Routledge, 2015, p. 132.

Bringing shame to light often illuminates a needy part of self (the exile) who is despised by a tough, perhaps ambitious, independent part (a manager). Listening respectfully to both parts and helping each find compassion for what drives the other brings balance and harmony to the whole system. Within this attuned emotional holding of "Self to part", hidden aspects of our inner system slowly become known, cared for, and integrated. The brain heals itself with a "we-ness" of compassion.

Shame and *Phantom of the Opera*

Sheila Rubin describes what happens at the end of the famous play *Phantom of the Opera* and how the process of healing shame showed up:

> The heroine sees the Phantom first in his kindness to her, and then she sees how he has harmed people and sees him in his cruelty and his acting out. She says, "I did love you. Now I'm confused." He proclaims how bad he is, which allows her to look deeper. When she looks deeper, she sees his pain. When she sees his pain, she sees it from a non-judging place. She does not poke him in that painful place, but she does not ignore it either.
>
> For her to really see him allows him to step out of his shame. He breaks into tears. He is seen for the first time. He goes from the emotion of shame into the emotion of grief, and finally the freeze that shame has had on him begins to unravel as these two emotions begin to unwind. We are deeply touched.[13]
>
> Dr. Lyon writes, "This expansive and accepting love—attachment, connection—is the cure for shame."[14]

---

[13] Sheila Rubin, LMFT, www.sheilarubin.com http://www.healingshame.com/articles/Unmasking_Shame Phantom_of_the_Opera.pdf.

[14] Bret Lyon, Ph.D. http://www.healingshame.com/articles/Melting_the_Shame_Freeze_in_Disneys_Frozen.pdf (Author's note: This excellent article explains shame and the power for its healing via myth and metaphor)

This connection starts within ourselves and grows to include others. In the process of healing shame, you do not want to be in a rush to receive it from without. Unless it is with a therapist who is helping you to give it to yourself.

Healing Turnarounds for Horsemen 1 and 2—Criticism and Contempt

Communicating criticism and contempt within and without are at the source of much negativity in our lives and in our culture. It is also a large aspect of what has caused so much of the feelings of shame within. What is the antidote?

Words of Kindness, Acceptance, Compassion, and Love: The Gottmans say learning to treat others and ourselves with respect and build a culture of appreciation is the antidote. But if we've grown up in a world that knows so much of this negativity, judgment, and other forms of harshness, where do we start?

We start with a shift in orientation. Think of the transformation of your vulnerable, wounded Inner Child (or exile) as you would an outer child who has been abused. The extra care, kindness, gentleness, listening, and/or time of attention you'd give to someone outside of yourself should be given to *you*—and to the wounded or neglected parts within you. This requires an extra focus when you're in the early phases of working with your inner wounded self.

For a while, err on the side of over attending to the child's needs for a specific amount of time. Again, it's like the recovery of an abused or neglected child—one that may have been shut in a closet or found under the bed. This can be where a therapist will often find their client's Inner Child hiding from early traumas. No one (including the client) has heard this child or allowed it to speak for many years. That Inner Child needs an inordinate amount of gentleness, acceptance, and attention for a time.

Healing a Traumatized Child—You

To begin healing your own trauma, the first step, Key 1, is paying attention to—and allowing for the existence of—whatever feelings you might have previously shunned, made wrong, kept hidden, or shoved underground. Key 2 requires you to Witness how you respond to these emotions or any other patterns of behavior and refrain from judging of any kind. Simply notice and be mindful.

The critical third step—Key 3—involves the conscious reversal of all critical self-talk or complaining, replacing it with accepting, allowing, or compassionate words. Even if you were successful at not judging what you witnessed, go beyond that and respond with loving compassion. This can be hard because you may never have had this demonstrated in your life—especially given the fears, concerns, and standards of the other protector/manager parts of yourself. When one demanding manager doesn't like the actions or emotions of another part, it can really get on your case. But Witnessing (noticing dispassionately) comes first, followed by actually saying something to yourself that reverses or counterbalances what you just heard in a kind way. Your inner dialog might look like this:

Harsh voice: "You are so stupid. You did that again! You made that mean remark to your coworker and now you are giving him more reason to reject you!"
Loving voice in response: "It's okay. I love you anyway. You're in a learning curve, and no one does it perfectly right off the bat."
Harsh voice: "You are so fat and look horrible in that dress."
Loving voice: "You may have more weight than you want, but I know you're truly beautiful no matter what. You are lovable to me and to our higher power."

Consciously reverse every negative statement with a loving one. You begin to see each part as an abused or neglected child that needs love, care, attention, and gentleness.

Truth and Lies

Chances are parts of you are kicking and screaming right now. You may be saying, "It's not true! Why should I lie to myself? If I believe I am, do, or look bad, flawed, or just not good enough in any way, then it's a lie! Besides, I need to crack the whip, or how will I be motivated to change?" Wrong!

Although this harsh strategy might work for some, it won't work for any already-abused, neglected, or abandoned inner parts hiding and frozen in space and time. It's those exiled inner parts that carry your joy, creativity, and aliveness. They need a safe space. And you're the only one who can provide that safety by changing your way of being with them.

Here's the truth: To your Self (and to the Higher Power, God, Divine Mother, or whatever name you prefer), loving words are ALL TRUE! But up to now, the ruling parts of the managers and firefighters have "blended"—that is, covered over the Self. From this, you may have become unaware of the Self's presence. To grow its presence, you might ask "other" formerly protective parts to step back. You could say it directly in words and even hear your Self say, "Step back." If it doesn't ring true, then fake it till you make it—*although this action is never fake*. The Self does feel and believe other positive points of view. However, you may not have sensed its presence. Dominating "other" parts believe they have to use certain unkind strategies and behaviors, but that's misguided. Any strategies that may have helped earlier are usually keeping you unhappy or feeling unloved and unlovable today.

Note: Many of the 7 Keys feature practices that help make space for the Self to grow in prominence. But "standing up to the negative voices" even before doing the full IFS Dialog process in Chapter 13 to transform them, can help expand the space for the Self to become a stronger leading presence in your life.

The negativity of these "other" often well-meaning but misguided protector voices don't always show up as specific negative words. They can be found in feelings of being shamed or made wrong without words going off in your head. It can come forth in many other feelings, like overwhelm, consistent anger states, weepiness, or general inferiority. That's when you witness any sly operations at work. As you sense them, you say something loving to yourself. Even before you do the full IFS Dialog process, you can soften these negative internal voices and attitudes. If it feels odd, strange or fake to say kind, all accepting things to yourself, its because its new and unfamiliar—do it anyway!

> **Forming New Neural Pathways**
>
> Before I even learned about the IFS work, I focused on transforming the voices in my head with an intention to do so. After a while, inner negative thoughts fell away as if they couldn't find a hook to hang their hat on. They no longer felt at home in my head because they didn't have the space to speak to me as they once had.
>
> I was glad to learn neuroscience's neuroplasticity research is proving the human brain can and does change memory to form new neural pathways. This requires conscious intention and attention until new pathways are fully created, but it means we can heal—we can change our lives for the better!

Healing Turnaround for Horsemen 3: Defensiveness

As you transform your inner voice to a loving, kind, and accepting one, any need for defensiveness will melt, because you'll no longer feel like a victim of your own internal parts. This is true especially after you transform a protective part to use its positive qualities and resources to support you. What a shift from activities that demean and undermine you in its zeal to protect you with its misinformed ways!

When do the feelings and experiences of defensiveness transform? Not only when you stop speaking this way, but when you see and take responsibility for how you contribute toward their occurrences. If you can witness your own victim-contributing behaviors—not speaking your truth, engaging in defensive, victim-oriented conversation—and then practice the 7 Keys, you can completely shift this harmful orientation.

Healing Turnaround for Horsemen 4: Stonewalling

When the harsh, demanding, self-hating, or high-expectation type of inner conversation has gone on for a long time, the inner expressions and emotions of the exile completely shut down. It's understandable. If you're constantly being told how you do things wrong or how worthless you are, why bother? You could totally give up, feel helpless, and go into a state of shut down.

Stonewalling usually starts when there's been Developmental Trauma in childhood. It occurs from ongoing neglect, lack of connection, missing attunement, and the need to be seen and have one's feelings accepted that has not been met. Or it occurs from Shock Trauma due to forms of physical abuse, witnessing abuse, accidents, and sometimes surgeries.

All of this creates the core Shame response discussed previously, along with shutting down inner communication. When it gets to this point, I recommend working with a therapist, especially one versed in IFS or some form of somatic work. (See resources at the end of the book.) The added Self energy of the counselor helps bring forth the Self of a shutdown person. It's also important to create a safe, loving space for the buried emotions to be received. There, the parts may also need "retrievals" from their shutdown places in the psyche after being there for so long.

Today, an MRI can reveal that when a trauma experience is reactivated, parts of the brain go off-line—that is, they don't light up on the MRI as they normally do. This indicates a shutdown is occurring. Shutdown aspects usually show up in the evolved parts of the brain (e.g., prefrontal cortex) or on the pathways to these more rational and conscious parts. So when someone is triggered by something related to one of these trauma wounds, the person goes into the fight-or-flight response of the more primitive parts of the brain while losing access to the more rational aspects of the brain.

When someone is in a triggered state, this work can become inaccessible because it requires the use of the prefrontal cortex. Top-down therapies integrate understanding from our higher mind into the healing process and utilize cognitive witnessing, mindfulness, and sensitivities to internal images or subtle responses. When these are coupled with bottom-up therapies—that is, working with energetic holdings in the body that occur in all forms of trauma, also called somatic work, it becomes possible to release and transform deeply held trauma. IFS is one of therapy modalities considered both top down/bottom up.

Note: All the 7 Keys and practices in this book support these therapeutic approaches. And these therapies support the practices to become much more effective. When a person can integrate both the deeper therapy as stated above with a commitment to personal awareness and practices, positive life transformations are not only possible and long lasting, but they can occur faster and more assuredly.

Forgiveness and Re-Parenting

If you have been involved in a 12-Step program, then you may already have a good start on forgiving yourself and others for their inadequacies and mistakes. The key is to use forgiveness daily in your internal conversation—that is, you'd say something like "I forgive you (as your Soul Self to other parts of you) for not being perfect" or "I forgive you for making that mistake" or for anything that falls short of what your managers expect or might otherwise like to see.

When you Witness what's said inside yourself, you might catch yourself saying judgmental, demanding, or high expectation kinds of things on and off all day long. That's when you state a forgiveness and/or add kind, supportive remarks. If you're frequently hearing or feeling negativity within, then it can act as a frequent reminder and opportunity to voice forgiving, kind, loving messages to yourself often. The more you notice and do these turnaround practices, the quicker your life will shift toward more joy and ease.

Some call this practice re-parenting ourselves—that is, replacing the inner critical, harsh, or abusive parent with a nurturing parent. Even if you have no idea how to do it, act as if you know. It may feel fake at first but in time, it will become natural.

Internal Family Systems Therapy—a Powerful, Specific Self-Love Practice

IFS therapy involves a detailed, powerful way to extend love and then transform every part of yourself. This is taking self-love to an advanced degree. I suggest working with the Dialog process as mapped out in Chapter 13. Of course, learning this process while working with an IFS therapist would be optimal. Yet before going to that level of transformational work, you can always practice Self Love, Compassion, and Loving Kindness with yourself as noted in these Medicine Tasks.

☀ Medicine Tasks ☀

Integrate any of these self-love practices/activities into your life—daily, weekly, or at least monthly. Pick any one or two to focus on before adding others. When you practice any of these regularly, you will notice a distinct change in the way you feel, your energy level, your courage to take risks, and your ability to express yourself. In addition, recent research is finding they will release the feel good internal hormone, Dopamine into your system.

1) Actively Loving Yourself Practices

Be Present
Give yourself a few minutes of focused quiet time each day. You might meditate, rest, stare out the window, or spend a few moments paying attention to what you are feeling in your body or emotions.

Fun Time
Set aside time to do activities that you and your inner child believe are fun. You can lose track of time when doing them. You don't have to have talent in the chosen activity nor does it have to serve a purpose beyond enjoyment.

Creative Expression
Find an avenue of creative play such as singing, dancing, music, art, poetry, or writing. Commit yourself to doing this a specified number of hours each week on your own or take a class. Classes will teach you new skills, and you can share the joy of doing what you love with others.

Nature Time
Spend time in nature. Scheduling a specific time each week or month to do this enhances the likelihood you will break out of your routine.

Listen
Listen to what's happening in the recesses of your mind and emotional body. Ask, "What am I feeling right now?" When you get a response or any other

communication from your inner being, don't discount your feelings. Instead, practice "compassionate listening" as discussed earlier.

Honor Feelings
Heed your internal messages to the best of your ability rather than dismissing them as unimportant, impossible, or otherwise invaluable. This may involve negotiating, risk taking, or rearranging priorities.

Speak Kindly
Listen carefully to your internal dialog. When you hear harsh or judgmental words, derogatory tones, or other unloving expressions, counterbalance these with kind and loving words.

Take Time to Write
Carve out time to write down your thoughts. This can either be done as 1) pure stream of consciousness with no thought or concern about content, or 2) a dialog between different parts of you (e.g., you and your Inner Child). You can always bring in other aspects/parts to the conversation. Simply identify the part—aware Self, loving parent, harsh parent, particular fire fighter or manager, critic, scared or adapted child, nurtured child—and start writing to find out how various aspects of you view a situation. Do this dialoging spontaneously without editing.

You'll find that gaining clarity and honoring the feelings of various parts and aspects of yourself to be nurturing and balancing.

Taking Tiny Steps Forward
Choose something you want to accomplish, be it a large long-range goal or something smaller like cleaning or organizing your space. Take 10 minutes to do something towards it. If you want you can do more, but only ask of yourself a small time frame. Each time you accomplish even very tiny steps it has been proven that dopamine will be released into your body's system and sometimes other positive hormones as well. This creates feelings of self-love, appreciation and positivity. As long as you don't get on your own case for not

doing more, than the short time intended. It also opens the door to continue on and do more if it feels good to do so.

2) Exercises to Enhance Self-Love
Intuitive Dialog
Set up a pillow, chair, or seat in front of where you're already sitting. Let this be the seat for your Inner Child. Move back and forth between these seats and have a discussion between you and the child (or have a trusted friend ask you the questions). When you're in the child's seat (or answering as the child when supported by another person), assume a posture that best imitates the child's. The more you allow yourself to role play the child, the better. Do this out loud in a soft voice or whisper. Perhaps put on some gentle music that supports the process.

You could also put a stuffed animal in the child's seat to address your questions to (or in your arms if someone is asking you as the child). Imagine that your Inner Child is sitting there as you speak.

The following is a list of questions to ask your Inner Child, then let your intuition guide you regarding how you respond. If you're doing it alone, ask a question and then move into the child's seat and speak for her or him. Write down key insights or commitments after you finish.

Possible questions:

- Are you willing to tell me what you're feeling?
- How can I help you feel safe enough to talk to me?
- How have you felt unloved by me?
- Have you felt I have discounted or ignored you or your feelings? If so, what are those feelings?
- What can I do to make you feel more loved by me or to honor your feelings?
- What can I do on a regular basis that you would enjoy?
- What changes would you like to see?

When you hear the child's responses to your questions, listen compassionately. Do not negate or discount any suggestions or feelings. Conclude with loving remarks or hugging the stuffed animal. Then make a list of the child's requests and do your best to make changes that feel appropriate to you.

Have dialogs like these periodically. They can be especially effective after an emotional release (as described in my previous book *Express Yourself*, Chapter 9), as part of the IFS dialog process when working with the exile, or during challenging emotional times.

Ideal Nurturing Parent

Find a comfortable, quiet spot, then close your eyes and relax. Allow an image to come forth of an ideal loving mother or father. Notice the hair, clothing, tone of voice, and so forth. Imagine yourself being held by him or her. Feel the way you are rocked.

Next, have this mother or father speak to you, telling you things you may have always wanted to hear from a parent. Perhaps say something about what makes you feel bad about yourself. Hear the accepting, loving responses.

You can enhance this exercise by having a friend you trust actually hold you. That person can even respond as the nurturing parent, using his or her intuition. If you do this exercise alone, you can hold a stuffed animal or pillow and imagine it is you being held by this loving parent.

Doing this exercise especially during times of distress can leave you feeling soothed and nurtured as if a real parent had supported you. Doing it *repeatedly* will make an imprint on your emotional body to permanently raise your level of self-love.

Being Seen in Our Expression

Children love to be seen or heard in their creative expression. Most likely you were not, or you were seen but only through someone else's critical eyes and words, or else someway inappropriate. Pick an activity you find enjoyable such as dancing, singing, painting, skating, yoga, and so on. It doesn't matter how adept you are or are not at the activity. Instead, let go of any self-criticism you may be holding and do the activities with your enthusiasm and enjoyment. Ask a trusted friend to watch you from the most non-judgmental and accepting place in themselves.

Being Seen in Our Beingness

Sit facing someone you trust. Look directly into his or her eyes. Rather than staring, let the focus of your eyes be soft. Notice your tendency to smile or laugh at first. As you settle in and get beyond initial feelings of discomfort, you'll find it to be amazingly soothing. Tears might arise from this level of vulnerability. Just let them flow as they are part of the healing.

This exercise is even more powerful if you have a group to work with. Spend a few minutes with one person then switch to someone else. Have one person call the switch so you can all change at the same time. Create a nurturing environment with soft music or someone gently playing guitar.

If you don't have a group or another person you feel comfortable with, you can start by making a regular practice of looking in your own eyes in the mirror. As you do, notice the tendency to think judgmental thoughts. Gently switch them to accepting loving thoughts or simply say, "I love you." This may seem difficult at first, but stick with it and you will notice positive results.

Acknowledge Yourself

Make a list of everything you can possibly think of that you can acknowledge yourself for—traits, qualities, talents, physical features, capabilities, etc. Read this list to yourself often. If you are with a group, have each person take turns acknowledging you. Either stand in the middle and receive this, or lie down with your eyes closed. Have them gently stroke your arms, legs, belly, forehead, face, and hair as they speak to you. They will either talk out loud or whisper in your ear. Each person can take turns receiving in this way.

Answer in Writing

On average, what percentage of your time is:

_____%   To fulfill obligations (shoulds, have to's, musts)
_____%   To solve problems (health, money, work, children, and/or relationships)

_____% To become more _____ (a form of ambition)
_____% By choice
_____% For fun and enjoyment

Write 10 activities you love to do. Beside each one, list the amount of time (by the day, week or month) you do these now. Then another column for how much you *will* do these things.

Committing to Practice

Make a commitment to regularly do any of these exercises. Try putting stars by the ones you will be doing at first. You can add or change them over time. They say it takes 21 days or 3 weeks to make a new habit—which equates to making a new brain pathway.

When you do some of these regularly notice how you feel after a month of consistent practice.

Are you feeling lighter, with more of a lift in your step?
Do you laugh or smile any more than usual?
Are you more willing to talk to people you wouldn't normally speak to?
Has it become easier to speak your truth?
Are you more willing to try new things or do things differently?

Write down what you notice has shifted after each month for 6 months to a year of doing these or any of the practices in the 7 Keys.

Chapter 7

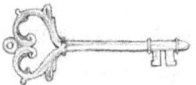

Key 4 The Art and Power of Surrender—Integrating the Spiritual

This Key sits right in the middle of the 7 Keys for a reason. The other Keys support this delicate art of letting go and Surrendering—Key 4—while one's growing ability to do so facilitates mastery of the other Keys, like a feedback loop.

Though Surrender could be called an ability, the word "ability" implies a "doing" of something. Yet true Surrender is a "*not* doing." It's a "be at peace and wait or trust" kind of thing. *Not* taking action when all of you wants to jump in and do something—to fix, answer, change, eliminate—is difficult. You're attempting to make something "how you want it" rather than be with "what is" or wait for what will organically shift.

Of course, I'm not saying never take action. But in our culture, *action* seems to be the only valued course. It's rarely balanced by *inaction*—the yang being valued over the yin. Being able to wait, allow, let go, and accept aspects of "what is" aids in our ability to take more effective, empowered action.

As noted earlier, it's important to restore the balance of yin and yang on our planet, our culture, and our lives. Did you notice how each of the Keys so far involves something "yin"? That includes:

Key 1: the honoring of feelings
Key 2: the simple witnessing/noticing and cessation of critical judgment in exchange for an all-inclusive accepting orientation
Key 3: the practice of love and compassion
Key 4: the non-linear practice of Surrendering to what we don't know or don't like, and to what is powerful yet unproven and completely unseen

A certain Buddhist philosophy says all suffering comes from "attachment to" (resisting change) or "aversion of" (intensely want something to change). Both sides of this coin lead to inner tension, stress, and turmoil. And the more we engage on either side of this pendulum, the more turmoil we create. We feel the opposite of peace and ease, either from the fear of losing what we're attached to or creating drama over what we don't want.

But releasing addictive patterns requires an inner opening that comes from:

- feeling our feelings
- letting them exist within us without judgment
- expressing them healthfully to ourselves or others
- loving, allowing, and finding compassion for all parts of ourselves and extending that to others

All of these build connection and create an inner relaxation that comes from the practice of Surrender. Its opposite—attachment and aversion—leads to deep tension and angst.

Aspects of Surrender

The practices in Key 4 help you create more joy and openness, which fosters more relaxation and a greater ability to trust. In turn, having a greater ability to trust creates more inner peace and with it a sense of freedom. This upward spiraling feedback loop cycles among the practices of allowing, trusting, and opening.

Each of the three main aspects of Surrender enhances the deepening of the other two. They are:

1) Trusting in a Positive Higher Power
2) Finding Peace in the Unknown
3) Letting Go of Control

Like an upward spiral, practicing elements of each Key deepens your ability to trust and Surrender. As you Surrender, you're able to accomplish more in each of the other Keys. Similarly, each act of trust gives you more confidence to take bigger risks and trust when dealing with challenging, high-stake situations. This spiral becomes a familiar theme.

The realm of Surrender embraces paradoxes and the unknown, which are difficult concepts for the linear, logical mind to understand. The linear mind often gets in the way of learning the art of Surrender because what it requires challenges the logical point of view. From the perspective of heartfelt knowing, however, it makes all the sense in the world. It's in this middle ground between the two (linear and non linier), that miracles are born. And as we embrace Surrender, we can experience ease, peace, and deep rest.

In discussing the three aspects of Surrender, note how the first one facilitates the other two.

Trusting in a Positive Higher Power
This form of Surrender is about trusting that your personal form of a benevolent, loving, higher power will catch you. You believe you'll be okay no matter what, and that whatever transpires is for your highest good, even if a part of you judges it as the worst thing.

Essential to Surrender is a belief in a universal power that works within, around, and through us. I use the word Spirit or Divine Source; other names for this energy are God, Higher Power, Goddess, Great Mother, Universal Life Force, Christ, Buddha, Great One, Allah, Mother Earth, or as I sometimes say, the Benevolent Forces of the Universe. On the 7 Keys path there are no exclusions—that is, you're free to believe whatever honors your truth and feels right. Some say, "We are one with this Higher Power" while others say, "It is greater than us." From whatever perspective you experience this wise and loving energy, have trust and faith in it as a powerful, benevolent, and creative source.

After all, life is exhausting when we try to do everything on our own—to make things happen or stop things from happening. This source of energy wants only our greatest good—and ultimately, the greatest good for all humanity. As we Surrender to it through trust, we gain an ever-increasing ability to let go of the need to "hold the fort" ourselves.

No Longer Pushing the Boulder Up the Mountain

In the past, I tended to be impatient and unable to trust that things would work out if I didn't do everything myself. That lack of trust reflected a lack of faith within myself and a disbelief that I would ever be supported from without. I'd have to carry the load myself and make life happen. Trying to push the boulder up the mountain on my own led to a lot of futile effort. Plus, I ended up with late-phase adrenal exhaustion from all that pushing.

But by working with the tools presented in this book, I've gained a deeper sense of trust. Learning the fine art of Surrender brought me to a place where I had faith in the flow of life and the support of a greater benevolent energy. From this new place, much of the struggle and stress in my life has disappeared; instead, I spend more of my time in a state of peace and ease. My outer circumstances have miraculously reflected this back to me. My point is this: *I can't expect the outer things to shift and THEN I will be peaceful.* The peace is gained in the trusting, then the outer changes I manifest line up with the open, relaxed state of trust I have come to experience.

Greatest Potential for Freedom

Achieving this level of let go is a tough yet easy, complex yet simple art—an art that's subtle and incorporates many paradoxes. Embracing all aspects of Surrender—especially a trust in something great and unseen—holds our greatest potential for freedom. It allows for our connection to a divine presence as well as a sense of joy, ease, flow, creativity, expression, and a true place of service in the world.

Because we tend to attach value to things of the known world, we have little training and few role models for how to surrender to this unseen force. Instead, we tend to base our reactions on fear and specifically fear of what we can't see, know, or control. Beneath our conscious awareness exist feelings of emptiness, worthlessness, or loneliness that keep this level of fear locked in place (as explained in previous Keys). It's our willingness to be in touch with these feelings that allows us to step into the world of the unknown and surrender to that place where our connection to all of life resides. When we allow ourselves to go to those deep, dark places of hurt, sad, scary, or shameful feelings, we come to know that we can not only survive it, but even feel open, released, freed. This in turn creates a sense of safety and trust in our Self and a connection to our own concept of a Higher Power. (Look at Key 1 as a powerful step toward embracing Surrender and trust in this unseen, benevolent force or energy.)

You are Loved No Matter What

Many organized religions aim to convince you that, to be loved, accepted, supported, "God" (or their concept of a Higher Power) needs you to do, not do, or be this or that. Based on your indoctrination, if you need a punishing God to keep you in line, then you certainly can keep that, for we're talking about a God of *your* understanding. However, consider another understanding—one that a growing number of people are deeply experiencing on their own without coercion or fear of punishment. It's a knowing that feels "right" on a deep inner level.

What is this understanding? That you are loved and accepted no matter what! That anything you feel shame about or have accepted blame for is all mistaken thinking.

Forgiveness

No matter if you've considered that some evil has transpired through you, at your core, you are one with pure consciousness and the love associated with it. Pure consciousness carries no judgment of anything, it just is. And you are forgiven the minute you fully accept that truth, and you can forgive yourself for any transgressions. Continued self-punishment is not necessary!

Yes, you could continue to punish yourself until the day you realize you have the power to let all that go—to forgive yourself and be forgiven. You have that power because you have a direct connection with the Self, which is always a part of you, and its link to the higher all forgiving benevolent force of the Universe. With an earnest plea, you can ask this higher energy to forgive you, yet it is important that you also ask for help to forgive yourself!

Notice the upward spiral. If you act in a less-than-perfect way (in your eyes), then you would pick yourself up and forgive again. Rather than the beating and berating, shaming and blaming you may give yourself due to downward-spiraling mistakes and fallbacks, you go straight to your trust in that Higher Power. There, you know you are loved and worthy of forgiveness. Knowing you are connected to this Higher Power, you forgive yourself yet again. You can know and trust that you're forgiven instantly as soon as you ask and give it to yourself.

The more you trust and forgive, the lighter and freer you feel. The lighter you feel, the less likely you are to do what you'd prefer you didn't do, including addictive behaviors. You're choosing to align yourself with benevolent (higher) energies rather than malevolent (lower) energies.

Realize that nothing about you is bad. Rather, it's a matter forgiving actions of the past along with recent choices you made regarding who or what energy you want to align with. If you want more of what feels truly good—more health, less drama, less pain in relating, more people who feel good to you and have a greater ability to connect, more forward movement—then make choices that align you with the benevolent energies—your Higher Power.

However, when you make choices aligned with malevolent energies and repercussions occur because of it, don't believe you're being punished as a bad person. Simply realize you chose to align with malevolent energies. Quickly forgive your mistakes and move on. This altered way of holding your actions is another way you Surrender to a higher positive power. This creates an upward spiral that can pull you out of the quicksand of addictions or other challenging situations. In the eyes of this Higher Power, you are loved and accepted no matter what!

Beyond this is extending forgiveness to those around you, for everyone is part of the same field of consciousness. Quantum physics calls this the protomorphogenic field. In spiritual language, it's the background sea of God consciousness or Love. With this, what you extend to others also comes to you.

Story of Tony Davis

Tony Davis exemplifies the miraculous healing and transformative power of forgiveness. His story is becoming well-known through a book, a movie, and write-ups in major newspapers.

A minister and singer, Davis and his wife were pillars in their community. Out of the blue when he was picking up his wife, someone shot multiple rounds of bullets onto his car. The police came, took his statement, and left. As his car was being towed away, the same person let out a hail of bullets again—this time hitting him. After seven hours of surgery, Tony died on the operating table. Thinking he'd been dead for about 30 minutes, the attendants went to cover his head with a sheet when suddenly he took a gasp of air and opened his eyes. The doctors had never seen someone come back from being officially dead for so long—ever.

Tony later stated that he went to a place that felt so beautiful and loving, he would have been happy to continue on that path. But he heard a voice telling him it wasn't his time, and he needed to go back. He felt being pulled back to the table in the hospital and was quite distraught about this. When he came to, doctors told him he'd have to have his leg amputated. They also said he'd never sing again because some of his vocal chords had been severed.

Tony prayed, "Why, God, why did you bring me back again?"

Later that day, he was scheduled to have his leg amputated. Then he heard God tell him, "Forgive. If you forgive, I will make you whole again." After noticing the conflict in his mind and heart, he chose to forgive. When he did, immediately he felt a warm feeling going to his leg that slowly spread up to his throat. He then fell asleep. When the doctors came to get him for the amputation, they said his leg seemed to be alive and they wouldn't have to amputate. Two days later, Tony could speak!

Today, Tony Davis can walk, talk, and sing. He speaks to youth at inner city schools and gang intervention programs. He had seen a glimpse of a young man behind a tree when he was shot, so he later went back to the area to try and find the shooter and give him redemption. It turns out the shooter was unable to receive this blessing because this misguided young man had been shot and killed by another gang member.

The essence of this story reveals the amazing miracles that can occur when we let our pain or anger be transformed into love and acceptance of another person. It doesn't mean condoning the behavior, though. Rather, it requires separating the person from the behavior.

We have been given the tool of forgiveness to make every act of love real. In the case of forgiving others, the surrender comes in surrendering our emotional pain and judgment to a higher power, and asking for help to transform them into something powerful and positive.

Note: When you do the full IFS Dialog process (Chapter 13), in part, you'll be offering understanding, acceptance, and forgiveness for every part of you, regardless of how their previous behaviors may have hurt you.

Finding Peace in the Unknown

This requires being willing to not know an answer to a problem or question or not know a next step, and yet remain peaceful and open. It also requires being patient and trusting that situations, people, or answers will show up when the time is right. They can't be forced. If they are, we pay a price through stress and struggle.

I used to ask myself, "How do I go about *not* doing?" The answer is, "Joy, you don't." It's not something you just do. But if you sit back and do nothing, or you do what you've always done, that doesn't work either. You can't learn this in an academic fashion. Although intellectual understanding helps, you master this fine art through a deep knowing acquired through consistent practice. Again, it's like an upward spiral that builds upon itself and can start with small leaps of faith.

In his book *The Path to Love*, Deepak Chopra describes being in the unknown this way:

> Reality is always on the move, shifting the known out from under us and bringing the unknown into view. Dying to the known brings knowledge that cannot be acquired any other way. The scriptures have called this "dying unto death."[1]

The Familiar vs. Freedom

When you let yourself dwell in the unknown, you're faced with the uncomfortable feelings associated with not having answers. You're also faced with another kind of unknown—leaving behind your world of perceived safety and security. No matter how much pain or dissatisfaction your current reality may cause you, it is known; therefore, it feels secure and appears desirable.

But anyone's life that's based on this type of security becomes a prison. Even though a maximum-security prison provides the basic needs for prisoners—food and shelter—it represents the ultimate loss of freedom. Similarly, when our inner being tells us to let go of something or try something new but we choose what appears to be security over the unknown, we give up our freedom and the ability to lead creative, fulfilling lives.

Show Empathy First

The ability to be comfortable with not knowing can be cultivated. Begin by not developing solutions or answers to your own questions right away. Instead, wait in the unknown to give new possibilities time to surface. Do the same thing with friends who share their problems with you. Instead of jumping in with solutions, just listen and be supportive.

---

[1] Deepak Chopra, *The Path to Love: Spiritual Strategies for Healing*, Harmony, 1998.

You can do this by feeding back what you sense they are feeling about a situation with no attempt to solve their problems. For example, a friend tells you she just lost her job. At the same time, her car broke down and fixing it used up her cash reserves. Instead of offering a plan to deal with the situation or telling your friend what to feel, simply listen to the details. Empathize with her by reflecting back her words and how you imagine she might be feeling at this time. Say, "I imagine you must be feeling pretty scared right now." This often has the magical effect of helping the person feel better. But if you play Dr. Fix-it before you express empathy, it often leaves the person feeling more frustrated.

Not offering solutions requires coming to terms with our own feelings about letting something be without trying to solve or fix it. An inability to fix a friend's problems taps into our own feelings of helplessness. But we can step into the unknown by letting ourselves "be" in this undefined place of shared feelings. Holding a non-fix-it attitude is also a way to be with ourselves during times of challenges, questioning, or indecision. Ironically, looking for immediate solutions or ruminating about the pros and cons of a possible choice will keep the answers from emerging.

Answers from Your Heart

When you find yourself ruminating about an issue, consciously take the time to engage in activities that bring you back into the current moment, that put you in your right brain. This brings you into your heart and out of your head, allowing your answers to arise from a different place. They will show up as an inner "knowing"—a place you can't access if all your energy is focused on thinking and worrying. (Key 5 - Chapter 8 details ways to do this.)

Also let yourself acknowledge what you are feeling in response to a situation. Give yourself time and space to allow expression of those feelings. It helps to ask, "What am I feeling?" This feeling place is directly related to the unknown and is a source for creativity.

Being in the unknown means letting go of knowing the answers, trying to fix problems and determining what is "right, while simultaneously surrendering to our feelings and relinquishing ideas of security. When we allow ourselves to be in this trusting space without normal tension and mental states, problems will work themselves out over time or unforeseen solutions will arise. Often, we do not have all the details we need to make a decision. If we can keep our heart and being in an open, relaxed state while waiting for that extra information, it can come together later quickly and fluidly. Once you acquire this delicate art form and integrate it into your being, life will flow with more ease and grace than ever.

Letting Go of Control

Letting go of control is:

- the ability to "be with what is" regarding life's twists, turns, surprises (and especially another's behaviors), and stay relaxed with an open heart.
- the willingness to give up preconceived outcomes.
- not pushing too hard and intensely to "make things happen."
- Consciously releasing sense of urgency and its attending muscular tension

Your Reactions

How do you react when things do not happen the way you want them to or the flow of your life is interrupted with unexpected change? How do you react when others don't respond to you as you would like them to or don't do what you think they should? Think about monetary or material loss. When these things occur, what emotions emerge? What do you feel in your body—a tightness in your chest, a churning in your belly?

What you feel is an indication of how "in control" you are trying to be. Different circumstances trigger different reactions in various people. For some, issues about money could have more potential for upset; for others, the inability to elicit a certain behavior or emotional response from someone could cause anxiety; for others yet, issues of organization are important.

Sometimes, our behavior responds to external circumstances or internal feelings by attempting to control them. Yet all this controlling proves to be a waste of creative life force because feelings, other individuals, and life in general can't be controlled. We pay a price when we try to force ourselves on others this way or try to shut down our true feelings. In fact, the more we try, the further we disconnect from others and the more we stray from our essence. Yes, we can guide the direction we want things to go, but controlling it all—impossible. To enhance our joy factor, life force, and therefore freedom from addictive behaviors, it's best to shift this old, limiting life pattern.

Accessing your Witness (Key 2) will help you notice when you're trying to be "in control." Look for these clues in your body: changes in breathing (higher, faster, or not at all), faster movements, feelings of anxiety, frowning, voice tone changes (usually higher, faster, or louder), an emotional charge building up, or stomach tension. Look for these clues in your behavior: emotional eating, upset with others, focusing attention on and judging others' behavior, self-righteousness, being demanding or defensive, blaming others, or complaining.

Qualities Associated with Being in Control vs. Surrender

The degree to which you experience the qualities listed here will help you know whether you're trying to be in control or have opened to surrender.

> *Control*: rigid, limiting, fixed, hard, confining, dominating, fitting in, attached, manipulative, defensive, reactive, intolerant, having expectations
>
> *Surrender*: flexible, allowing, flowing, spontaneous, alive, radiant, forgiving, empathetic, compassionate, creative, soft, open, playful, lives outside the norm

When a controlling part tries to control circumstances or people, it does its job of "external controlling." When it tries to protect us from experiencing uncomfortable feelings—anger, sadness, hurt, fear, loneliness, helplessness, dissatisfaction, or not wanting to be here—it's doing its job of "internal controlling." By nature, experiencing our feelings is a nonlinear, out-of-control activity—that is, we have to be somewhat out of control, or at least in a different part of our brain, to really *feel*.

Using Do-aholism to Control My Feelings

For years, I didn't see myself as controlling, at least I didn't think I was trying to push people around. However, as I achieved a greater understanding of how controlling operates, I started to recognize how I *did* act to control things. I was showing tense, anxious responses to the twists and turns of life. When things didn't go as I expected, I became upset. When my daughter acted obnoxious, I behaved obnoxiously, too. When sudden financial crises occurred, I became exceedingly tense. In my relationships with others, I was often defensive.

Outwardly, many of these reactions weren't apparent and I appeared cheerful and friendly. But inwardly, I was feeling anxious. Often, I expressed that anxiety by going a hundred miles an hour. In fact, I had my life set up with so much to do that I had little time or energy to stop and feel what was going on inside. Do-aholism was my form of controlling my feelings. It created so many distractions that I could no longer experience my true feelings.

This is what happens with any addiction. It becomes a controlling strategy.

How did these controlling yet protective parts come about? Growing up, often one experienced elements of being out of control including having an alcoholic, abusive, fighting, or missing parent(s). As noted in Chapter 4, these parts protected us in important ways, especially from our own painful feelings, which had its advantages at the time. However, with continued use of this strategy, an intense defense against experiencing "bad" feelings becomes a blocking device to other more desired feelings such as joy, spontaneity, and love.

This way of controlling limits our connection with Spirit as well as access to our creativity and inner guidance. It does this by: 1) not letting us express our feelings that help us create our sense of aliveness, and 2) not allowing us to be spontaneous, which inhibits our free co-creative flow with the universe.

Our culture's normal way of operating—a desire to have everything in control—often breeds struggle, stress, illness, and suffering. But embracing

Surrender in the midst of modern living is key to turning our world around—not only our inner world and its outer manifestations but also our planet.

Remember, accepting and allowing doesn't mean to take no action when needed. Rather, it refers to an *internal* state that supports us in taking effective long-term action and helps us avoid burnout. By accepting what life brings us (good or bad) and allowing ourselves to feel deeply about what is transpiring, we open our lives to a flow, a sense of ease, and an inner peace.

> ### Joanna Macy's Work
> Joanna Macy is a powerful activist for sustainability and the environment. In her circles are people who care about the state of the environment, but they can also feel helpless to effect enough of the changes they aspire to make. Many experience burn out or stay stuck in an angry place.
>
> Joanna's work involved leading workshops that helped the participants feel their full range of emotions around what's happening in the world and within themselves. As a result, they were able to increase their effectiveness with their actions because she helped them lift their levels of internal control. They learned to let go of some of their rigidity and get unstuck emotionally. Some have even become high-empowered activists.[2]

Opening to Vulnerability

Learning to let go of control, be in the unknown, and Surrender to a Higher Power also involves opening to our vulnerability. In our culture, vulnerability has gotten a bad rap and is meant to be avoided at all costs. But, in fact, learning to be vulnerable has many benefits. As we let go of defenses blocking our emotions, ideas, and intuitions and discover it's safe to do so, we can walk through life without as many walls and facades. We then appear more authentic because we *are*. We also become stronger because we gain flexibility. That actually makes us safer than when we construct rigid walls for

---

[2] Joanna Macy and Molly Young Brown, Coming Back to Life: The Updated Guide to the Work that Reconnects, New Society Publishers, 2014 For more about Joanna Macy: https://workthatreconnects.org/about-joanna/

protection. Like any walls, when they're penetrated, they can break. Without the need for all these walls we can feel free.

When we come from a place of vulnerability, we have more resilience when challenging events occur. We're better off because it's impossible to completely prevent the storms of life from blowing. Like the willow tree, we bend but don't break in a storm. If we have feelings of hurt, loss, or frustration, they can flow through us more quickly and fluidly than when we try to defend ourselves against such feelings. In the long run, allowing vulnerability is gentler on us than blocking it.

In addition, being vulnerable helps us understand others' feelings better and creates opportunities to show compassion. Sometimes this leads to healing and harmony between people where discord had been. It happened for me as a final stage to a long healing process with my former husband. Allowing myself to be vulnerable to his feelings opened the space that let us finally be friends after 11 painful years of anger projected at me.

The Magic of Vulnerability

I had been working on the issues that our relationship brought up and trying to take as much responsibility as I could for my part—mostly through the intellectual process of understanding. But one day, I let myself experience sadness and remorse for the people I had shut out of my heart by my internal wall of defenses. From that place of vulnerability, I was able to both feel and understand what my former husband had been feeling when we were together. Sure, he did plenty of things I could be angry about, but I overlooked them in that moment and let myself feel events from *his* perspective. I didn't only understand his feelings; I actually *felt* them.

The day after this happened, he looked me directly in the eyes for the first time since early in our relationship. I never said anything, but somehow I had opened a space in my heart that he could feel. A few weeks later, I told him what I'd felt and shared my remorse for how I had contributed to the downfall of our relationship. I saw and explained that though his ways of being hurtful may have been more obvious, my subtle ways were just as hurtful to him.

> As a result of being vulnerable, the wall of hate he'd held for me finally lifted.
>
> Not long after this, nothing short of a miracle happened. We joined forces in a business venture and even lived under one roof as friends for a while. Though other steps in this healing process played a role, I believe it was my vulnerability that had the greatest single impact on this situation.
>
> I know for me *and* for you that it's worth the risk. Being vulnerable can open real magic in your life.

Decision-Making Challenges

Surrender can be extremely powerful in decision making as we find the balance between the head and the heart. Indeed, our best decisions come from a healthy combination of the two. Commonly, we get confused about what's guiding us—head or heart—thus making a choice can be challenging. When we feel the subtle urging of the heart, our minds want to discourage seemingly irrational actions. In this way, our minds tend to keep us frozen and unable to act.

How can we discern the difference between messages coming from the head or heart? Simply ask, "Which one has a 'should' in it?" It's the head (in association with controlling, demanding parts) that communicate with "should," not the heart. Instead, our inner knowing gently urges us to *do* or *not do* something.

Certainly your mind can help you evaluate which thoughts are worth considering and which are just old limiting beliefs holding you back unnecessarily. Once you uncover the "shoulds," ask your Higher Self to assist you in coming to a resolution. This process of discernment by separating out the "shoulds", then bringing in prayer or request for help, will help you gain balance between the head and the heart. Hence, you make decisions that are closer to a deeper truth, guided by Self rather than by what different "parts" might be demanding or pushing for. Doing the IFS process in Chapter 13 can help you separate out the parts and their messages from Self, as well.

"Do Something Fun"

My daughter had a major life decision that she ruminated about for some time. Each choice made sense to be the one to go with; no one choice outweighed the other. New points kept coming in that bound them evenly and made it all seem impossible to pick the "right" one. I was trying to "fix" her by helping her make a logical choice.

I finally reached that point of impossibility and remembered my own advice. I said, "Go do something fun for a few days and don't let yourself think about it." She only did one thing—played basketball—then she called later to say not only did she know the choice she wanted to make but a later call confirmed it was her best choice.

We aren't always blessed to receive such a quick confirmation of choice as my daughter did. But know this: If it comes from the Self, our centered heart, ultimately, it's best for all concerned. That's true even if it doesn't first appear that way to us or to other parts of ourselves with their beliefs and agendas. This is another reason the work of transforming the parts is important. Then the parts don't make our choices; rather, the Self leads the way.

Do these kinds of "be in the moment" activities often until the way is shown or felt. If it takes longer than you think it should, use this time to keep Surrendering while asking/praying for the highest and best answer or a resolve. Make continued statements of your trust in the higher benevolent forces. For example, you'd say, "I trust you have the best way to resolve this situation; please send that resolve now. I trust you will guide me to make the best choice for all concerned." Even if you can't see how it is best for you or someone else now, when you get the sense of the way to go, then trust it will ultimately be the highest and best choice for all concerned.

The Role of Surrender

Surrender, Key 4, is the center pole of the 7 Keys, with the first three Keys dealing with our humanness (and much of it the Shadow side). The two following, Keys 5 and 6 bring forth and further align us with our Soul Self side. They also uplift the dark or difficult aspects of dealing with the pains of our humanness. Those two Keys not only make it easier to be with the hard stuff when it arises, they support the whole process to be more enjoyable.

Key 7 represents how we put our humanness together with our spiritual side to ultimately give back to the world. We extend our love in ways that feel good to our soul, and it comes back around for us to feel more joy, love, and peace within. There's that non-linear upward spiral movement again!

When we learn to Surrender in these three ways, Trusting in a Higher Positive Power, Stepping Out into the Unknown, and Letting Go of Control, we become more open to the flow of life. When we let ourselves be supported we're caught by an invisible safety net. Support may appear as things we manifest from our own efforts as well as help from others, creative inspiration, or serendipitous circumstances that occur miraculously. As our references for being caught increase in number, our sense of trust grows. As our trust grows, we let go more and experience a greater sense of ease. After a while, the concept of struggle becomes a thing of the past. Our experiences feel easy and even fun. From this relaxed and open place, the opportunities for clean living, creativity, and full expression are heightened.

Embarking on such an adventurous journey might require an appealing carrot at the end of the stick. With the confidence I and others have gained through experience, we know that nothing yields greater results in life—both inner results of peace and outer results of balanced success. Learning the subtle yet powerful art of Surrender and letting go of control holds a magic key to living authentically. As we fully live every moment in co-creation and concert with our divine connection to Spirit, we open the door to our creativity, passion, and aliveness.

☀ Medicine Tasks ☀

The practices of listening and silence help us open to those unknown, creative places in life. They cultivate receptivity within us. When we change our outgoing energies into a state of receptivity, we create an openness that invites something fresh or unexpected to occur.

The more we can be with the open spaces in our mind and not always speak the answer or the thought, the more comfortable we'll be with the uncertainties of waiting for the unknown to reveal itself. Silence also promotes a state of inner peace and a sense of internal relaxation.

Try these practices to cultivate your ability to listen and be silent.

1) Notice if you spend a lot of time conversing, whether related to business, homemaking, or simply talking to friends. If this is so, set aside time daily or at least weekly to be alone and quiet. If that seems impossible, make an agreement with people in your life to allow you to be silent for a certain period. Tell them not to expect dialog from you during that time. It could be a day, an afternoon, an hour, or only 15 minutes. Just let it be focused time.

2) Notice if in conversations you spend a lot of the time being the talker. If so, practice spending more time as the listener.

3) An extremely powerful move is to learn a meditation technique. (More about this in Chapter 9 – Key 6.) When starting, meditate for a minimal amount of time—about five minutes at first—so any resistance to it will be lessened. Once you establish meditation as a habit, then do it for longer periods as you feel so inclined. But don't push, for too much pushing will end the practice as other parts of you resist being pushed.

4) Next time you feel the urge to "fix" friends' problems, Witness yourself doing this. Then consciously ask, "What must they be feeling in having this problem?" Trust your intuition and then say, "I imagine you must be feeling _____," repeating what they told you back first. This helps them

feel heard. Don't tell them what they're feeling; offer a guess to show your willingness to empathize. This is a powerful relationship tool in *any* situation. After it seems they're feeling heard and understood, then ask, "Would you be interested in some of my ideas of what to do about this?" They might say, "Not right now." Perhaps they want to wait until something in their life reveals an answer. You can always ask again later but honor that request and acknowledge them for their ability to wait.

5) Next time you find yourself in a tough situation or making a difficult choice, honor your feelings and then ask, "What am I feeling about this?" It's helpful to write out your answer in the first person from an inner part of you. Let it be spontaneous. Maybe your emotional part is so angry, it wants to curse and be mean. Allow that to happen without censorship or righteousness. Or perhaps it's scared, concerned, or worried. If your vocabulary for emotions is limited, look online for lists of emotions to give you ideas.

Sometime after or during this writing exercise, go to a place in nature or do an activity that brings you pleasure. (See Chapter 8 – Key 5 for ideas.) Let yourself totally be in the moment of doing that activity. Take in nature without thinking about an issue of concern. With discipline, tell yourself, "You can think about it later but not now." Feel the breeze or the sun on your skin, the ground under your feet. See the beauty of what you're looking at or marvel at the blessings of the natural world. This brings you into your right-brain less-linear Self where you can *feel* or *sense* fresh answers rather than mentally figure them out.

Chapter 8

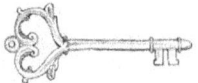

Key 5 Right Brain Integration—Soul Food

Living our lives with all the pressures related to survival and day-to-day details, we tend to spend most of our time functioning in our left-brain, which is the norm in Western culture. However, indigenous or nature-based cultures know a secret. For centuries, they've integrated movement/dance, voice/song, music/rhythm making, and other right brain, creatively expressive activities into their daily lives. They also included rituals, praying, or creating art together.

What Nature-Based Cultures Know

People in indigenous cultures understand how these right brain activities bring balance to the challenges of daily living, open minds in problem solving and foster connection within the community. They also bring health to the body and aliveness to the soul. These right brain activities are meant for everyone to participate in, regardless of skill level. Some may be more talented than others, but they all engage, usually with the whole community.

Remnants of this kind of activity such as singing in church still exist in our culture. But as people become disillusioned with more dogmatic forms of expressing spirituality, it's lessening in frequency. Communal expression occurs in a distorted form in bars through drinking and sometimes dancing. Therefore, it's not surprising that alcohol and drug abuse run rampant in these environments, which are main options for social engagement. Watching sports provides another community ritual, but this activity doesn't provide full participation for the observers. (Though I do acknowledge there is some through the joint enthusiasm.)

It seems there are few other means for communally channeling the tension of daily living. Moreover, stress is enhanced with many mandates put on our behavior and yet few outlets for healthy releases through creative self-expression.

With many right brain activities, we tend to fall into the category of either performers or spectators. This leaves most of the population only *good enough* to sit around and watch. But healing and transformation comes through participating—that's the magic!

Feeding Your Soul Self

Dr. Stanislav Grof,[1] a well-known neuroscience researcher and creator of Holotrophic Breathwork™, has researched altered brain states for over 35 years. He says the human body has an organic desire to heal and bring itself into balance, hence when in a naturally induced trance state, healing will automatically occur. He devised his form of breathwork to bring people to this trance/altered state using the breath. Due to its effectiveness, many other forms of breathwork have followed.

Key 5 discusses options that can create this right brain and balancing altered state naturally. It can be most anything—singing, dancing, music making, writing creatively, gardening, theater, nature immersion, and more. My indigenous oriented teacher calls this Soulcraft because it feeds your centered Soul Self, brings it to the forefront, and thus makes it more prominent in your life.

Have you ever noticed how differently you feel when you take off from your normal life and do something you love? (I am not speaking about an addictive habit.)

---

[1] http://www.stanislavgrof.com/

Three Main Criteria

There are three distinguishing features to these activities that heal and transform.

1) You need to participate. (Watching has some benefit but not nearly to the degree that participating does.)
2) You do it for the sheer enjoyment of it and *not* for a goal such as having to become great to prove something (though you might in the process), or you have to make money or lose weight from doing it. (This might happen but the "have to" isn't there.)
3) You're totally immersed in the moment in the activity. (You lose track of time, meaning you're totally present.)

Creative Expression—The Joy of the Journey

When right brain activities fit the three transformational criteria, I call them Creatively Expressive Activities. Creativity and this altered healing state can also come through any activity such as sports, daily chores, work, volunteering, or social projects. Though this state of creativity can be expressed in any area of life, I refer mainly to artistic forms of expression. Much of the healing that occurs relates to surrendering to the moment, for which these creative endeavors provide excellent practice. In addition, they are fun or at least uplifting and speed your path of transformation *away from* depression, anxiety and addictive behaviors and *toward* freedom.

Practicing any form we choose provides a greater opportunity for creative and healing energy to come through us. Gaining more experience gives this energy more freedom to create through its vehicle of expression—you. However, it's also possible for it to express through you *without* skill or experience on your part. You only need to get your mind out of the way and refrain from judging the outcome. You'll likely experience the most creative freedom by finding a balance between structure and no structure. When you've gained enough structure/skill that you aren't struggling with basic capabilities, you can be more fully in the moment, and may even feel the spirit working through you.

"Become One with the Medium"

When I asked an artist friend his definition of creativity, he said, "My measure of creativity is how much you become absorbed in the process so that you become one with the medium through which you are creating."

When you are fully present, every moment is creative. In athletics, it's referred to as being "in the zone." Though full absorption is not a criterion for creativity, it does help you manifest what you're creating. Paradoxically, creating is not about the result; it's about the process.

While having skill and expertise help, they don't always assure creativity or this state of absorption. Accomplished artists, musicians, and writers can sometimes lose their in-the-moment fresh expression and, with it, the joy in their art form. At such times, their art may be reduced to mechanical replications that rely on repetition of past successes. Their skill might allow them to produce something that's acceptable by society's standards, but it lacks soul, depth, and the ability to touch viewers or even the artist themselves. By comparison, I have witnessed audience members moved to their core by beginners who wrote and sang their own songs, which emerged from their soul center of creativity.

Creativity Lost and Found

When *have to* replaces *want to* or *love to*, an important element for creativity gets lost. Creativity isn't just about performing or producing; it's about surrendering to its spirit. That's when something powerful and beautiful can result, especially if you learn not to judge it by worldly standards.

Our judgments and expectations cause us to lose our capacity for spontaneous creativity. They make it difficult to experience the unknown of the moment where true creativity is born. Often, we don't know how to surrender to the emptiness and openness of the moment—where the magic is. We become attached to an outcome and fear we won't meet idealized standards—our own and those of others. In effect, attachment and fear close off the flow of creativity. Even if we manage to be open long enough to let something happen, we often judge the outcome as "not good enough." Thus, learning to disarm our inner critic/judging parts (as discussed in Key 2) is essential to creativity.

Going into a Trance

When we become extremely absorbed in the moment and in the process, we often go into a *trance*—that is, functioning from a primal portion of the brain. Indigenous cultures have used trances for eons because of their healing and balancing properties. Being in this type of trance also enhances their ability to create a deeper connection to others, life, and Spirit. People commonly induce trances through repetitive actions particularly with sound that might include chanting, dancing, singing, drumming, playing special instruments, or using specific breathing techniques.

Though these forms of expressive arts are therapeutic, almost any form done with full focus can induce a healing trance state—especially when we no longer have to rely on our left brain to perform the activity. When we let go of our linear thinking and move into the moment this way, we access a connection that brings us ever closer to a state of peace and balance.

Not only is the trance state healing to the body, psyche, and emotions but when we add intention, the trance intensifies the intention itself! For example, say you affirm your intention to heal a certain part of your body or to be free of a certain limiting pattern. If you state this intention before going into a trance or during it, amazing miracles result—particularly if you repeat the experience on different occasions. Typically, rituals induce trances through sounds, smells, candles, environment, and invocation. The participants then set their intentions through prayer, singing, or proclamations—affirmations stated out loud.

This concept of an altered state brings up the use of substances, for which indigenous people have a healthy viewpoint. Natural plant substances from the earth (rather than made in a lab) are used on occasion under the guidance of a shaman—a respected healer and spiritual guide. Shamans support people in using plant medicine by integrating it with spiritually oriented rituals for insight, growth, and personal transformation. Please understand the difference—they are not using these substances for simple fun or escape.

Instincts Suppressed at an Early Age

In my workshops, most participants have experienced a specific suppression of their innate instincts toward any artistic or creative endeavors. For example, some loved to sing when they were children and then were told, "Keep your voice down; you can't sing." Others loved art projects but were told not to make messes, or they thought their pieces were not as good as others. Some loved to dance but were told they had "two left feet."

In high school, I enjoyed rhythm and had natural abilities with music. I wanted to take up drumming, but drumming was taboo for girls at the time. I wanted to sing and took singing lessons with a woman from down the street. But the songs she made me sing felt so corny and strange that I quickly lost the desire. Plus, I believed I couldn't sing the songs right anyway. When I was forced to take piano lessons from an uninspiring teacher who didn't make it fun, I lost my desire to learn to play. Consequently, I dropped the exploration of music except to listen to what others have created. Yet over most of my life, I harbored a futile longing to make music myself.

Later in life, though, my interest in music resurfaced. I took classes and learned hand drumming well enough to teach others. Then I taught myself to sing, play piano, and play flute well enough to play with others. I don't consider myself a "star" at any of this, but it makes no difference because playing music even at this level, has brought me so much joy and connection with others.

People can be jokesters with a propensity for wit and humor, but they never even thought about cultivating it by writing comedy or taking an improv theater class. We hear about frustrated poets who, on rare occasion, put something heartfelt on paper, only to be stuffed in a trunk. This sentiment was exemplified when one man said, "I don't know if I will continue writing because I don't know if I am a writer." Of course, he's a writer, just as I am a singer and someone else is a dancer or poet. We are not to be acknowledged as such by our culture's narrow standard of acceptable artistic expression but by our innate heart for it. Consequently, expression of this type is mostly limited to the few who meet society's high standards. Even those who try hard to meet these standards often lose their personal sense of creative expression in the process.

Think of all the possibilities for artistic creative expression. The key is to pick anything that catches your fancy, even if you're not sure you want to stick with it. No matter how unskilled you believe you are, trust your intuition and experiment. Remember, creative expression is about the process, not the product!

This concept may be difficult to grasp in a society that rates everything according to performance, ability, appearances, and so forth—and creates much unhappiness for many. However, countless stories from others concur with my own experience of how relaxed, satisfied, and joyful I feel after doing favorite right brain activities—no matter what other upsetting life events are occurring.

The attitude "if you don't do it great, don't do it" can get people stuck in unsatisfying left-brain ruts. It's common to buy into the propaganda about doing something for the product rather than the process. Sadly, this belief keeps many people from ever even beginning to express themselves creatively, and we *all* have the capability within us. So let's rebel against the concept of keeping the expressive arts for the "talented few" and be part of bringing it forth for the innately creative many.

The Capacity to Create

In the workshops I facilitate, we play with improvisational singing, rhythm, movement, and words. At first, this seems intimidating because people have preconceived ideas of how they're supposed to perform. But it's exciting to see them set aside their internal critic and just go for it. What emerges is an aliveness, playfulness, and spontaneity that often produces amazing results. When the pressure of judgment and "supposed to be" is lifted, they're astounded by their innate capability to create.

Amid expressing themselves and playing in a safe space, deep truths emerge easily and spontaneously. It's beautiful to see how a profound

> awareness and shift can occur while having fun. Afterward, participants feel vitalized, inspired, and transformed. Moreover, once they've had the experience of suspending self-judgment so something creative can come through—responding to the magic of the moment—they have a point of reference for doing this elsewhere. They understand they are indeed creative and can apply their creativity to anything they do.

Express Creatively and Focus on the Process

Many possibilities for creative expression abound: taking a tap or jazz dance class, a drum class; joining a chorus; doing sketching, painting, sculpturing, photography, creative writing, acting, or improvisational comedy. At age 44, my sister took up ice skating. A woman I know in her 60s takes an Afro dance class. Others start to learn new skills in their 70s or older. It's never too late to start. Although private lessons are great, there's something wonderful about learning a skill with others who also enjoy doing it.

I was a closet car singer for years. Because I couldn't sing perfectly on pitch, I never sang in front of anyone. Mostly I sang on long trips in the car. Tears would roll down my face when I heard certain singers perform because I'd think, "That's me. I'm supposed to be able to do that! I got a bum deal and wasn't born with the pipes."

At different points over the years, I have taken singing lessons but quit because I didn't seem to improve. Clearly, I'd been hung up on results. I finally decided to accept my voice the way it was and just enjoy singing, whatever came out. With this new perspective, I've come to *enjoy the process* instead of striving for perfection.

Once I made that decision, I was internally guided to do different exercises, which led me to *acapella* improv singing. Because of this new attitude and what came to me, my voice actually began opening. Though my singing isn't the quality of a recording star, I don't care. I can now hear the pitches, make up harmonies and have fun with it. I am even expressing myself with my own songs and sounds.

After becoming more playful, putting less pressure on myself, and being willing to be seen without being perfect, my voice opened even more. I then began leading group song circles, participating and performing in an *acappela* singing group, teaching improv singing, and then doing solo performances of songs I have written. Ultimately, I created and recorded 2 CDs of songs I wrote related to these 7 Keys—at first the songs were using other singers and later with me singing my own songs!

This to me is a miracle, not only because of where I started, but because of the great joy it has brought me. In addition, the opening that transpired with singing has crossed over into many other areas of my life.

Getting Lost in the Moment

I encourage you from my heart to begin a creative endeavor. Letting go of your judgment may be the most difficult part, even more challenging than learning the skill itself. If you can let go of the judgment, however, not only will you enjoy yourself tremendously, but you may even discover you have a great deal more talent than you realize. For example, during a singing class, a woman had stood up to perform her piece. In her attempt to go for it in the way the teacher suggested, this woman judged herself when she made sounds she thought weren't beautiful. But after receiving feedback that we could see how her judgments held her back, she let go and quit worrying about what her voice sounded like. As a result, her singing came out not only powerfully but beautifully and deeply expressive.

When you attempt creative expression, it doesn't matter if you call what happens talent or not. What matters is letting go of your idealistic expectations and getting lost in the moment. Though it might seem difficult or scary to persist, a part of you will leave the experience satisfied, fulfilled, and genuinely happy.

Most people report that the satisfaction derived through creative efforts spills over to other areas of life, allowing even humdrum work to be performed with enthusiasm. *And that supports recovery from any unhealthy addictive behavior or disabling emotion,* for inner happiness will transform any experience.

Joyfully Charged by Dance

At one point in my life, I was an aspiring dancer struggling in New York City to make it professionally. Then suddenly I realized that, though I loved to dance, all the fun had gone out of it. The joyful experience of dancing for its own sake was no longer present. Drained and exhausted, I decided to quit it as a professional endeavor. Now when I dance, it's for fun—improvisational and creative with no rigid standards to meet. And when I dance, I am joyfully charged by it.

Multiple Benefits

Consider other benefits of creative expression as well. My improv singing teacher said many women reported to her they'd lost weight while taking her class—without even trying. Apparently, something had happened to their psyches that had caused a shift. They let their voices be heard and became willing to be seen nonjudgmentally by themselves and others. What's the takeaway? *The more opportunities you give yourself to express creatively—to focus on the process rather than the product—the happier you will be.*

Another great benefit is finding answers to challenging questions with more clarity and assuredness. Einstein said, "Solutions to our problems cannot come from the same mind that created them." Creative expression helps you access a different part of your brain, so you can come forth with entirely different solutions than you might otherwise have thought of or choose.

Many different programs exist for inner-city and at-risk teenage youth involving art, student created theater, or wilderness rites of passage. These right brain-oriented programs have a high success rate in changing the attitudes and lifestyles of the participants. From this we can project a strong potential for dealing with social problems by making expression through the arts and ritual more available. How can we make arts and other expressive activities a normal part of our culture, including our own lives?

Make Your Journey Fun!

Committing yourself to a program of creative expression makes your journey through life and personal transformation more enjoyable. Since lightheartedness is an important attribute of an enlightened, happy, and whole individual, start working on this fun part now. Even making a commitment to creative expression for just a few hours one day a week will support you on the rest of the journey. It can give you self-confidence, inspiration, strength, and an optimistic outlook that will support you with other challenges you may face.

Along with assisting other deeper work right brain creative expression (especially that fit the 3 criteria on page 163), has the capacity to forever shift depression, anxiety and numerous forms of addictive behaviors. Even if it seems like you have to force yourself to do one of these things, do so. Think of it as medicine, at first maybe hard to go down but in time you will want to take it for all that it does for you.

Becoming more expressive in one area of your life carries over into other areas. Soon you'll find it easier to know and express your feelings and truths to others. Ultimately, this leads to more personal power, which not only helps you to express your personal truth but allows you to take the risks involved in expressing that truth (see Key 7 – Chapter 10).

Expressing your truth as well as your creativity enhances enthusiasm and motivation, which helps you go for what you want in life. It's a self-supporting cycle rather than a stagnating downward spiral that depression or addictions pull you into. As mentioned in Key 4, aligning ourselves with the benevolent forces feeds and brings forth our Soul Self. Artful, in-the-moment activities do just that, thus making it easier to transform addictive behaviors of any kind. After a while, your whole life becomes a fuller expression of who you truly are, including what you put forth into the world.

Bringing art forms alive in your life—together with learning to express your truth—is a winning combination for creating a more fulfilling, passionate, and expressive life, free of spiraling negative emotions and behaviors. Why? Because brain changes on a neurochemical level occur from a heightened state of living. Behavior patterns that move *away from* this heightened vibration simply lose their appeal. Know that you don't have to be "good" at the form of expressive arts you choose; just start. Take a class or return to something you once loved. It simply has to pique your interest.

Unknowing Truths

When I was about 18 and lived in San Francisco, I made a statement I'll never forget.

I had walked out of a huge gay bar where everyone including me was dancing with reckless abandon. When we came out dripping with sweat, exhausted, and exhilarated, I said to my friends, "Wow, that was worth many hundreds of dollars in therapy!" At the time, I had no idea the intense truth of the statement and how that concept would play an integral part in my life's soul work!

I also said, "We just danced our brains out!" Another unknowing truth—dancing ourselves out of our left brains into a healthy trance that took us to another place in our brains that naturally creates healing, balance, and joy.

Time to Start is Now

To begin Key 5 and cultivating a more creative, healthier life, pick any art form and play with it—whether it's music, dance, painting, writing, theater, singing, or other. Notice how the rules and judgments we apply to other aspects of our lives also get applied to these arts. We either stopped doing similar activities at an early age or never started. If we did begin but weren't "good enough" to be ranked high or bound for a career, chances are we weren't encouraged to continue, or worse, were told to stop.

Even if we were encouraged, our own comparisons and self-appraisals got in the way. Thus, we ended up leading "responsible" adult lives with few avenues for creative expression. It's no wonder depression, anxiety and addictions are rampant. Overly left brain lives can be boring and uninspiring! Notice the thoughts or activities that keep you from starting or continuing to do something creative. (witnessing – Key 2) However, you don't have to let it stop you from taking any small first step.

If you are depressed I understand the tendency to not want to do any of this. But just set a strong intention, perhaps call to your higher power or soul self to help you get yourself to do one of these positive and ultimately enjoyable activities. It will pay off in the long run. It is often easier to get yourself *to do* something than it is to *not to do* something. Then when your energy shifts from what you are choosing to do, it becomes easier and more natural *to not do* those things you would prefer you wouldn't.

The Soulcraft activities that you choose will "grease the wheels" of your growth and healing path, making your journey easier, faster, and a lot more fun!

Medicine Tasks

1) List one to three forms of expression that you are strongly attracted to but might have never done, did something with it at some point, or rarely do now.

    _____, _____, _____

2) Using each of your answers to number 1, fill in the blank and answer each question that fits:

    - When did I stop doing _____?
    - Who silenced me or stopped me from starting _____?
    - What was or am I scared of _____?
    - What do I believe to be true about me in relation to _____?
    - Is (what I believe that stops me) really true? Or does it have to be true forever?
    - What would it take for me to start or expand on what I do in this area? _____
    - Do I see taking care of myself in this way important enough to make it a priority and give up something else if necessary? _____ (yes or no)
    - What might I have to give up, move or let go of for now in order to make space in my life for this? _____

3) Pick one form of creative expression or type of right brain activity. Make a commitment to begin on a small scale and follow through at least once a week. Do this for one month and see how it feels. Extend it if you like the results.

Chapter 9

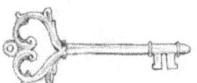

Key 6 Practices—Committing to Healthy Routines

Key 6 is about the power of committing to one or more healthy practices. Each practice you select has the capacity to both expand your Soul Self presence and increase your state of feeling good. Many people report that, after doing one or more of these practices for a time, it gets them high in a natural way. This natural high has them feeling better more consistently than other unhealthy avenues they had previously used to feel good (or less bad).

The Deepak Chopra Center for Well Being has a similar strategy on helping people get off their addictions or other detrimental habits. The center's patients are given so many ways to feel good that they don't want to dampen it with addictive habits or substances. They are told to not resist the addiction but "be with it" and witness the feelings that come up as they begin to feel the urge (Key 1: Witness). The idea is to feel so much better from all these practices that they don't want to ruin it using antiquated, unconscious ways to feel good. In the long run, the unhealthy addictive approaches pale in comparison because these behaviors don't actually get them to feel good, at least not for more than a very short time. In effect, they help avoid pain for that short time, but then they feel worse after. Whereas the feel good approaches the center uses has a lasting and upward spiraling effect.

Adding Positive Practices

Any positive Soulcraft, health or life practices you do will have you feeling lighter, more joyful, and ultimately better about yourself. Even if only a hardly noticeable amount at first. Each practice you commit to helps create an upward spiraling cycle. This draws you to move forward rather than resist what you don't want. It opens the door to positive feelings and self-appreciation, hence moving you on your way to greater vitality and ultimately the ability to move beyond your depressive feelings or addictive habits. (This is especially true when you simultaneously deal with the underlying psychological issues as discussed in this book.)

A word of caution: Don't be over ambitious. Make your practices easy and brief so you experience benefits that outweigh the efforts. Besides, over committing will lead to quitting. As I explained to my chiropractic patients about exercise, "Make the effort less than the reward you get from it." Then you're less likely to hear from the resistive forces within. And you'll feel much better than the energy output it takes to do the exercise or practice.

Of course, you can add or switch practices as your capacity to handle more grows. No rules; just know that the practices you stick with will pay off in many ways. As you fill your life with actions that expand your Soul Self, the less room you'll have for activities that take you in a direction you know in your heart you don't want to go. And as you begin feeling better from the added practices, you won't want to lose those good feelings you thought only came from negative habits.

Expansion/Contraction—a Fact of Life and Growth

Warning! An expansion/contraction principle is in force that works like this: As you do elements of the work—whether it's specific practices mentioned in the book or additional healthy choices—aspects of your body and your being relax. With these new openings, you'll feel better than you did before.

However, just as you allow yourself to become intimate with someone new by opening your heart and allowing that person in, a point of unfamiliarity and even discomfort sets in due to these expanded feelings of "goodness." Next comes a contraction in response to the expansion. That's when, in a relationship, you might push the person away, pick a fight, or shift your tone or do something else until things aren't lovely anymore.

We do the same thing within ourselves. We expand to feel great, then we *slip* and do something that leads to not feeling great anymore. It could be a full-fledged slip into an addictive pattern or something simpler.

What's the magic that will keep you from falling back into the abys? You refuse to shame yourself! In fact, as stated in Key 4 – Chapter 7, just the opposite happens. You want to bring compassion and understanding, knowing this expansion/contraction cycle is *completely normal!* It's how you stretch to make room for receiving more good, more love, more joy!

If your partner reached that tipping point of expansion-to-contraction before you, you'd handle it the same way in your relationship. Don't react with anger, self-pity, or shaming yourself or the other. Just accept it as a fact of intra-psychic life. You have to slowly expand your capacities for more goodness of every kind. Whether you are loving another or loving yourself in all the ways discussed in this book. If you don't judge another or yourself for a slip, and accept it as a learning and growth period, you'll stretch your capacities more and sooner.

When the contraction happens, simply witness it and say, "I know what's going on here. I will wait this out. I love you, I appreciate the growth and stretching you have done, and after a short break, (and even a fall back) I'll get back on the horse." Growth, whether in a business or within ourselves, is best achieved this way.

Time for Consolidation

For years, what I'd done was push, stress, work super hard, then push some more and finally burn out. When I hit a burnout, I rolled into sliding back to what sometimes was zero as in quitting, and then have to start all over again from scratch. But rather than continue until I burned out, I learned a more potent way to manifest and create change in a business training. It involves applying uphill energy at a pace I could keep consistently, and then allowing a period of backing off or what is called *consolidation*—a rest period with little or no efforting. This is the time to integrate what has been gathered and harness it so the change or new can sink in. After the consolidation phase, it's back on the forward-and-upward road again with a fresh energy, enthusiasm and wisdom.

In this expansion/contraction cycle of working with your own forward movement from negative emotions or addictive behaviors, if you take the contraction as a rest period after all the growth and expansion, it doesn't have to roll into a full-on slide-back contraction. Rather, see it as a relaxation period for allowing the new state of being to settle in. In neurobiology, it's a time for new neural pathways to take hold and become a true new road. It's like taking time to let the pavement firm up before running cars and trucks over it. Once the road gets ruined, it's back to the old potholes again. By giving it plenty of consolidation time without pressure, the new neural pathways can settle in. It becomes a new highway that takes you where you want to go.

When you've made progress but start feeling an urge to reduce your discipline or you have inkling to undo your recent good, then back off. Allow yourself to have that break time rather than go into ruination. Accept small backward movements or simply take a rest from going forward. Witness what's happening with no judgment of yourself, others, or the process. This contraction *will* pass if you wait it out without judgment or actions to attempt to avoid it. With this level of self-love and acceptance you *will* want to resume your practices again, sooner rather than later, had you gotten on your case for stopping.

Powerful Practices to Choose From

Most progressive recovery treatment centers include classes in many of the following practices, and I highly recommend them. Choose from this list, take a class or two, learn on your own from the internet or add others not found listed here.

Meditation

In countless studies relating to brain science, mediation comes up as a winner. In double blind studies on many different counts, when meditation is introduced, people's physical and emotional health improve. Seek meditation and teaching styles you like. Courses can be found anywhere from hospitals to yoga studios to corporations to television and YouTube.

Meditate between five minutes to an hour a day or for 20 minutes twice a day. Commit only to what's doable so you will actually follow through. Let me encourage you by saying this: "The days I meditate, I typically feel calmer and more energetic, and my day just flows better."

My personal style starts with a breathing exercise that includes affirmations I say in my mind. I ask for Earth Mother, Divine Father, Christ, and other powerful white light brother/sisterhood energies or personal guides or angels to walk with me this day. Then I start saying a mantra, which involve simple words carrying a higher vibration than normal that I repeat over and over. This helps calm and focus my mind and brings me into the present moment. I move between a few words such as *At Peace, Atma* (God, the One, or Divine Consciousness in Sanskrit, the powerful spiritual language of India,) or *Ahma* (a softer way to say Atma with more of the Divine Feminine). I also say *here now* to remind me to be present rather than letting my mind drift to multiple thoughts. I stick with one of these words for a bit and switch to another, saying one of the two syllables on the in-breath and one on the out-breath.

Eventually, I let all the words go and be quiet. When a thought about something comes back in (and it always does), I notice I'm thinking as quickly as I can. Then I bring it back to the simple in-out of my breath or perhaps the mantra of *here now*. The key is not judging that I'm thinking again. I simply notice and bring back my thoughts to right now. Eventually, the active brain "gives up," allowing longer and longer stretches of silence. With that comes a calming inside, plus a palpable feeling that something is letting go. It might take you a number of sittings to get to this place of letting go, or it might come on your first try. But if you just keep doing it as a practice, you *will* notice a shift in time. It becomes rewarding and completely worth the effort.

Another technique is to notice the space between the in-breath and the out-breath or the space between the thoughts. Watch as the spaces get longer. If you get caught up in thoughts again, then as soon as you notice it, go back to paying attention to the empty spaces between the thoughts. It's powerful if you can feel or hear your heart beat as well. This is another great focus for coming back to the present moment.

I'm of the school of thought that says "be gentle on yourself." Allow the quiet to emerge rather than force yourself into a rigid practice such as saying a mantra the entire time or counting from one to ten over and over. I also prefer eyes closed over eyes open.

You'll be fine in your meditation practice if you follow these instructions. Or research different techniques and try them until you find what feels best to you. Start with a short time goal—even five minutes—and extend the time when you feel ready. Watch any tendency to be over ambitious, and keep the time commitments short so you can experience success early. You can always sit longer if you feel like it at the time.

Prayer

To be in prayer is to consistently hold the belief (in word and thought) that this positive organizing principle (some call God and a host of other names and ideas) will organize and create around the way you see it, feel it, and believe it can be with the depth of your heart. Even when you don't see the evidence in your own life or never have, it's possible for all manner of miracles to occur simply from the consistency of those "prayers" or statement of intentions (especially when stated in the present tense or accompanied by the words I Am).

One way to pray is this: "God (or whatever name resonates for you)—Divine Light—Christ—Christ light—Benevolent force of the Universe—Great Pure Consciousness, I trust you. I trust you to help me _____ (fill in the blank). I am so grateful for _____ (what you are working on manifesting such as a healthy motivated life, financial freedom, comfort, flexibility, etc.).

Prayers are answered more fruitfully and easily when asked in the affirmative. Instead of praying by mentioning what you *don't* want, pray for what you *do* want. Rather than say, "Please help me over this addiction" you'd say, "Please help me become truly healthy in mind, body, and heart. Rather than help me out of this financial hole I am in, pray to be lifted to a life of enough—more than enough—and even excess to share and help others."

There is no specific time to pray. In fact, the more often you pray throughout the day, the better. Every time you hear yourself complaining about a financial situation or a person who drives you crazy or your physical aches and pain, say a positive prayer. It can be stated as a request. Yet even more powerful is stating your prayer as gratitude for what's already happened. "Thank you, Great Spirit, for this perfect health and energy I am experiencing and for all the tools and knowledge you have sent and continue to send to help me get there. Thank you, Divine Mother, for the most amazing loving partner you are sending or have sent to me. Thank you, Christ, for that job I have been waiting for, that promotion or new direction. I *trust you* to provide!"

Never give up on your prayers; the Divine's timing is different than yours or mine. Keep holding that belief and trust you *will* be provided for in Spirit's or God's timing. It can be a test of your faith, but *do not* give up. Keep saying, "I trust You to provide."

Many Bible statements support these words about prayer, but I cannot quote them as my deep convictions and beliefs about the miracle power of the benevolent forces of the Universe come from the multitude of my personal experiences. They seem to grow with my growing level of trust.

You know you are in trust when you feel relaxed about what has not yet manifested or come to pass, even when it's a solution to a challenging situation. Keep saying, "I trust You to bring this to a peaceful or blessed resolve" and "I know in my heart of hearts that all is well."

So whether you hold it as there is a being in heaven that supplies you with your good—be it Christ, or God; or you hold it more metaphysically, (where your mind goes energy flows); or even from a Quantum Physics perspective that matter is manipulatable with the energy of our thoughts and emotions; or see it as a sort of synthesis of that which is spiritual and scientific; the bottom line is the more you align with positivity and hold a conviction in your words, belief, and actions you are guided to take, the more those things you desire in your heart will manifest.

Yoga

If you started yoga in 1970 when I did, you were considered a strange person. Today, yoga instructions and/or classes are found in almost every neighborhood, in countless books and online, and in every gym. You'll see aspects of it every place you look.

Whether you pick up a few postures (single yoga exercises) from a magazine article, follow along on TV or a video, or attend chanting, breathing, and advanced classes, at least commit a few yoga postures to memory. Include them in a routine you do regularly in the morning or at night. Though it might be optimal to adopt yoga's whole spiritual philosophy, you'll still experience powerful and lasting effects to do even a few postures on a regular basis.

For me, the regularity of doing even a small amount of yoga over many years, along with integrating the 7 Keys, has kept me pain free and flexible. It is much better to do a small bit over a long period of time than a long bit over a short period. As with any practice, regularity of even something short and easy, over an extended period makes all the difference, rather than pushing to do something extensive and then stopping.

QiGong and Tai Chi

Qigong is the grandfather of Tai Chi and the foundation of Chinese medicine. Tai Chi is only one of the many forms of Qigong.

Conventional medical science on the Chinese art of Tai Chi/Qigong shows what these masters have known for centuries: *regular practice leads to more vigor and flexibility, better balance and mobility, and a sense of well-being.* Cutting-edge research from Harvard Medical School supports the long-standing claims that Tai Chi/Qigong has a beneficial effect on the health of the heart, bones, nerves and muscles, immune system, and the mind. This research provides fascinating insight into the physiological mechanisms that explain how Tai Chi actually works. Harvard Medical School's *Harvard Health Publications* calls Tai Chi "medication in motion."

Tai Chi/Qigong is helpful for conditions including arthritis, low bone density, breast cancer, heart disease, heart failure, hypertension, Parkinson's disease, sleep problems, stroke, and *recovery from addictions*. Researchers are on the forefront of a form of care that could dramatically reshape the way drug addiction is treated in the United States. Their findings show that, with Tai Chi/Qigong, there's improvement in all categories. That includes reduced anxiety and decreased withdrawal and detox symptoms. Plus it's safe with no negative side effects or risks. Research also shows increased brain neurotransmitter activity, higher oxygen metabolism, and better sleep patterns. It also helps prevent relapses.[1]

Neurofeedback

This particular practice requires going to a practitioner or getting your own bio-feed back equipment. It is a treatment of choice with Developmental Trauma according to Bessel Van der Kolk, author of *The Body Keeps the Score*.[2] Psychotherapist Sebern Fisher uses it as a main staple in her practice which is explained why in her book, *Neurofeedback in the treatment of Developmental Trauma* and on her blog:[3]

> Neurofeedback is a computer program therapists use in their office, training clients on it to get them in touch with their own brain waves, learn what's good for the brain, and calm their thoughts."

The brain is organized from the womb in oscillatory patterns so with developmental trauma, early neglect and abuse have disorganized and dysregulated these young brains. Our fear circuits dominate. Neurofeedback can calm these erupting circuits and even grow neural connectivity, which

---

[1] Sheng Zhen Society, Master Li, ShengZhen.org Gregory Boster, LoveLightPower.com
[2] Bessel Van der Kolk, M.D., *The Body Keeps the Score: Brain, Mind and Body in the Healing of Trauma*, Penguin Books, New York, NY, 2014.
[3] Sebern F. Fisher, *Neurofeedback in the Treatment of Developmental Trauma*, W.W. Norton & Co., Inc, New York, NY, 2014.

helps us create a more coherent sense of self, so we feel safer and more centered."

I was moved to tears by Ms. Fisher's more recent interview "neurofeedback in the treatment of Developmental Trauma," as she described how deeply necessary love and attachment are to the creations of a human brain. It's because we crave the regulation of our nervous systems which love can bring, that our brains respond to neurofeedback signals which can have us feel calmer and even loved.[4]

Breathing Exercises

Like yoga and meditation, classes in breathing are offered in many areas throughout the country. Look for Kundalini yoga (mainly about the breathing), alternate nostril breathing (a calming form of breathing found in hatha yoga), breathwork (an emotionally releasing type of breathing such as Holotrophic Breathwork or Re-Birthing), and a technique called Gamma Breath.

This cutting-edge style of breathwork, Gamma Breath, taught in some recovery centers in Florida, focuses on four different breathing patterns that regulate brainwaves. It not only increases peace of mind by changing the chemistry in the brain, but it rejuvenates the billions of cells in our bodies, promoting healing of all systems on a cellular level.

Dopamine, Gaba, Serotonin, and Dimethyl tryptamine are important brain chemicals released into the system during gamma breathing. It brings people to a state of optimal well-being and higher brain and body function. It also processes non-supportive patterns and trauma charges from the past, which frees energy for more positive adaptation and authentic ways of thinking and being.

Gamma breathwork improves low energy states in all regions of the brain. On a physiological level, it also shifts brainwave patterns that perpetuate dysfunction, mood swings, anxiety, depression, disease, brain disorders, addictions, and more. Using this powerful breath sequence, the brain is

---

[4] http://shrinkrapradio.com/452-neurofeedback-in-the-treatment-of-developmental-trauma-with-sebern-fisher-m-a/

reprogrammed to function through a higher operating system that can bring forth significant life upgrades.[5]

Connecting with Nature

Being in nature helps us connect to our own essential nature. We call it "human nature" because we are part of nature and hence nature helps us connect to our essential Soul Self. There's something magical and powerful as well as deeply healing and transforming about time spent in nature.

I suggest you find a place that has trees, a pond, or a nearby trail and commit to walking or sitting in a special place as often as possible. If you can, go at least once a week. Also take extended time—a day, a weekend, a week—to be in "wild" nature. That could be camping in the woods, walking on a beach, or hiking a trail in a county, state, or federal park.

I urge you to check out Animus Valley Institute, an organization founded by Bill Plotkin, Ph.D., that offers guidance and ways to connect deeply with nature. Programs range from comfortable workshops at retreat centers to longer vision fast experiences involving back packing and days and nights of solo journey in the wild. It may feel scary, but AVI provides enough structure to ensure participants are safe. With these Animus vision fast quests there is important group work led by experienced guides that occurs before and after the actual vision fast experience. The entire experience integrating nature, group work, the wild and our fear of it organically brings up so much for clearing and deep change. I highly recommend this work as it is some of the most profound I have experienced. It takes being in nature to another level.[6] See for yourself at the web site below.

Classes in a Creative Art Form

Key 5 – Chapter 8 discussed the value of creative expression and any right brain activity. Participating in any form of art or creative expression—drawing, writing, painting, music and more—helps you move *away from* addictive

---

[5] https://www.youtube.com/watch?v=UZ-rV0M9BSg
[6] https://animas.org

patterns and move your life *toward* more balance, joy, and health. It can center you, bring you into your right brain, energize your body, calm your nervous system, and help you connect with your Soul Self. Making time for even one of these activities is essential to include in your holistic self-created program.

Ecstatic Dance

Ecstatic or Free Dance (aka Barefoot Boogie) can be extremely liberating for the Soul Self. It's Free Dance because it's alcohol free and judgment free. With this form of dance you will find yourself moving in an authentic way to creative music (not always with lyrics or familiar tunes). The music, which can have flavors from around the world is played on a great sound system with strong beats that entice your body to move. I have sent clients to this type of dance gathering, and they respond by saying how positively it affects them. They experience it as fun yet deeply healing.

I have facilitated such events within other workshops and even men who never dance say how amazed they are at how great they feel. I have met many a man who goes regularly to this type of dance who say how much it has positively changed their lives!

To find this resource in your area, google "Ecstatic Dance." It's called Ecstatic because when you can surrender to it, you feel ecstatic. This practice can bring about a natural high that is transforming as I discussed in Chapter 8 when discussing natural trance states.

It's also sometimes referred to as Conscious Dance, because the consciousness around this type of dance is expanded beyond what you'd find at your local bar or disco. In fact, it raises your vibration and hence your consciousness. This is another one of those activities that has you feeling so good that you don't want to go back to those old dark habits. Clients have thanked me profusely for sending them because, along with the inner work they're doing, Conscious Dance helps to move them forward more rapidly and brings them a lot of joy!

Changing Your Food Habits

This practice requires a category of its own because in all situations, whether emotional issues, chronic physical conditions, or addictive behaviors, instituting healthy, neurologically supportive dietary practices should be included. In some cases, it could be that food *is* your addiction. Of course, this addiction is tricky because everyone needs to eat. However, there are some specific food substances that exacerbate the situation. Today, overeating groups, weight loss programs, and other organized groups are using the 30-Day Challenge. Mainly, it involves eliminating two main types of what's understood as inflammatory foods—gluten and sugar.

Experts in the natural health field have been addressing inflammatory foods for decades. Inflammation is often related to the gluten in certain foods and especially wheat. Gluten can irritate the linings of our intestines and our entire digestive tract and set up a cycle of inflammation that effects the rest of our body. If you've grown up on bread, you've eaten plenty of wheat, which is found in most processed food today. Original wheat carries only a small percentage of gluten, but it has been hybridized and altered so much over the decades that it now contains a high percentage of gluten.

How does gluten cause inflammation? In the intestinal linings are cilia—little waving seaweed-like things attached to the inner walls of the small intestines that move the food along. At the base of these cilia are microscopic holes that allow the nutrients from the (hopefully) pre-digested foods to be absorbed into the blood stream. But when the linings get inflamed and irritated from the gluten and exacerbated by the sugars, starches or other foods you might be "sensitive" to (and in some case full blown allergic to) then those normally flowing cilia form crypts. That means they swell up, curve over, and make lovely hiding places for the yeasts (candida) and parasites that thrive on the sugars and starches passing through. It's a vicious cycle because not only are the gluten and sugars inflammatory to the gut but they feed these small creatures that inflame the lining more, thus making everything worse. Plus, the more inflamed your intestines are, the more you crave inflammation-forming foods.

What happens next? With all this irritation and inflammation, the usually tiny holes at the base of the cilia get bigger, much bigger. Through those holes pass larger molecules of undigested proteins or other inflammation-causing items that then move into the bloodstream. This causes what natural doctors jokingly call blood sludge! And sludge it is. The red blood cells that, when healthy, bounce around as mobile circles, get sticky, and stick together to form clumps. So now you have these macro molecules of proteins (not fully digested for a variety of reasons) that went through the larger than normal openings in the small intestines, clumps of red blood cells and other miscellaneous items floating around in your blood stream that don't belong there. With the general western diet, and the blood sludge it creates, it's no wonder so many people feel sluggish and depressed.

We can generalize all these foreign bodies as *oxidants* because they oxidize your blood—think rust that forms when metal oxidizes. That's why you are always hearing about "antioxidants". Taking antioxidant supplements helps to some degree, but there's nothing better than eliminating what is inflammation-causing in the first place!

Once these irritating and inflammatory substances are floating around in your bloodstream, they irritate your joints, creating aches and pains. They can even end up in your brain, causing brain fog, depression, increased desire for addictive substances and foods, and other conditions that medicine has not been able to cure. What a big, messy, self-perpetuating cycle! Is eating bread worth of all that?

Mainstream medical doctors are discovering this cycle and telling patients to stop eating glutens and sugars. Autistic and ADHD kids are being taken off gluten. Even Walmart and Target sell gluten-free food now! But know these foods are really "gluten low" rather than fully gluten free. To balance your sugar metabolism, you want to minimize how much starch-oriented food you eat. Starchy foods—pasta, potatoes, breads, some grains are just one digestive step away from sugar, so they come in close to craving sweets. You can have a small amount of a starch option to appease your sugar cravings. You can use low-gluten options as a support for starch cravings but not as a huge part of your diet. Eating other more nutrient dense foods like those containing healthy fats and oils, and proteins is your best bet for curbing less healthy cravings.

The 30-Day Challenge

A former client came in for a "tune up." In spite of some emotional issues that had recently surfaced, she said she has never felt better physically. And she's never looked better. Though I had mentioned the gluten and sugar-free option to her in the past, she only recently had started on this popular 30-Day Challenge.

The 30-Day Challenge requires you to stay off of gluten and sugar (or anything else you're sensitive to, such as dairy) for 30 days. When you stay off these items for at least 3 weeks, you usually start to feel so good that you'd prefer to let go of the few food items that pull you down than lose that good feeling. Different organizations have various forms of support for those following this diet challenge. After taking the Challenge, another client said her brain never felt clearer, her skin was better, her eyes were clear, and she felt more grounded. Remarkably, though she didn't have time to exercise as she was her mom's full-time caregiver, yet she felt great physically.

How can you find the foods that you're sensitive to short of doing expensive tests? Basically start by eliminating gluten and sugar. These are pretty much a given for being inflammatory for a huge percentage of the population. Though mainly in wheat, gluten is also found (in lower quantities) in spelt, rye, oatmeal, and a few other less popular grains. Usually, though, you can eat rice, quinoa, and potato flours, and more. Corn (as long as it's non-GMO) can be incorporated as well, though corn is a food some are sensitive to as well.

You can often find substitute breads with these items along with tapioca. Still, an excess of starch can affect blood sugar balances. It's best to keep the starches to a minimum.

Experiment with Your Food

To discover other foods you might be sensitive to, you will be testing them out on yourself. To experiment on yourself, avoid a suspected common problematic food type (or two) for three to four weeks. Then reintroduce one food at a time for two to three days to see if symptoms such as nausea, gas, cramps, bloating, stomach pain, tiredness, brain fogginess, rashes, diarrhea or headaches return. Then try this with other food types. If you experience feeling better by being off any of those foods, then those are foods to stay off of long term.

Though I mostly stay away from wheat, refined sugars, and dairy, I've been able to reintroduce some dairy without problem. But if I eat too much bread or sugar, I'm exhausted and can feel pain start up in my neck area soon after!

I used to eat a lot of brown rice and felt sleepy after a meal. At one point, I did blood-oriented allergy testing and, sure enough, rice came up as an allergen. I've learned I can eat white basmati rice but not brown rice. Something about it didn't work for me, perhaps because I had lived on it when I was younger. Our bodies seem to not like too much of one food over and over. If you have an intuition about a food that might not work for you beyond the two biggies of gluten and sugar (very sweet fruit can fall in this category), then do this test.

In time, you'll find it isn't hard to eat gluten-free. For sandwiches, you can toast rice cakes, put on a little butter or Earth Balance butter substitute (normal margarine a no no—look up why online). You might enrich it with flax seed oil or olive oil, then add the items you want (e.g., turkey slices, chicken salad, avocado for the vegetarians, lettuce, sprouts, or nut butters—other than peanut.) Eat the sandwich open faced. You can also buy a gluten-free (gluten-less) bread for sandwiches. But I've lost interest in eating sandwiches myself. Instead, I eat the meat salads alone or on a green salad, or I put on slices of turkey wrapped up in a romaine lettuce leaf with olive oil.

Also, I suggest eating plenty of salmon. Some people frown on farm-raised salmon. But the farms selling to Whole Foods Market, for example, raise them in a more sustainable way than the normal grocery stores. This type of sustainable farm raised salmon (especially from Whole Foods) is less expensive than the wild caught, has a more delicious flavor, and is buttery and tender. Whichever type you get, salmon is fantastic for your nervous system and helps calm, soothe, and ground you. It is helpful, especially with any kind of mood or behavioral issues to take Omega DHA and EPA fish oil supplements. Though nothing better than getting these direct from the fish.

Be Sure to Nutrify

When weaning your diet off sugar and wheat, be sure to eat nutrient rich foods—flax seed oil, olive oil, salmon, avocado, some nut butters, some nuts and seeds, and of course vegetables in all forms. It's called nutrify! When you nurtrify, the food cravings lessen. If you think these foods are high in calories, trust that if you eat more of the good oils and fats than the starches and sugars, your metabolism will balance out. You can actually lose weight if that's what you desire.

For more suggestions on things you can and should eat look up and check out Mediterranean diet, Cave man diet, or Paleo diet. These are diets that work mostly off of meats, fish, oils, nuts and all manner of vegetables and salads. If you are vegetarian, there are ways that these can be adapted for you as well. For some a Raw diet is uplifting but I have found it does not work for all and is best used for healing conditions for a certain time. So again, experiment with what works for your body and pay attention to your inner guidance about what is right for you. But you pretty much can't go wrong starting by eliminating wheat, sugars and high amounts of starches, and for some, dairy.

When you make these dietary shifts, your energy lifts and becomes more consistent, your brain functions with more clarity, and life feels more worth living. In most cases, depression will be positively affected by this as well.

Whatever addictive patterns, depressive states or recovery programs you've experienced, know this: Eliminating toxins such as gluten and sugar from your diet and choosing a few practices to do regularly from Key 6 and others from this book, will be integral in ensuring you have a freer, happier, more balanced and purposeful life!

Chapter 10

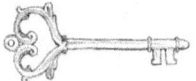

Key 7 Foundation of Trust— The Ability to Take Risks

The result of these Keys: *Developing a foundation of strength from a new relationship of trust with Self, that gives you the courage to take risks.* These risks are necessary to create a life that fits *who you really are*. When life feels true to you, and with that purposeful, the distraction of addictions lose their appeal, heavy emotions lift, and we finally feel connected. It's a sense that all is right with the world, whether things are showing up exactly as you would have them or not.

I've experienced the truth in this from my work with many others—that the outcome of integrating these keys is developing a relationship of trust with Self and Spirit. If you do the work, this happens! I used to live in fear and inner anxiety before I started integrating the 7 Keys and had grown a sense of trust in my life. The foundation of strength this yields gives me the courage to risk going for the kind of changes my inner Self tells me to make.

That means any of these can apply to you, too:

- speaking your truth to someone,
- making a major shift in how you live your life,

- letting something or someone go,
- going for a new form of creative expression, or
- taking a major leap of faith to go for a new livelihood or passion.

You simply can't take the risks necessary if you don't have this inner strength and relationship of trust with Self and Spirit.

The Journey Outward

Much discussion in this book has pertained to inner work. Now let's direct our journey out into the world. Earlier chapters focused on gaining the trust of our inner being through the practices of accepting our feelings, witnessing, listening to our inner self, speaking kindly to ourselves and others, finding multiple forms of nurturing behavior, making time for creative expression, choosing and implementing empowering practices and connecting with nature. We also might have found a wise, compassionate individual to work with one-on-one.

As we do this work, the voice of our inner being becomes clearer and more specific about what it desires and what it wants to avoid. To further increase the clarity of this inner voice and expand the presence of our Soul Self, we take risks by trying new behaviors. We go against the norm if guided, and we stand up for ourselves in ways we perhaps never have. Such practices are essential to creating a life that's true to who we are. It has us feel so "right" that we don't want to act in our old, addictive ways.

The ongoing process of developing a trusting, loving relationship with ourselves gives us the courage to stretch and take ever more challenging risks—that yield ever increasing improvements in the quality of our lives. These two powerful risk-taking actions can help to up-level everything related to our relationships and the outer world: 1) standing in our truth and 2) setting boundaries.

1) Standing in Our Truth

In previous chapters, we learned to hear our inner messages and know what our truth is. Then we learned to honor our truth by suspending our judgments and desire to talk ourselves out of it. We're now finding ways to incorporate our truths into our lives.

The next and riskier step is to *stand in our truth*—that is, holding firm to what we believe is right and true, even when challenged by others or difficult circumstances. The more we practice standing in our truth, the more our courage grows.

It's common to spend time giving in to the desires of others or conforming to their needs or standards. In growing up, we probably learned to set aside our feelings and desires when they conflicted with the expectations of family, friends, or society for fear of losing their approval or being left alone.

In addition, we've been taught that focusing on our own desires is selfish and therefore bad. Consequently, any time we begin putting our desires first or we think someone might be adversely affected by our actions, a reflex reaction occurs. That reaction either stops us from pursuing our choice or causes us great internal conflict. Witnessing is called for in such situations.

Once we become aware we're basing our actions on the desires of others or fearing their responses, we can decide to make choices centered on our own truth instead. That requires listening for our own inner knowing and facing the consequences when we act on our truth. This is where the *courage to take risks* comes in. Hopefully by now, we can draw on a foundation of inner strength from our previous work.

Fear of Consequences

At times, standing in our truth will cause adverse consequences. More times, the consequences are less horrible than we'd imagined. We fear that people will dislike us, be mad at us, say bad things, or abandon us if we do what is true in our hearts instead of what we think they'd like. Sometimes our fears are justified. Still, others are often more accepting than we think they'll be, or what occurs isn't that bad in the long run.

Survival fears come up when we take risks involving our livelihood. But often, I see the courage to make a leap of faith met by miracles that support that leap. I've also seen circumstances in which an inner-directed change was resisted because it meant giving up a certain standard of living or letting go of prized possessions. In these cases, I ask the people, "Are you willing to give up your Soul for your stuff?" (A 2016 documentary *Minimalism: A Documentary About the Important Things* brings this point home. It's easily found on Netflix.)

Assurance
Whether the consequences are nonexistent or severe, standing in our truth comes with an assurance. When decisions and actions are based on our inner knowledge and guidance, they ultimately work out for the better. The Soul Self with its direct link to higher energy knows what's in the ultimate good for all concerned, even if it doesn't look that way at first. When we look back over time, almost always we can notice it.

To stand in our truth starts by feeling into and listening to the Self. Yes, it can be confusing whether we're hearing the Self or a part. The mind can get caught up weighing all the pros and cons of the situation. Making a decision with the mind alone can be difficult and leave us frozen, unable to move in any direction.

I recommend allowing ourselves to "be in the unknown," making it a practice to stop the back-and-forth thoughts relating to the pros and cons. After initially evaluating all the sides of the situation, we calm the mind and let go of the issue. I find it helpful to stop the flip flopping thoughts in midstream and say, "I'll know when I know." Experience has given me confidence that the truest answer surfaces through either feelings or life circumstances.

Particularly when dealing with weighty decisions, the mind can cause us to play a crazy-making mental tennis game. Awareness, self-discipline and engaging in Soulcraft activities can stop this bantering and allow the creative space of the unknown to be a guide as we practice surrender. (See Key 4 – Chapter 7 for more on this.)

Holding a Question Guides Your Direction
What can help guide us in the right direction? Holding a question. It usually goes like this: "What is the highest truth in this situation? Give me the strength to stand in this truth. Give me the patience to wait for this answer."

Then we repeat it periodically every day until the answer is revealed. Although it may take a while for the answer to become clear, by cultivating an ability to be in the unknown, this waiting period doesn't have to be stressful.

The busy workings of the mind leave no room for messages from our Soul Self. Consider this: *The left brain relates to the mind, and the right brain relates to the heart.* If too much is going on in the left brain, messages from the right brain and heart can't get through.

Remaining in the unknown will open space for our highest truth to come through. Right brain activities help us cultivate this ability, including being in nature, art, music, song, dance, fun sports, exercise, or any form of play. Doing what nurtures us in times of stress can take discipline, especially if we're shut down and don't feel like participating. Just as it requires self-control to stop the internal dialogue about a decision, it takes self-management to stop what we're doing (however important it may seem) and do something enjoyable. That's when truth becomes evident.

Asking for Strength to Stand in Your Truth

The process of standing in your truth often works like this: First you have a sense of knowing about what you are feeling, what you are to do, or how you are to be. This will happen through either subtle internal senses or life's circumstances showing you a direction. Once you have this sense of knowing, your ability to stand in your truth comes into play. Although you may have a good indication of what path to take, your fear of the immediate consequences can overpower any decision. This is where extra support from your Soul Self may be required.

Asking daily for the strength to stand in your own truth can help, even in the most challenging situations. Sometimes willpower or desire to improve isn't enough to move you through a difficult situation. Regularly seeking support from your Self and/or Spirit gives you the strength to face the fear of consequences that could come from standing in your truth.

A client of mine had the unfortunate circumstances of having her car stolen when she stepped out of it with keys in the ignition, to say something to a friend across the street. This was not in a city but in a quiet neighborhood! She is a single mom and her livelihood depended on her car as she had been cleaning for a living. She had very little funds to buy another car, but her truth was, this time it had to be a good condition well running car.

She had to go through a lot of difficulty while trying to find and waiting for the "right" car. But wait she did, while holding her questions and repeated requests of her higher self to bring her this car. She held patient, trusted and stood in her truth that she deserved nothing less, even for the simple $2000 she had to pay for it.

Then it happened. Somehow, she met an elderly gentleman who had hardly used his car who would sell it to her if she could just wait another month. This act itself was a feat of inner strength given all the juggling she had to do regarding her child and getting to her multiple jobs.

She ended up with a great car for the funds she had. She has used this same type of standing in her truth and courage when she let go of the cleaning work to transition over to her Soul work—"right livelihood" as discussed in the next chapter.

The more times you move through this process, the more your strength, courage, and "knowingness" will build.

When we risk standing in our truth, we leave many knowns behind, and with them a sense of security. However, true security lies in our ability to tap into and be directed by our Soul Self. When our Exiled parts are fully vibrating because we allowed ourselves to get to know them (IFS has the tools to do this), they can directly link to information from our Soul Self. Said another way, the inner child connects us to our intuition. The healing process of getting to know and feel the old feelings of our inner child (our Exiled parts) awakens them. That's how we can come to know our current feelings and truths more clearly.

Therefore, the more we cultivate communication with our inner parts, the more we can feel connected to a higher source. And the more connected we feel, the more courage we have to take risks and face the consequences of our decisions. This doesn't mean we don't experience fear when taking risks. However, we know that the consequences of our decisions are worth the price of growth, self-expression, joyfulness, and—as my indigenous teacher calls it—living a life of Soul.

One Big Episode of Standing in My Truth

A turning point in my ability to truly support my inner child and stand in my truth came shortly after the death of my father. I was scheduled to give a weekend seminar to a group of doctors. Doing so was quite uncomfortable for me because the environment I'd be in and the image I believed I had to uphold felt rigid. This was opposite to my innately creative nature. But the fee was good, and I had spent a long time cultivating the opportunity to be hired for such an honorable position.

Before my father's death, I had been flying frequently from Hawaii to California and Florida for numerous projects. After my dad died, however, I decided my incessant doing had to stop. I wanted space and time to feel my feelings about Dad's death and whatever else might surface. Consequently, three or four weeks before the seminar, I called the head of the organization and told him because my dad had passed, I was in no condition to stand before a group of doctors. He answered, "Well, if it had happened the week before I would understand, but you have three weeks to get it together." Not wanting to cause problems, I backed down from my truth and agreed to show up.

After another week, my inner self let me know that teaching this seminar was a big mistake. Every time I thought about it, I got a sick feeling in my stomach and felt tired and depressed. Because I'd made time and space to allow deep feelings to surface, my inner being was beginning to reveal hidden emotions. I know all the activity to prepare for and then go to the seminar would interfere with my grieving process. Thus, my truth became glaringly clear—I could not go.

One of the most challenging acts of standing in my truth was calling the head of the organization and telling him, "No, I absolutely cannot do this." My sense of responsibility to my worldly commitments has always been important to me, so backing out seemed irresponsible. That message came from a manager part. However, from my Soul Self, I knew I was finally being responsible to my inner self, not just the world. My relationship with myself had often been put on the back burner for the sake of productivity, both worldly and domestic. It had always been important to take care of everything else over my deepest relationship with myself. Now I was proving to my inner being I could be trusted to put myself first when necessary. Although I certainly don't advocate breaking agreements, sometimes when we are out of balance in one direction, it takes overcompensating in the other direction to attain a healthy middle ground.

When I told the director I would not teach, he responded negatively as I had expected. His words reflected my inner patriarchal part and voice that only valued productivity. However, I knew I had to Stand Strong for My Truth, even in the face of his accusations and legal threats. I also had to stand up to my own inner critic, who wanted me to feel shame for being irresponsible. I cried deeply when I hung up the phone.

Suddenly I felt totally naked. My sense of value (called an identity) was tied to being a respected, responsible, and productive individual. Now I was dropping this persona and not letting myself be led by the part that held this identity. Instead, I was accepting that my essential being was enough. I could love myself for just "being" and not for what I did. On one level, I felt scared and vulnerable. I had just let go of my defense mechanism with its identity that my protector part had held deeply. On the other hand, I felt a renewed sense of trust in myself.

A few weeks after the seminar was to have occurred, I checked with the sponsoring college. I learned the event had very low enrollment. Consequently, by taking the risk to stand in my truth, I succeeded both in improving my relationship with myself and helping the sponsoring organization by saving it money.

Although standing in our truth doesn't always end with everyone happy, it rarely causes harm in the long run when the choice has been made from an inner truth and directed by a higher power. Other people involved may not approve of our choices, and even when things do work out the best for all concerned, they may never admit it. Nevertheless, acting from our own authenticity is ultimately more valuable than gaining outside approval.

2) Setting Boundaries

As we practice being in our truth and standing on that truth, we engage in a practice called "setting boundaries." This term has many definitions depending on the orientation of those using it. So does the term "codependence." Here's how I interpret these two terms as they apply to the 7 Keys.

Codependence means being dependent on another person's love or approval for a sense of self-worth and/or safety. If we are codependent, we won't risk doing anything we think might result in the withdrawal of that love or approval. We do what we believe will get that love, even if it goes against what's true for us.

The person or people we are co-dependent with most often represent key figures from childhood and where we try to get what is called "redemption." This means, via current people in our lives, attempting to accomplish helping, saving, or making authentic connections with those people from childhood that they represent, and where it felt impossible to do so at that time.

Codependence also means giving up what is true for us, by altering our words and actions to avoid another person's reactions. We may be trying to protect them or ourselves from experiencing a particular feeling. To play the codependence game requires ignoring our Soul Self voice that's telling us to break free of the prison the codependence is keeping us in. We also have a great aversion to feeling our deepest feelings because being hooked in a codependent loop is a type of addiction that helps us avoid those feelings—that is, until the dam breaks and we find ourselves in a flood of feelings equal to the intensity of the denial.

Escaping the Cycle

How do we get out of this cycle of codependence—internal numbing to exploding or breaking down? Through the practice of setting boundaries. Codependence and boundaries go hand in hand, with codependence being the culprit and setting boundaries the antidote.

In this context, setting boundaries means knowing our inner truth and then putting limits based on this truth. This might take the form of saying "no" to people when your tendency (though not your truth) is to say "yes." Or it might involve setting limits of allowing others' behaviors we find unacceptable such as a spouse's drinking. Although we can't change another's behavior, we can limit how much of a particular behavior we'll allow in our life, and then act accordingly.

Here is a personal example of my setting a boundary on a codependent loop with someone close. This person had been carrying an attitude toward me for a while. I finally asked what was going on and she said I had been laying a guilt trip on her when she said no about certain things. I knew I was fine about those no's and even appreciative that she would speak her truth. She didn't believe me. I set a boundary and said, "you may be feeling guilty inside about your no's and though I may experience some disappointment, I am Ok with that. I would rather have you be in your truth. I assure you there is not a guilt trip coming from me, so if you choose to feel guilty then you go right ahead as I am not buying it is coming from me." I said it in a way that was "congruent", meaning everything lined up with in me as it was my truth and hence believable. Everything shifted and lightened up after I set a boundary on what I was going to have projected on to me.

Of course, there's setting that final limit on what behaviors we will allow of ourselves in our own lives. The 7 Keys and practices in this book, along with a good therapist or support person, help us accomplish setting boundaries and limits with ourselves. As a result, we'll feel more like we're being pulled *toward* something better that we do want, rather than just resisting something we *don't* want.

When we set boundaries with others, immediate repercussions may follow. For example, if we disrupt an old dynamic between two people, resistance ensues. The other person will push every button they know to attempt to return us to the old game using such tactics as guilt, criticism, or emotional or physical abuse. Maintaining boundaries requires inner strength. Calling for divine assistance can help. Plus, once we've integrated any of the 7 Keys and/or have the support of a good therapist, our inner strength to accept the feelings associated with another's resistance will be greatly enhanced.

Dynamic Shifts

Inevitably, when one party of a codependent pair sets a boundary, the dynamic between them is altered. The other individual either rises to the occasion, raising awareness and growth in the process, or the relationship shifts. It requires risk-taking, for the codependent relationship protects both from facing their deep issues and feelings.

Fear of disruption often keeps us from setting boundaries or standing in our truth. However, often this fear does not manifest, and the other person responds to meet the challenge. At these times, it helps to ask, "Would I rather have the relationship the way it is with its apparent security or the life of my soul?" Breaking out of a deeply codependent knot can catapult us to the next level of our inner journey toward spiritual mastery. As stated in the Soulcentric Developmental Wheel, (Chapter 2) a difficult break up is often just the "crisis" that can spur us to connect more deeply with our Soul Self. Thus, leading to a Soul centered and enriched life. Although things may seem shaky while in this process, setting a particular boundary that's inspired by inner knowing ultimately leads to expansion and happiness.

Inner Trust Must Be Present

To effectively set our boundaries with others, we must have already cultivated a good deal of trust within ourselves. Our inner self trusts that our Soul Self will be present for it on all levels. Yes, we can set boundaries with others before this occurs, but our ability to do so is enhanced by having a strong base of trust in Self. Indeed, one action feeds the other: Setting boundaries helps cultivate the trust in Self, which in turn strengthens the ability to set boundaries. A well-established relationship between our inner self and Soul Self makes challenging situations less stressful. As my indigenous teacher said, it becomes a matter of being Soul-centric rather than ego-centric. When the parts are in their extreme roles (as IFS describes), they are aspects of ego. As they become transformed and trust the Self, they function in support of the Self rather than the other way around. Thus, we have a meeting of the minds with both indigenous ways and modern psychology ways of looking at it. Ego becomes the servant of Soul or, as IFS states it, we become Self led.

> **Your Greater Authenticity Changes Relationships**
> As you become true to who you are, your circle of friends' likely changes. When you put out something different, you attract people who are aligned with that. As you express yourself more authentically, you attract individuals who resonate with that. Those who can't accept the "new you" will fall away.
>
> Remember that relationships approached from an authentic place will ultimately be more satisfying. When you consistently take care of yourself, stand in your truth, and set boundaries, your relationships become richer and more intimate and fulfilling.

Substituting New Behaviors

A critical step in the process of freeing ourselves from addictive patterns is the risky business of altering behavior. Through willingness, awareness, and insight (see Witnessing in Key 2 – Chapter 5), we've opened ourselves to what's not working for us. Possibilities include nonproductive behaviors with others, addictions of any kind, belief systems that run our lives, and/or hidden feelings that plague us when they surface, demonstrating a part still needs work. Once we've uncovered these aspects and parts, worked with each part (see IFS Dialog Process Chapter 13), and integrated other aspects of the Keys into our daily lives, then we can plant the seeds of change in the form of new behaviors.

When fully established into our lives, intentional changes lead to making desired outer-world shifts a permanent part of our reality. As the adage says, "If you always do what you've always done, you'll always get what you've always got." Therefore, to get different results, we must do things differently.

New behaviors can include practices mentioned in Key 6 – Chapter 9. We can also choose different ways to respond to and reach out to others, such as seeking out new friends who resonate more with us now than those from our previous world. We can restate our commitment to do whatever it takes to move forward, re-accessing our willingness to make the selected changes. As with learning any new skill, the process of learning a new behavior requires practice and focus until it becomes second nature.

A warning—let's not use changing behaviors as another opportunity to judge and berate ourselves. We can give ourselves lots of time and room to fail. At the same time, let's acknowledge ourselves for the work done so far. Before we step out into the treacherous waters of changing behavior, we can take in our own credit, love, and support for our accomplishments. Understanding the learning process, as described in the Four-stage Process of Learning, helps us practice patience, compassion, and self-acceptance.

Four-Stage Process of Learning

In psychology the **four stages of competence**, or the "conscious competence" learning model, relates to the psychological states involved in the process of progressing from incompetence to competence in learning a new skill.[1]

1. *Unconscious Incompetence.* This is when you don't know that you don't know. In this stage learning or changing behavior is not possible. Related to self growth, it could be called denial. The individual must recognize their own incompetence, and the value of the new skill, before moving on to the next stage. The length of time an individual spends in this stage depends on the strength of the impetus to learn.

---

[1] https://en.wikipedia.org/wiki/Four_stages_of_competence Gordon Training International by its employee Noel Burch in the 1970s.

2. *Conscious Incompetence.* In general, this is when you recognize the deficit, as well as the value of a new skill in addressing the deficit. In other words, this is when you know that you don't know. For example, you may know that you want a different result in a certain aspect of life and you become aware of your limiting beliefs. But you don't yet have the ability or know any actions or tools to change the beliefs. Although you can catch yourself saying things you wouldn't have noticed before or perceive other limiting behaviors, you don't yet know how to change them. The making of mistakes can be integral to the learning process at this stage.
3. *Conscious Competence.* This is when you're learning something new with intense concentration. You start instituting a change, but it requires a good deal of attention to maintain the learning. At this step, you may intermittently slip into the old pattern. It's important not to say "ah, forget it" here. This is where the downward spiral of relapse can happen unless you've learned the fine art of self-compassion, acceptance, and self-love (Key 3 – Chapter 6).
4. *Unconscious Competence.* This is when you just do something without much extra thought. You know you know, and you don't have to think too much about it any longer, such as when you have learned a skill so completely that thought is unnecessary. At this stage, you find your life becoming a reflection of your new beliefs, actions, and behaviors.

It takes time to learn anything new, and we can never expect to succeed instantly. We tend to think that, once we're aware of a limiting action or belief and have put a new behavior into practice one time, we have mastered the change. When we revert to an old pattern, we might have an underlying feeling of "you should have done better" or "there you go, you blew it again." We can regard this as a chance to practice Key 3: Self Love and Compassion.

Finding Balance in Opposites

Cultivating balance means balancing extremes or smoothing out our unhealthy edges, then bringing them to a centered place of harmony and health. To do this, it's helpful to ask ourselves, "Does this belief, philosophy, behavior, or approach to life accentuate an imbalance I'm already experiencing, or does it make me more centered and give me greater peace of mind?" We can seek balance in any aspect of life.

How we approach our work is one example. At one extreme are people who are unmotivated, put in minimal effort, and "live for Friday." The other extreme is when people work hard in a non-stop fashion because they believe they have to "push to make it happen." When we are out of balance on this end, we commonly experience burnout or discover we're spinning our wheels without a lot to show for it. Or we might have a lot to show for it materially, but our relationships, health, and state of mind are suffering.

Finding balance in our work is both an internal and external process. The balance manifests as working with energy and focus, while simultaneously letting go and trusting "we'll get there when we get there." This allows for doing creative, pleasurable activities between projects or at least working in a more relaxed, open way.

Then there's the balance between work and play. When people say, "I can't afford to take time off," looking at the bigger picture, I often tell them they can't afford *not* to take time off. Success is not just how much money we make; it's also how happy and fulfilled we feel in all aspects of life. Unfortunately, people forget this when they put on their money blinders and think that career and finances totally define success. It's the balance that's important.

Achieving balance involves balancing the yin (non-linear, heart-centered, feminine) with the yang (logical, rational, masculine) aspects of our natures. This is reflected in making decisions from the head or the heart and approaching our lives through control or through surrender, as mentioned earlier. We also see this yin/yang issue in our tendency to "do" compulsively versus being comfortable with "being." It also shows up in isolating versus connecting and in being fixed about things versus the ability to be flexible.

Accessing Our Emotions

Another type of balance comes from listening to feelings versus working with our minds. It's about how we approach life in general. If we live mostly in our heads spending time mentally processing things, we diminish our capacity to access our emotions and subtle feelings. When this is the case, feelings tend to emerge as an expression of overload—with crisis points and periodic blowups. The swing will be from *no feelings* to *excess emotion*, sometimes along with destructive behaviors. An extreme version would be the quiet, mild-mannered guy in the back office who turns out to be a killer. At the other end would be the person who's excessively emotional and overreacts to things that appear insignificant.

Working with the mind can also help us transform our belief systems, change our self-talk from critical to accepting, and shift our perspective about something—reframing it. Although making these transitions in the mind is essential, working *only* with the mind can result in denying our feelings. We must fully feel, accept, and transform the underlying emotion before we use the mind to help us transform our thought and action patterns. (See Chapter 13: IFS Dialog Process) Consequently, both *feeling* and *thinking* need to be integrated into our growth process. In the world of therapy and especially trauma work, they call this *bottom up—top down*, with the most respected modalities in trauma work (including IFS) accessing both.

Integrating these opposites requires noticing imbalances while dropping judgment. We then work with our behaviors to achieve a balance. We can adopt an opposite mode for a while as a counterbalance. It will eventually bring us to a middle ground.

You Deserve Positive Acknowledgment

When you fall back into an old behavior or repeat a pattern you thought you'd eliminated, be loving and gentle with yourself. Give yourself credit for having the intention to change your behavior and know that any progress, however small, deserves positive acknowledgment. Your loving acceptance is an additional opportunity to enhance your relationship with your inner self and parts.

You'll soon find that the time from becoming aware of an old negative behavior to activating a new, empowered one gets shorter and shorter until the process becomes natural. After doing the deeper work, the parts worked with are ready for the changes and wont resist. It's then only a matter of learning the new behavior as described in the conscious competence model. You'll become *unconsciously competent* in your ability to practice the tools and institute the new desired behaviors. You'll find the rewards well worth the effort.

The greatest benefit for taking the risks of time, energy, and focus to change behaviors (including balancing your opposites) is a heightened sense of spontaneity, creativity, and aliveness. As we become true to ourselves, life becomes true to us. This evolves from a practice to an automatic way of life. That's when expressing *who we are* becomes easy and natural. We're living authentically.

Medicine Tasks

A. Standing in Your Truth
1) Write down the truth about three issues or circumstances that you have not yet expressed to a significant person or people in your life (or if you have expressed it, you have done nothing else about it).
2) Ask this question and write down your answer: "What is one step or action I can take to begin to express these truths, or take action towards?"

B. Setting Boundaries
1) Ask this question and write down your answer:
   - "What am I tolerating from others?" and "What can I do to begin to set a boundary regarding this?
   - "What am I tolerating regarding myself?" and "What can I do to set a boundary regarding this?"
2) Return to questions 1 and 2 periodically. Notice if you have taken any steps regarding them or if there are any new answers and actions to be taken.

C. Inventory of Patterns and Tendencies to Take the Risk to Change
Use the list below as a guide to isolate your tendencies and patterns, then add anything else you become aware of. Make a list of any tendencies that seem fixed or heavily weighted to one side or the other.

1) Self initiative and action orientation
   - Are you self-motivated to take action, or do you need outside influences?
   - Do you consider yourself a do-er or a couch potato?
   - Do you find you rarely sit still and you're always doing something, or do you sit around a lot, reading, watching TV, relaxing, and doing very little?
   - Are you a compulsive "do-it-nower," or do you tend to procrastinate?

2) Relationship to others
   - Do you spend much of your free time with others or alone?
   - Do you enjoy being with people or feel more comfortable alone?
   - Do you tend to be very open with others or closed and cautious?
   - In a relationship, do you prefer to be with the other person most of the time, or do you tend to want independence?
   - Do you experience ease with and enjoy intimacy, or do you tend to want distance?
   - Do you often take care of or help others, or do others take care of you?
   - Are you the initiator in connecting with people or the receptive one, waiting for others to step forward?
   - Are you talkative or quiet and shy?
   - Do you reach out or hold back?

3) Material world
   - Are you fastidious, or do you feel comfortable in messiness?
   - Are you always the capable one taking care of business, or do you need others to handle things?
   - Do you collect possessions, or do you have only a few things?
   - Do you spend money with little regard, or pay attention to every penny?
   - Do you believe only spiritual things matter and shy away from dealing with material possessions, or are you very attached to and material oriented?

4) Modes of operation
   - Do you easily access and focus on your emotions, or are you rational about most things?
   - Do you express your feelings a lot or prefer to keep them to yourself?
   - Do you act on impulse or think things through before taking action?
   - Are you usually optimistic and overlook the downside of things, or do you usually see what is wrong or why something won't work?
   - Are you overly trusting or overly cautious?
   - Do you talk, eat, and move quickly, or do you move slowly?
   - Do you spend a lot of time in your head, thinking about the future, planning, or worrying, or do you spend excessive time in your emotions easily upset or feeling anger, etc.?
   - Do you complain a lot, or are you constantly cheerful?
   - Do you frequently put others' needs and desires before yours, or do you tend to think of your needs first?
   - Do you work all the time taking little time for play, or do you play all the time and find it hard to stay focused?

D. *Counterbalancing*
   1) Choose your tendencies
      Look at your list of key tendencies from the list above and choose which most describes you. If you feel you have a good balance between the two sides, then skip that one, but do be honest with yourself.
   2) Take a deeper inventory
      With each one you listed above, write down answers to the following questions:
      - How does this tendency cause problems or hinder you?
      - How does it affect the quality of your relationships or ability to connect or to experience intimacy?
      - What new behavior might help you balance out this pattern?
      - If this appears to be a large undertaking, ask: "What is the first step I can take that will initiate a change toward balance?"

Chapter 11

Key 7 Continued The Give Back—Worldly Soul Expression

An important step on the road to recovery from any difficult emotional state, addictive substance or behavior pattern is to move your life toward a fuller expression of who you are in your outer world. By now, I hope you've been working the 7 Keys on your own or with an IFS, somatic, or other therapist. You've likely come to the place of spending more time living in your truth—honoring your feelings, expressing what's real for you, and taking necessary risks.

By this time in the transformation process, it's not uncommon to experience a deep desire to change jobs or careers or simply offer a "giveback" in some way. The desire might have been there for some time, but at this point, having truly engaged in the work, it will be accompanied by a willingness to do what it takes to bring about this change. This "giving back" of our gifts—in the indigenous way of holding it—is part of the natural cycle of life. (See Chapter 2.) Without this sense of connection to our core Soul Self and perhaps something greater (the Earth, the Divine), along with a meaningful way to give of ourselves, it can still feel like there's an empty place inside. It's this core emptiness from lack of purpose that is a significant part of what leads to addictive behavior, substances and inhibiting emotions. Therefore, a full recovery should include meaningful ways to give back.

Transitioning to Right Livelihood

"Right livelihood" means doing work that expresses the truth of who you are, what you love and in some way serves. It's not necessary for you to derive income from this, so don't get hung up on the cultural beliefs that only what makes money has value. Rather, if you're feeling fulfilled and joyful in what you give without a return, you'll be provided for. Or even if you cover your basic needs by doing something that's simple or mundane, you'll have joy in your heart and a lift in your step when whatever else you do feels good. This is especially true when you have a loving relationship with yourself.

Anything we do can be seen as a gift; it depends on how we do it. Buddhists call it "Chop Wood Carry Water." This means the most basic tasks can be a spiritual practice and raise the vibration around you, depending on our attitude and way of being when doing it.

A Natural Journey

I get excited when I hear someone is embarking on this stage of the journey because I strongly believe it's a natural process. More than that, it's our human right to find joy in how we express ourselves in the world. We're frequently taught that we have a work life—which can be often boring or stressful—and then we have life outside of work, which is supposed to be great because it's not work! But this isn't a reality. The unfulfillment we feel from doing work we choose not to like can carry over to our personal lives and vice versa.

This doesn't mean our inherent happiness depends on what we do for a living. After all, part of the journey is discovering peace and fulfillment wherever we find ourselves. However, when we're expressing aspects of who we are through our work or a form of giveback to the world, we find life fun and fulfilling. We notice a natural progression on this path—that is, after working on ourselves and moving through our issues, a natural desire to serve others follow. That's why "right livelihood" is also called "doing your service work."

If what you're doing brings you joy, then you are being of service to the environment, if only in adding a positive vibration to your surroundings. And it can work in reverse as well. For example, you might love being a competitive athlete (or did love it at one point), but then you become so hard on yourself to perform or win that you no longer feel the joy in it. This can inadvertently undermine the service aspect and the vibrations around you.

Doing what brings joy can serve the environment around you, even if the direct effects aren't immediately apparent. That's an aspect of how doing healing work to uplift yourself can be of service to those around you as well. It raises the vibration—the life force frequency around you. Imagine, if each person did it, how much it would affect the whole!

Transitioning to Expressive Work

There are many different ways to make your transition to expressive work. If you're one of the fortunate who love your work and feel fulfilled in it, you're probably not interested in making a change. But if you're among the majority who feel stuck, consider this option. It starts with a willingness and clear decision to make a career or job change or to express yourself through a creative project. As noted in Chapter 10 on risks, this choice comes with challenges, but take comfort in knowing your inner guidance will indicate when it's right for you. In time, it will be! And when it is the right time for taking risks, just know you will have the inner strength, courage, and connection to your Soul Self that you'll need.

On a practical level, you don't have to know exactly *what* you'll do or how you'll make this change. However, many people get stuck here—in the unknown. Because they don't have a clear image of what they want or assurance about how things will turn out, some give up before they start. They say, "I just can't" or "I will when the next job is waiting for me." A common story is this: "I'd love to get out of this job, but for financial reasons I can't." Although such a view has a basis in cold reality, other possibilities exist if you hold a strong intention and an open mind.

Although life offers no guarantees, many wonderful things happen when we take risks and work hard. They can also occur through "grace"—those miraculous opportunities bestowed upon us by Spirit (though I sometimes believe these are life rewards for other good work we have done). Still, many people wait for such miraculous opportunities but then never take action. They remain dissatisfied in their place of perceived security.

Practicing the art of being in the unknown (see Key 4 – Chapter 7) gives you the tools you need for the first step, which is to strongly tell your Self and Spirit you're ready and willing to make this change. That's true even if you don't know *what* it is or *how* you'll get there. You simply know that what you're doing now no longer serves you. It's not allowing you to use your talents to serve others.

Feeling the joy of service can be a motivating factor to support your willingness to change. This begins with your ability to be okay being in the unknown.

What Comes After Willingness?

Suppose you've clearly decided to move toward your right livelihood and giving back, and you've expressed your willingness to yourself and the forces at work. What's next? If you have no idea what you want to do, read *What Color is My Parachute* by Richard Bowles, *Do What You Love and the Money Will Follow* by Marsha Sinetar, and/or read and do exercises for discovering what you want in *I Could Do Anything If I Only Knew What It Was* by Barbara Sher or read Carolyn Anderson and Katherine Roske's *The Co-Creator's Handbook: An Experiential Guide for Discovering Your Life's Purpose and Building a Co-creative Society*. For sure, do the exercises in the Medicine Tasks throughout this book and in particular in this chapter. They may be all you need. Reading books on this subject can inspire you, help you choose, and get you back on course as they did for me.

Barbara Sher's book helped me see that giving up on my dream came from my fear and my deep programming that put financial security above all else. From doing her exercises, I was able to renew my vision and follow my dream—fulfilling my Soul and expressing myself joyfully.

Once you gain a degree of clarity (even if you still don't know exactly what the picture will look like or how long it will take (see Chapter 2 Stage 4 the Wanderer), take initial steps without worrying about being on the right path. Just put your energy in motion. If you're heading down Path A with a good deal of energy but it turns out to be the wrong path for you, all is not wasted. Eventually, Path B will emerge from the energies you've put forth. You'll have the momentum already going to advance down that new path. Sure, you may have to follow side roads with twists and curves until you get to the highway that takes you where you want to go. But don't think you're wasting time, energy, or resources. *You are putting energy in the energy bank.* And all your efforts will have a bearing on your original intention, which is to be of service in a way that's an expression of you.

Process of Applying Energy and Effort

By contrast, if you never invest in getting started, you'll never be anywhere other than where you are. Your willingness to apply energy and effort—and not struggle—in the direction you're initially motivated is critical.

The process is this:

1) Access your strong willingness to make a change.
2) Feel into or research a direction for that change. (until something hits a Soul chord)
3) Take action steps however small, even if you only have a general sense of direction.

These action steps might require enrolling in community education classes or taking workshops that teach you about your subject of interest. If you have special skills, you might do community service or offer to teach a class. To learn more, you could volunteer in a place that focuses on what interests you. You don't have to give up your job or do anything rash to begin making the change. Just start *somewhere* and trust the process.

As you take action, you'll notice a greater clarity about your course. When the puzzle pieces begin fitting together, more specific planning becomes appropriate. However, don't be too attached to any one plan. Even though you may be taking larger steps, unless you have total clarity your course is still likely to change.

Plan to Save the Money You'll Need

Start planning now for the money you will need to comfortably make the transition. Whether you need time for a job search or launching something of your own, know it will take longer than you think. Even if you're unsure of the path, still start saving or planning for how you can acquire the funds that will allow you to be without income for a while. See where you can cut expenses and save little by little. (check out *Minimalism: A Documentary About the Important Things*[1] to give you ideas.) Even if it seems it will take five years to save enough money for the transition, you're demonstrating your commitment to the change, which often sets forces in motion that make miracles occur. The transition can happen faster or slower than you planned but moving toward it will bring forth a new spirit of joy and enthusiasm that can make even drudgery seem easier.

Doing Whatever It Takes

At a certain point, you know what you want to do and you've prepared financially for the transition. That's when you need to make a bigger commitment—to do "whatever it takes." On the path of the 7 Keys, this can mean facing all the issues standing in the way of manifesting what you want. In the case of transitioning to right livelihood, it also requires doing something you've never done before. That something might be scary or involve considerable energy output and risk. But it's your commitment to this that will lead you where you need to go and make miracles happen.

This famous quote by W. H. Murray says it well:

> Until one is committed there is hesitancy, the chance to draw back, always ineffectiveness. Concerning all acts of initiative (and creation) there is one

---

[1] Joshua Fields Millburn and Ryan Nicodemus, *Minimalism: A Documentary About the Important Things*, 2016. https://minimalismfilm.com/ https://www.netflix.com/title/80114460

elementary truth, the ignorance of which kills countless ideas and splendid plans: that the moment one definitely commits oneself, then Providence moves, too. All sorts of things occur to help one that would otherwise never have occurred. A whole stream of events issues from the decision, raising in one's favor all manner of unforeseen incidents and meetings and material assistance, which no person could have dreamt would have come their way. I have learned a deep respect for one of Goethe's couplets: "Whatever you can do, or dream you can, begin it. Boldness has genius, power and magic in it."[2]

My Story of Doing Whatever It Takes

Because I have created and owned businesses since I was 25, I have many stories of doing whatever it takes to start something new. Here's how I got started leading retreats and workshops.

From having taken retreats myself and experienced my own growth as well as growth for many others, I wanted to lead experiential, growth-oriented classes. I had no idea what would be involved or where participants would come from. The odds seemed against me; I had never done this before. An unknown in this field, I didn't even have my Ph.D.c at the time.

Nevertheless, I set an intention to do this. Soon after, a friend approached me about forming a women's group, where a different woman would facilitate each gathering. My friend and I decided to co-create one of the evenings. Between us, we had so many ideas, we ended up creating two different full one-day workshops. We offered our first classes on a donation basis.

Doing something for the first time requires stretching and risk-taking. Once I was over the first-time hump, I created other opportunities, offering my services wherever possible. Eventually, I became more comfortable leading workshops and planned a week-long retreat in a natural setting in Maui where I'd experienced much healing myself. This time, I teamed up with another woman who was not only a good teacher but quite the networker as well.

---

[2] https://en.wikiquote.org/wiki/W._H._Murray

As it turned out, though, I had only partially committed to this (equal to no real commitment at all). I realized I was leaning on her to fill the retreat, and though I did some outreach marketing, I did nothing outside my comfort zone to market our retreat. She also had not fully committed herself either due to her involvement in other projects. Consequently, our efforts led to nothing. Only one person registered.

This marked a turning point for me. I would either let this "failure" defeat me or use it to give me greater determination. After a few days of deliberation, I was ready for a big shift. I told myself and Spirit resolutely, "I will do whatever it takes; just show me what to do." After that, miracles started to happen. First, the retreat center I'd booked gave me a second chance, even though they lost money when I canceled the original retreat. Next, by a series of serendipitous events, I connected with a talented facilitator who had been leading workshops for years and had his own following. We had mutually supporting strengths and similar paths, so we teamed up. I then met a woman who had successfully marketed seminars for a well-known teacher and hired her for a few consultations. (Spending money on people who have accomplished what you want can prevent waste in both time and mistakes and give you a great jump start.) I became so committed to making this dream a reality, I even moved to a more supportive location than where I lived.

Then, armed with my ideas and a willingness to put out energy, I pounded the pavement, so to speak, to fill the workshops we'd set up. Less than one year after making the firm commitment to do "whatever it takes," we held an extremely successful retreat, not only in terms of results for participants but in the number who came. This could be taken as a miracle. Neither of us was well known, I had little experience at the time, and participants were required to invest a lot of time and money. However, the retreatants were amazed and in awe of how profound these retreats were, as we integrated not only deep transformational process, but singing, dancing, nature immersion, ritual and other elements that made it both fun and life changing. As

> we put on these retreats over the years, they got better and better, and I continued to grow in my abilities.
>
> A number of other projects I'd started followed a course similar to these initial retreats. Sometimes I had to make a living at something less desirable while working on my new vision and the ability to take the leap to go for it fully. But happily, each new endeavor has been a beautiful, yet fuller and more "naturally right" expression of me and my gifts in the world.

Some people may be blessed with knowing their path; they go straight for it without deviation. For others, it's a gradual progression. There is no *one* way to make a transition that's fulfilling and expresses who you are, but I suggest using the ideas in this book to help you along the way.

Pitfalls to Manifesting Your Dreams

You'll face dozens of pitfalls when manifesting your dream. Notice if you're holding some of the beliefs and attitudes mentioned here, then work with yourself using tools in this book to move beyond them. In doing so, you can face the feelings associated with limiting attitudes and transform the paralyzing effects they create on your ability to pursue right livelihood.

Pitfalls to watch out for include:

1) Putting a lot of attention on why you say your dream can't be achieved
   "Too many other people are doing it."
   "I'm not good or experienced enough."
   "Others are so much better at it than me."
   "It will take too long to get going."
   "There is too much competition."
2) Lack of strong intention or willingness to do whatever it takes
   Even if you don't know the exact result, with a strong desire and intention to move in a particular direction, doors will open, opportunities will arise, and helpful people will appear. Willingness and strong intention can carry you through all the unknowns and give you the energy

to follow through on what you wish to do. Many people never actively seek change but believe that someday, magically, their "ship will come in." Due to lack of intention, they never start or persevere. And again, to have the level of commitment needed, one has usually mastered (or been working on) some or all of the 7 Keys.

3) Lacking persistence or ability to hold a long-range vision

If you have the willingness to start but don't have the ability to persist, you won't be prepared to deal with the challenges that invariably arise. You may resort to telling yourself why it can't be done, then quit rather than use the challenges as fuel to fire your determination. If you have already put out a lot of energy, it's good to periodically rest and integrate what you've done. This helps to prevent burnout and gives you a second wind to begin again. Also, if you like to start projects but not necessarily maintain them, work with partners who excel at long-haul maintenance. They can carry your endeavor when your start-up energies need a rest.

4) Waiting for everything to be perfect before starting

Not moving until you have complete information, all the money you need, and approval or support from everyone close to you (or others) will stop you from manifesting your dreams. You don't have to know exactly where you're going to get started; having a strong sense of what you want to move toward can be enough. Getting started helps build momentum that will clarify your vision.

5) Believing it's not okay to change your mind

Not starting for fear of doing the wrong thing is more likely to lead to the wrong thing than not starting at all. Move down Path A to generate enough energy to manifest Path B or C, which could be more appropriate. If your intuition or circumstances are telling you Path A isn't right and you continue on that path—because you believe it's not okay to change your mind or have wasted time, energy, money—then it's been a true waste of time. Often, Path A is a necessary stepping stone to where you're going by providing either the training you need or useful connections.

6) Using excessiveness as a shield
   Excessiveness means filling your life with so much that you can't experience having enough. This leaves little room for exactly what you do want or for the simplicity that supports focus. When you bite off more than you can chew, you can't accomplish anything. Don't mistake movement for true action. In working with this issue, look at your core beliefs to discover if one of them implies, "I'm not enough" or "there's not enough." When this happens, you tend to overfill your life with too much and you also collect a lot of material "stuff" you don't really need.
7) Being overwhelmed by the vision
   Remember, achieving a dream is a marathon, not a sprint. If the vision seems too big, you can use stepping stones along the way. Aim for the ledge just ahead of you while holding the vision of the mountain top. Let your focus be on what's do-able so you can accomplish plenty of wins and successful learning experiences. Remember, there is no such thing as a failure, just an opportunity for refinement. Define what success means for you, and if it seems impossible to attain, redefine it to something that will allow you continual wins. For example, go from "success equals making money" to "success equals learning something useful."
8) Unwillingness to trust
   This is being unwilling to trust yourself or your intuition, which makes you unwilling to take risks. It may also mean being unwilling to trust Spirit or the flow of life. Practicing letting go of control comes in, too. It might also mean it's time to go back to the drawing board of the 7 Keys. For when you have gained enough progress, your level of trust in Self and Spirit gets anchored. In addition, the more you trust and experience positive results, the more references you have for believing that life will support you and even take you where you're going. All of this gives you the courage to take risks, which is essential to manifesting miracles.

Pursuing right livelihood often requires working with many of the tools in this book: knowing your truth, being willing to express it, standing in that truth, taking risks, feeling the feelings that come up along the way, and working through negative beliefs. Transitions aren't quick and easy, but if you commit yourself to this path, over time you'll have more ability to express your passion in life and through your work.

☀ Medicine Tasks ☀

Discovering Your Right Livelihood

A) *What do I love and what do I have to offer?*

To discover where your heart and soul would thrive and where you could most fully express your uniquely creative self in the world, answer the following questions by writing them down. If you prefer, share your answers with another person. That can be more powerful to help get the answers out of you rather than just going over them in your mind. (Credit for this series of questions, first Co-Creators Handbook by Carolyn Anderson and Katherine Roske.)[3]

- What gifts have I been given to use, either natural talents I came in with or those that I have been blessed to have acquired in this life?
- What do I love to do?
- What gives me great satisfaction?
- Have I ever done anything that felt like I was making a contribution? What was it?
- When have I felt totally successful and joyful? What was I doing?
- What worked for me then that I could use in other aspects of my life now?
- What am I really good at?

---

[3] Carolyn Anderson with Katherine Roske: The Co-Creator's Handbook: An Experiential Guide for Discovering Your Life's Purpose and Building a Co-creative Society, 2001. The Co-Creator's Handbook 2.0: An Experiential Guide for Discovering Your Life's Purpose and Birthing a New World, Global Family, Penn Valley, CA, 2016.

- When have I been able to sustain a high level of performance with a high level of personal energy? What are the characteristics of these times: the work, the people, the physical environment, and the results?
- If money were no object, what would I be doing with my days?
- If all the conditions were right (family, education, time) what would I be doing with my life?
- What do I feel really passionate about?
- If I had only a few years to live, what would I do?

Sit with your answers for a while and let your ideas bubble up. Do not judge them as being too difficult, too expensive, too much competition, or otherwise not do-able. You are brainstorming—letting creative ideas flow—which must occur without judgment.

If you don't get many ideas at first, keep the answers to these questions in mind for a longer period and eventually something will pop up. It's best to first work with the 7 Keys and other exercises in this book so any underlying beliefs and emotions don't sabotage your good intentions.

B) *What do I not want?*

If you have too much resistance to being straightforward about what you want, try this back-door approach laid out by Barbara Sher. Looking at what you *don't* want often leads you to what you *do* want.[4]

- "What would be the worst possible job I could think of?" Include the types of people involved, hours, pay, location, environment, what you'd be doing or not doing—as many details as you can think of.
- "What do I dislike most about the job I do now or jobs I have done in the past?" Be specific.
- List the specifics of your ideal job based on the *opposite* characteristics you described above. Do not worry about being practical by thinking of

---

[4] Barbara Sher, I Could Do Anything If I Only Knew What It Was, Bantam Doubleday Dell Publishing, NY, NY, 1994.

job possibilities you already know about. Just describe the qualities and details that counterbalance what you specifically dislike.

C) *Grounding intention*

Integrating your answers from the previous questions, respond to the following:

- "What am I here to do?"
- "If I knew I could not fail, what would I do?"
- "What are possible livelihood options through which these things (answers to previous questions) can express?" Be creative. It doesn't have to be a previously known job or anything someone else might hire you for. Instead, it could be something entirely new that you create.
- "What are the first steps (either small or large) I can take to move in this direction?"
- "What could be my long-range game plan for moving in this direction?"

D) *Holding the Question*

In addition to answering this series of questions, be sure to hold the question—that is, repeat it daily like a prayer saying, "How can I best serve?" or "What are my best gifts, and how can I bring them forth to serve in the world?"

Chapter 12

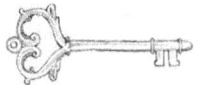

Magic Happens—Where You Have Been and Where You are Headed

When does the magic happen? Once you have opened lines of communication by . . .

- being willing to feel your feelings and emotions
- honoring them by taking actions they've motivated
- finding healthy alternatives to express those feelings
- developing the Witness enough to be aware of adaptive strategies or hidden parts
- having transformed the critical voice or other operations of managers or firefighters
- extending love and acceptance to each previously judged part of yourself
- letting go of the need to control life by trusting the flow more
- allowing others to be *who they are* or do *what they do* even when it displeases you
- forgiving others for the above and yourself even when self-honoring means letting go

- prioritizing time in nature or engaging in a creative endeavor regularly
- integrating healthy practices into your daily life.

. . . something magic happens. It's the magic of more ease, more inner peace, and greater ability to take the important risks necessary to bring about significant life changes. It's also the magic of more authentic, satisfying relationships, more feelings of aliveness as well as health issues clearing up without even knowing what you did.

All of this magic begins when you take the time, energy, and focus to integrate all aspects of the 7 Keys. You then feel that you cannot *not* do what you want! And now you have a platform from which to take your leaps of faith.

When you engage in Key 7, which is taking risks, you're magically transported to a new life—one that's richer, healthier, more vital, authentic, meaningful, and passionate. Most important, you're free from the weight of negative emotions, depression and the compulsion of the addictions that covered your previously buried pain.

That's not to say life suddenly becomes pain free or without its challenges, but feeling it all fully—with all Exiled parts of you by your side and moving undefended (or at least less defended)—opens you to more ease, vitality, and fulfillment than you've ever imagined.

Adding one Key at a time and practicing them slowly so they build on each other, makes it easier to add another. It raises your vibration as it increases joy and inner relaxation from an increased level of trust in life, Spirit, and Self. You could say a raised vibration vibrates away all manner of infirmity, physical conditions, pains, stiffness and emotional pains. Even negative life conditions shift as the vibration raises. The 7 Keys create flexibility in body, mind, and heart while increasing physical energy and JOY—which ultimately heals all.

Going Full Circle Back to the Culture

I began this book commenting on how we're the products of a disconnected culture. This type of culture has been going on for so many centuries that it's firmly fixed in our habits, lifestyles, and ways of treating each other and ourselves. The negativity and blame energy that's a part of it isn't healthy nor does it lead to true joy or happiness.

I want to share with you an excerpt from an article in *YES Magazine*, a completely reader-supported periodical, that points out the positive changes in the culture—changes happening at grassroots, person-by-person, and community levels. In "The Election: Of Hate, Grief, and a New Story" Charles Eisenstein speaks about what's happening on a sociopolitical level relative to U.S. President Donald Trump. (Supporting or opposing him is not the issue here.) This piece expresses how changes we're making *within us* need to show up on an outer cultural level. As this shift happens, we will finally see the outer world make important changes and stop repeating the negative legacies that have led people to their addictions. Eisenstein wrote:

> We are entering a time of great uncertainty. Institutions so enduring as to seem identical to reality itself may lose their legitimacy and dissolve. It may seem that the world is falling apart. For many, that process started on election night, when Trump's victory provoked incredulity, shock, even vertigo. "I can't believe this is happening!"
>
> At such moments, it is a normal response to find someone to blame, as if identifying fault could restore the lost normality, and to lash out in anger. Hate and blame are convenient ways of making meaning out of a bewildering situation. Anyone who disputes the blame narrative may receive more hostility than the opponents themselves, as in wartime when pacifists are more reviled than the enemy.
>
> . . . That is why, as we enter a period of intensifying disorder, it is important to introduce a different kind of force to animate the structures that might appear after the old ones crumble. I would call it love if it weren't for the risk of triggering your New Age bullshit detector, and, besides, how does one practically bring love into the world in the realm of politics? So let's start with empathy. Politically, empathy is akin to solidarity, born of the understanding that we are all in this together. In what together? For starters, we are in the uncertainty together.

. . . We are entering a space between stories. After various retrograde versions of a new story rise and fall and we enter a period of true unknowing, an authentic next story will emerge. What would it take for it to embody love, compassion, and interbeing? I see its lineaments in those marginal structures and practices that we call holistic, alternative, regenerative, and restorative. All of them source from empathy, the result of the compassionate inquiry: What is it like to be you?

It is time now to bring this question and the empathy it arouses into our political discourse as a new animating force. If you are appalled at the election outcome and feel the call of hate, perhaps try asking yourself, "What is it like to be a Trump supporter?" Ask it not with a patronizing condescension, but for real, looking underneath the caricature of misogynist and bigot to find the real person. (My note: Just as the 7 Keys asks us to do with each part of ourselves.)

Even if the person you face is a misogynist or bigot, ask, "Is this who they are, really?" Ask what confluence of circumstances, social, economic, and biographical, may have brought them there. You may still not know how to engage them, but at least you will not be on the warpath automatically. We hate what we fear, and we fear what we do not know. So let's stop making our opponents invisible behind a caricature of evil.

We've got to stop acting out hate. I see no less of it in the liberal media than I do in the right-wing. It is just better disguised, hiding beneath pseudo-psychological epithets and dehumanizing ideological labels. Exercising it, we create more of it. What is beneath the hate? My acupuncturist Sarah Fields wrote to me, "Hate is just a bodyguard for grief. When people lose the hate, they are forced to deal with the pain beneath."

I think the pain beneath is fundamentally the same pain that animates misogyny and racism, hate in a different form. Please stop thinking you are better than these people! We are all victims of the same world-dominating machine, suffering different mutations of the same wound of separation. Something hurts in there. We live in a civilization that has robbed nearly all of us of deep community, intimate connection with nature, unconditional love, freedom to explore the kingdom of childhood, and so much more. The acute trauma endured by the incarcerated, the abused, the raped, the trafficked, the starved, the murdered, and the dispossessed does not exempt the perpetrators. They feel it in mirror image, adding damage to their souls atop the damage that compels them to violence. Thus, it is that suicide is the leading cause of death in the U.S. military (and among youth). Thus, it is that addiction is rampant among the police. (as well as youth and many more). Thus, it is that depression is epidemic in the upper-middle class. We are all in this together.

Something hurts in there. Can you feel it? We are all in this together. One Earth, one tribe, one people.

We have entertained teachings like these long enough in our spiritual retreats, meditations, and prayers. Can we take them now into the political (outer) world and create an eye of compassion inside the political hate vortex? It is time to do it, time to up our game. It is time to stop feeding hate. Next time you post online, check your words to see if they smuggle in some form of hate: dehumanization, snark, belittling, derision, some invitation to "us versus them." Notice how it feels kind of good to do that, like getting a fix. And notice what hurts underneath, and how it doesn't feel good, not really. Maybe it is time to stop.

This does not mean to withdraw from political conversation, (My note: or cultural change) but to rewrite its vocabulary. It is to speak hard truths with love. It is to offer acute analysis that doesn't carry the implicit message of, "Aren't those people horrible?" Such analysis is rare. Usually, those evangelizing compassion do not write about politics, and sometimes they veer into passivity. We need to confront an unjust, ecocidal system. Each time we do, we will receive an invitation to give in to the dark side and hate "the deplorables." We must not shy away from those confrontations. Instead, we can engage them empowered by the inner mantra that my friend Pancho Ramos-Stierle uses in confrontations with his jailers: "Brother, your soul is too beautiful to be doing this work." If we can stare hate in the face and never waver from that knowledge, we will access inexhaustible tools of creative engagement, and hold a compelling invitation to the haters to fulfill their beauty.[1]

This brings us full circle from where this book started in discussion of our culture being at early source for our ills. However, when we make changes within, we then carry them into our outer world. When enough of us have found self-love and compassion for every previously despicable part of ourselves, not only do *we* change, but our *outer world* changes. When enough of that happens, those in generations to come will change and ultimately will influence change in our cultures. There will come a tipping point. Though it is not for us to ask *when* but *if* we will engage in this process and trust that in time our efforts will affect the whole.

As an optimist, I have faith in the work embedded in these 7 Keys. They represent not only my take but also the multitude of variations that countless others are communicating and practicing. Taking this journey will ultimately change our whole world. It's not too late. But more and more of us need to apply ourselves, fervently and with a "whatever it takes" commitment. We don't have the time to try and fall off again and again. Now, we'll just do it!

Getting Support

However, I recognize that the old negative patterns run deep, both culturally and personally, plus achieving change on one's own isn't easy. I highly encourage you to find others on a similar transformational path and get their support.

Yet in our culture, we're not programmed for reaching out for support and we value doing things alone. Instead, go for support—be it a therapist, a yoga instructor—private or group, a lifestyle or diet coach, a naturopath or chiropractor, a body worker, a biofeedback technician and more. There are so many possibilities for support that can speed the process.

---

[1] Charles Eisenstein, "The Election: Of Hate, Grief, and a New Story," re published in YES newsletter November 10, 2016, charleseisenstein.net. Author of *Sacred Economics* and *The More Beautiful World Our Hearts Know is Possible*. Yes Magazine: http://www.yesmagazine.org/

We live on this planet to help each other, so don't attempt to make changes totally alone. It would be slow going if it goes at all. Make yourself a priority by being willing to spend time and money on your health and growth. You intuitively know the next step, whether it's working on your emotional body, physical or energetic body, the spiritual aspects, or through workshops, classes, or private individuals. Work on more than one area at once if you like, but don't bite off more than you can chew. Be sure you go back to at least something simple that keeps you moving forward. It *will* ultimately free you.

Remember to make changing and growing fun. Hold the attitude that change is exciting rather than the old idea that it's scary. The *new* is giving you energy rather than taking it away. If you can bring at least one right-brain activity into the mix, it will energize the whole upward spiraling movement and speed the process . . . plus make everything a lot more FUN!

May you enjoy this journey, whether you feel like you are winning, sliding back or even stagnant for a while, don't let those phases throw you off course. Allow every setback to function as a motivator to your deeper commitment. As long as you keep your intention for positive change and growth in your heart, you are still moving forward.

Thank you for choosing to be a part of this Great Change in our culture. Blessings to you. With love, compassion, and encouragement,

Joy Lynn Freeman

Chapter 13

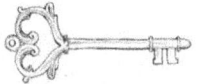

IFS Dialog Process—Moving from Egocentric to Soulcentric

This summarizing chapter serves as a workbook as it addresses in detail the Internal Family Systems (IFS) process to bring self-love and compassion to every previously unlovable, judged, and often hated part of ourselves. This process is particularly important when trauma has occurred, especially Developmental (ongoing childhood) Trauma.

From a neurobiological standpoint, the evidence-based IFS work has been shown to have the capacity to change neural pathways. These are extremely grooved pathways in our brains developed from past and then re-occurring circumstances that has made it hard for people to change—even those with the greatest intentions.

The many practices in the 7 Keys can accomplish a lot in terms of life shifts. However, taking these specific steps as laid out in the IFS Dialog Process can bring more compassion, love, and understanding independently to each of these previously troublesome or unhappy parts, especially those that continue to plague you. This, along with other work of the 7 Keys, can transform these parts to *move beyond* causing problems. Instead, they become critical supports on your life journey.

All of the practices in this book are intended to bring maladaptive parts to the place—as my indigenous teacher described—of becoming servants of Soul rather than players of ego running the show. Ego parts cover or push the Soul voice to the background. This transformational work makes the space for the Soul voice to emerge, thus moving us forward from egocentric to Soulcentric.

I have witnessed amazing transformations using the IFS model through my work with others and myself. In addition, when witnessing other therapists working with their clients, I can speak with confidence that this model is extremely effective to transform one's orientation to life. With that comes a person's level of authenticity, creativity, expression, peace, and joy, especially when coupled with other practices in this book.

IFS Dialog Process Outlined

Understand, though, that when an IFS counselor or therapist works with an individual, no one session can look like another. However, I'll do my best to provide the overall context to this process so you can use it yourself on some level. Naturally, it's best to work with someone versed in the work; however, if you understand the essence of each step and intend to come from your Self, while keeping the Self present (even when answering for a part), then miracles happen. Just trust your intuition.

You will find it helpful to have a trusted friend ask you the questions and be witness to your answers. If you do it alone, be sure to write down your answers as more information seems to come though when you write than when you only think about it.

Let's begin!

1) Choose a Target Part to Work With

What is not working in your life or causing you deep challenges or emotional pain? If there are several, pick the one that tops your list. What patterns of behavior contribute to this problem? Sometimes it takes a back-and-forth conversation or writing to find the specific part to work with.

Start with a Protector, either a manager or firefighter (explained in Chapters 3 and 4) before going to the part with the deepest hurt feelings—an

Exile (see Chapter 4). Otherwise, you could face a backlash from those Protectors if they haven't come to trust your Soul Self enough to be ok with you accessing your vulnerable parts or to keep you safe from some of the other protector's behaviors. Without this trust in your Soul Self, your protector parts fear what might happen when the Exile opens to its feelings or other vulnerabilities that might come up in the Dialog Process.

When a Protector "gets" that there's a Soul Self present in you—and it has been accepted and honored for its positive intent and ultimately given a new job—it usually gives its permission for you, with your soul Self present to approach and work with an Exile.

Choose a Target Part Example
Statement of the challenge: "I've been trying to succeed at different projects I want to create for myself, but I always give up or stop at a certain point. I just can't seem to stay with it."

Next, ask for behaviors that might contribute to this: "I tend to do all kinds of things that distract me such as cleaning, eating, watching TV. Sometimes I smoke pot."

Discussing what isn't working right now and answering the background questions below will help you choose a target part to start working with. More back-and-forth discussion might be needed before you decide on a target part for this session.

Answering the following questions help support the IFS process. Though not a formal step in the process, giving your answers brings details into your conscious awareness for when you embark on the Dialog Process. You can also ask questions that come to you intuitively. Then from that intuitive place, write or state whatever comes forth whether you have actual memory of it or not. Even before birth we have feelings about what goes on and sense it from within the womb. Whether pre-birth or infant, though they don't have the capacity to express in words or even have linear memory at that time, feelings are stored in their bodies and energy fields where it plays out in life later. (As described earlier—this is implicit memory.)

No matter what details come up, no blame is meant. Instead, consider it information to work with. When it all comes together in the Dialog Process, many things will make sense without having to figure it out. The more you trust what comes through in these self-guided (or friend-supported) sessions, the more it works on a deeper level. Later, you'll feel and see the changes in your life.

Background Questions

Answer the following questions on paper or tell the person who's supporting you:

- What was the prevailing energy or mood in your family of origin?
- What was either lacking or too much of? (ex. no attention with attunement missing or was it more like engulfment—smothering)
- Did it feel safe? If not, in what way, or why?
- Were there boundaries set? If so, were they set kindly? If not, why not, and how did that play out?
- Did you have to act like an adult before growing up? If so, in what way?
- What style(s) of protection or support from within (certain behaviors or attitudes) showed up to help you?
- About how old were you or what was transpiring when you first noticed this style of protection happening?
- What was it protecting you from or helping you to do? (though it may have caused challenges throughout life, this attempt to help is called 'positive intent')
- What has been the cost of this style of protection or help in your adult life?

After answering these questions, if you feel like changing the target part you've chosen, feel free to do so. You can do the practice again with as many different parts as you like.

Remember to start with Protector parts rather than your vulnerable Exiled parts because up to now the Protectors have kept the Exiles under lock and key. These protectors have held the exiles down from expressing who they truly are or have distracted them so intensely for so long, that sometimes they don't feel safe enough to come out and let you know what is going on. That is, until they have observed the transformation of the protectors and get a strong sense of your Self's presence.

Review of Protectors: Managers and Firefighters

Managers are pre-emptive. This means they try to win us love, acknowledgment, attention, and so on to try to help us avoid or *prevent* painful feelings from arising, that are hidden from earlier experiences. How? By making us look good, do good, and be good especially in the eyes of our parents, caretakers or other important people from our early years. The more difficult the experiences endured, the stronger the traits and efforts to accomplish the goal of "being or looking good." These efforts carry on throughout life. Though there are positive aspects to these behaviors there are always other negative consequences that sometimes can be less noticeable.

Firefighters react *after* the Exile is triggered—that is, after an explosion of emotional flames or an ongoing intense state of difficult feelings. They come in when the managers' work has proven ineffective. The firefighters douse the fire of the Exiles, by distracting or dissociating from it. Their behavior tends to be frantic, reactive, impulsive due to a heightened state of arousal (via sympathetic nervous system dominance) with obvious negative consequences. They feel they cannot stop until the Exile feels fully safe or healed. Of course, this never happens until the deeper work occurs. That's why relapses happen.

Common firefighter activities are to binge, work, shop, and overindulge in sex, food, drugs, alcohol, rage, danger, self-mutilation, illness, and even consider suicide. Managers and firefighters share the goal of containing and "protecting" Exiles. However, firefighters and managers are often polarized in extreme opposite ways of going about this. Managers want to look good and be respected; firefighters don't care about that all. They just want to escape the feelings in any way—no matter how bad it makes them look or other havoc it causes.

(Revisit Chapter 4 for more details on the two Protector types: manager and firefighters.)

2) Naming the Chosen Part

As you learned in Key 2 – Chapter 5, put a name to the quality or job of the target part you chose to work with. i.e., Ms. Perfection, Mr. Bossy, Ms. Angry Bitch, Missy Pretty Thing. Or maybe add a catchy person's name such as Danny Distractor, Connie Care Taker. Or include a specific behavior in the name such as Ms. Wants Extra Attention from Men.

Giving the target part a name makes it easier to address it as a viable energy that you hold as other than yourself. Though it's part of you, it's still distinctly separate from the Self of you. Addressing it with a name brings clarity to the role it has been playing.

Simply seeing the part as a separate energy helps provide space for the Soul Self to emerge more fully. It also lets you witness its operation more clearly when it does, to separate yourself from its behaviors, and to recognize "this is not really *you* doing these activities." Rather, it's an adaptive part of you that came to this for various reasons. Your consistent awareness helps anchor in the transformation.

3) Finding a Physical Feeling in the Body (Somatic Work)

While thinking about what came up in answering the previous questions or about more recent circumstances related to the initial issue/target part, do this exercise:

a. With your mind's eye (optimally with closed eyes), scan your body and see if you can sense one area that stands out, even if subtly. Don't worry if it feels vague at first. This can take a few minutes, but sit quietly and use your mind to slowly scan each area top to bottom. Especially focus on the throat to torso (heart area, below sternum (solar plexus), belly, etc.).

b. Notice if anything stands out slightly above the rest—a place of tension, a shot of pain, or something even subtler. Occasionally take your mind back to the circumstance for a moment. Reactivate it, then go back to scanning your body as you look for something that may not be easily obvious. When you find something, put your focus specifically into that area.

c. In a metaphoric way, ask, "What is this feeling like and where exactly is it located?" This means, compare the feeling to something else. For example, is it like a block of wood pressing down from above my chest. If so, what space does it cover—a little spot or covering the entire chest? Is it like a lead blanket you find at the dentist, or is it a ball of rope knotted inside my gut, or is it like a knife that goes through from front to back, or strange bubblies or prickly feelings, or flames moving around in my belly? Are there little sparkles darting about with intensity in my chest area? Or is it nebulous like a black cloud of smoke, or perhaps a blank empty hollow encompassing the entire chest area? Or is it a small, hard, dense, lead-like ball or even a dark hole in my heart area?

Taking it Deeper

The more in your right-brain "feeling" body you are, the more you have access to your intuition, and the more powerful transformation you'll feel through the IFS process. Being in your right brain helps your answers come from a place you don't normally access and that might actually surprise you.

This Taking It Deeper step of somatic work is especially helpful when working with an Exile, which is discussed later. You can skip to the next step if your exile feels triggered to begin with. Just explain to that part that you will be back to work with it after you have worked with the protectors involved, because you are wanting to make it safe for him or her. Whether you use this step now or later, this is a very potent step. The practice is this:

a. With your hands in front of you in the air, match the quality of the sensation you are feeling in your body with some movements of your hands and arms. This doesn't mean to literally act it out; do this metaphorically. For example, if you feel a deep tightness in your gut, then let your hands make a tight fist. Or if it feels like a knife in your chest, then your hands, arms, and forearms can get straight and stiff.

b. Then say, "Now exaggerate that, so it involves more of your forearms and arms." Say this a few times until it includes more of your upper body and/or face and neck.
c. To go deeper, do this: Make a sound that matches the quality of this feeling.

For many, this last step of adding sound, is quite a stretch, but don't worry about being embarrassed. This can take you to a deeper feeling or awareness related to the issue. It works powerfully because sounds are universal—that is, a person's moan in one place is the same as a moan or a whimper or a growl in any country in the world. No left-brain interpretations into words are necessary. As a result, feelings will arise that you may not even know exist or the extent to which they do.

In Case of Overwhelm

You can practice the IFS Dialog Process without first going into these powerful body-centered practices, although each level you use helps the work go deeper. However, it's standard procedure to use at least the body scan. But if at any point (even if you intend to work with the Protectors first) you trigger *too far* into the feelings of an Exile (child/vulnerable/wounded part), you'll need to pull back rather than deepen. You will know you are in an Exile if strong feelings of sadness or grief arise or anything that has you cry uncontrollably or become intensely angry.

If that happens, call on your Soul Self with a strong prayer or stated intention. With the Self present, tell this Exile part you *do* want to know what he or she feels, but get it to agree to let you know in smaller doses that won't *overwhelm* your system. Let it know it will be better and safer to express more fully *after* you have the Protectors on board to support the Self in supporting this Exile in expressing its long-held truth.

At any point, you would clearly say, "It's not okay to overwhelm our system, yet I *do* want to know what you are feeling. It *is* okay to express these feelings little by little. Yet first, it's best to transform the Protectors who may have been mean to you, kept you shut away, or unknowingly caused you harm. You want them to be supportive of you rather than making it all worse."

Having another person, especially an IFS therapist skilled in deeper somatic therapies, helps the process for sure. But I have done a lot on my own with the knowledge in this book and my Soul Self supporting my intentions for growth and healing.

4) Create a Metaphoric Image

Whether you stopped at the first stage of finding the feeling of the target part in your body or have taken it deeper, now that you've named it, it's time to ask (or tell) this part to step outside of you. I find it helpful to have your eyes closed by now (or in between reading of steps) if they weren't already. You want to consciously place it off to your left, right, above, behind, etc. Put it where you can see it or at least know it is there. Say, "Please step back." Then say, "You don't have to leave the room or go away; just step aside so we (or I) can get to know you better."

Next, ask in your mind for a symbolic image to come to you that fits the name or energetic sense of the target part. It can be similar to what came up when describing the feeling, but often it's different. To do this, tap into the essence of how the part operates, both how it feels in your body and how it behaves. Then allow your intuition to conjure up a picture.

People are blown away by the accuracy of these images in expressing the qualities and energies of the parts! That's true even for those who don't consider themselves highly intuitive. If you can open to an image, include it when addressing the part. It helps reveal other images you might not have had access to before. However, if nothing comes, don't worry; just notice where you sense the part is sitting. If it stays super close, then ask it to step back until you feel it energetically "off" you.

The name you choose can be based on behaviors, but it's also sometimes supported by the image that comes up. You can enhance the name or change it based on what shows up. It also helps to have an image when working with the part in daily life, as in the practice of witnessing it. The image will change by the end of the transformation process. Later, you'll anchor the new image daily. However, if you can't get an image at this point—just move on.

Here are examples of images from some of my clients: a Jack in the box (like a boogey man that suddenly pops out of nowhere on a big dark cloud), a clinging vine called Ms Clingy, a wet dirty limp dishcloth, Gary give up, a being in a big dark cape—sort of Darth Vader-like, a huge pillow—later called the Smotherer, a big green giant that could step on you.

Don't try to make something up or figure out what might seem to fit. Just allow your intuition to present something to you. Again, closed eyes can help this. It might take a moment, but if you are still and open, usually a metaphoric image appears, and it often this gives more clues about it or deepens the experience. If nothing comes at all, it's okay. You can continue the process knowing that an energy with the name you gave it is over there—outside of you.

Knowing it's separate from you and speaking to it from this vantage point is critical.

5) Befriending

Once you've homed in on a Protector part you want to work with, whether a manager or fire fighter, the next steps to bring self-love and acceptance to a part is by "befriending" it. If a highly emotional part is "up," let that part know you'll be back to hear it, get to know it, and give it love. Let it know that with the intention of giving it safety, though, you'll work with the active managers and firefighters first. While a Protector part does have *its* positive intentions, Protectors can inadvertently be harsh, critical, or demeaning. They can otherwise undermine your progress as an aspect of an upside-down protective strategy. That's why you work with Protectors first.

To begin the step of befriending, be sure you have at least some of your Self present. This can be determined by asking,

- *How do I feel toward this part?* (or if a support person is asking),
- *How do you feel toward this part?*

If other parts are stepping in you'll receive an angry or judgmental remark. Blending means the part has taken over and is covering the naturally curious or compassionate place of Self. The Self is not pushy. So if another part is in front of or covering the Self, it takes your intention to get it to step back to reveal the Self again.

This intention can be a statement said to that part of you such as,

- *Please Step Back. We may come and talk to you later but for now, please step back.*

You do this because you want to know and understand the part you're working with—the target part you've chosen. You can't do that until you are in your Self (or at least a good percentage of it). When you're in your Self, you'll know because then you won't feel so angry or disgruntled at the part you're trying to understand.

After telling the intervening part to step back, wait a moment and then ask again,

- *How do I (you) feel toward this part?*

If you have a sense of curiosity and openness to want to know what's gone on, then you have some Self present and can proceed.

If you still feel closed or angry, then you can say a direct prayer to what your personal understanding of a benevolent power is. Say something like, "Please help me bring you forth so I can find out a deeper truth and come to a place of compassion for this part."

When you can answer the question about how you feel about this part from an open state of mind, then continue. You may need to ask other intruding parts to step back periodically as you are having a conversation. And that's okay. Just repeat any of these steps as needed, stating a prayer or asking an intervening part to step back.

Once you know that Self is present, then fully separate yourself from the target part again if needed. If it crept back super close, tell it again more firmly,

- *Step back now!*

Repeat that until you determine it's off at least two feet or more, perhaps to the right or left of you. If it doesn't go willingly, then use your will and the help of Self (if needed) to place it someplace other than *in* or *on top of* you. Acknowledge to yourself where it is located. Once it ends up someplace other than *in* or *on top of* you, you'll feel the energy lighten or see the image off to one side or the other.

If it's still very close, then tell it to move back a bit—at least at arm's length. Having the conversation from a distance helps you clearly understand that *this part is not you*. Rather, it's an energetic that resides with you and, as such, is mutable.

Next, have a conversation that helps you to get to know this part better. Here are the steps:

- Let it know you'd like to get to know it. If you are in your Self, you will have found the curiosity.
- Does it know you are here to get to know it? You can ask it directly. It may hesitate or not be sure this is happening but will get it in a while.
- Find out what it wants you to know about it and how long it's been around.

You or your helper will use your intuition about which of these questions to ask and in which order:

- *When did you first show up in my life?* Sit quietly for a moment and wait for it to tell you something rather than trying to make something up. You might get an image of something happening, certain people, or circumstances. Trust whatever comes up and work with it. If it only tells you something more recent. That is fine you can start there.
- *What are you afraid would happen if you didn't do your thing* (referring to its strategy or operations).
- *What are you afraid the Exile might feel?*
- *How have you been protecting me* (us, the Exile, or your whole system)*?*
- *What might be your job/role? What do you hope to accomplish?*
- *What are your strategies to accomplish this?*
- *How long have you had to do this job/role?*
- *What might have caused you to take on this job/role?*
- *How did you learn to do this? Whose voice do you hear or actions did you see?*
- *Is there anything else you want me to know about you? Or about some other part?*
- *How do you feel about this job/role you needed to undertake?*

- *What bad thing do you believe might happen or might you lose if you leave this job/role?*
- *What price have you had to pay to carry out this job/role all this time?*
- *How do you feel now after doing this job/role for so many years?* (The parts are often exhausted and sick of their jobs/roles but know nothing else.)

Now ask,

- *Can you see how this part has protected or helped you in some way, even if those strategies are not working so well now?*

When you get it, then let the part know and acknowledge it for this. You'd say,

- *Thank you so much for helping me* (whatever it is it has been doing for you) *all this time.*

Give the part genuine appreciation or gratitude and/or also validation and credit by saying things like:

- *That makes sense to me.*
- *I know how hard you have had to work.*
- *You have had such a responsibility to carry.*
- *You have sacrificed a lot.*
- *All your efforts were on my behalf.*
- *What you did for me when I was a child . . .*
- *What you have been trying to do for me throughout my life . . .*
- *I so want to give you my acceptance, appreciation, compassion, and love for your efforts to keep me* (safe, loved, acknowledged, not so lonely or other painful emotions).

During this conversation, check in with the part periodically and see how it sits with being asked about itself, its sensibilities, its motivations, and its being heard without being made wrong.

Remember, you don't have to agree with its strategies, as they have probably caused some great losses by this time, you are just befriending and having it learn to trust you—the Self of you.

Once you acknowledge and appreciate what it's been doing (even though it's not working for you any more), it relaxes.

Checking in can involve a simple question or two your helper asks you such as:

- *How is the part sitting with all this now?*
- *How does that land on the target part?* (You can use the name you came up with.)

Or you ask the target part directly:

- *How does it feel to receive this acknowledgment?* (rather than mostly being made wrong for its ways) *Or how is this sitting for you?* (to the part)

At this point, you should feel it relaxing and opening (even a little) and sense it's beginning to trust you—the Soul Self of you. In the midst of this, if you get there's another energy that's still judging or angry at this target part, then another part has stepped in. The Self is no longer out front. Simply go back and regarding this new energetic, ask:

- *How do you feel toward the part?*

The answer to that will let you know if there's anything other than kind feelings of curiosity, acceptance, appreciation, etc.). It could mean another part has dropped in. So you'd say to this intrusive part:

- *Would you be willing to step back?*
- *Please step back.*

If the part resists, you'd say:

- *Step back now* (more emphatically) *as we want to hear from the Self again.*

If it seems this is an important part to hear from, then let it know you will be back to have a conversation with it later after you complete with the part you are talking to now. Make note of who or what this energy is to come back to later. When the Self is present again and acknowledges the target part, then relaxation follows.

6) Finding a New Role

Even though the way in which the Protectors have operated no longer serves and has caused challenges or created results you may not like, each Protector also has a strength or positive aspect to its way of being. For instance, a manager that's been unrelenting and dogmatic in ruling your life may also have the quality of determination to see something through. It could possess great forbearance to get through challenging circumstances. Or a firefighter that gets you to forget about your challenges by having you unwind to daily alcohol, pot, or video gaming might really know how to chill, relax, or just have fun.

Finding the upside or positive qualities related to each of our troublesome Protectors is an important part of the process. When they feel ready to release their current roles—after feeling completely heard, understood, and appreciated by the Soul-Centered part of you—they will agree to take on using their true strengths in other ways. These strengths are a more positive version of the misdirected qualities and roles they previously hung on to, no matter how tired or exasperated they feel.

Before leaving the target part, share with your support person or write down the answer to these questions:

- *What are attributes or qualities that this part possesses that could be used for the goals or desires you and your Soul Self would choose?*

After the befriending part of this process, you've come to understand why the parts have been doing what they've been doing and their positive intentions. Now, tell them not only do you appreciate this positive intention, but you no longer need this way of helping you. Your Soul Self is part of your life now and, with the target part's input and desire together you'll find a new job/role for it. It might go something like this:

- *Thank you for keeping me small yet safe* (or seen or getting kudos, etc.)!
- *Thank you for keeping me from feeling all that sadness* that was so overwhelming when I was young. (*substitute fear, anger, loneliness, worthlessness, etc.)*
- *I understand what you're trying to do for me. But as well intended as it is, I need support in a different way now.*
- *I'm no longer a child. I no longer need protecting in the way you have been. I have access to my wise Self now who can help protect me—but in different ways. AND I still need you to support me in ways that will use your natural abilities and be more fun for you.*
- *Would you be open to entertaining a new job or role that will be a lot less exhausting and even enjoyable?*

With the thoughts in mind that came up with the question about the Protector's attributes and qualities, ask your Self to come up with new tasks. You want to reassign a new job to this oh-so-Loyal Soldier (see Chapter 5)—the Protector—where it can remain a faithful servant to the Self yet in different ways. If you sense the part wants to be involved in this choice, you can directly ask the part these questions:

- *What new role or job would you like, as it is no longer necessary for you do what you've done for so long?*
- *Is there anything you need from me that would make you feel better or safer to do this new job?*
- *I understand that you might need to see proof that things are different before you totally let go to the new way. Or you might need time to learn how to do things differently. It will be okay to go slowly and/or not do the new job perfectly all at once.*

Once you sense the Protector is open to a new way, then let it know you'll be working with the part it's been protecting (the exile). It will later see for itself that it no longer needs the kind of protection it had been giving any more. However, you will need to get its permission to work with the Exile.

On some occasions, if the Exile's feelings are coming up strongly, it might become apparent you need to work with the Exile before finishing this new role for the Protector. If so, you can go back and finish after your work with the particular Exile is complete. Typically, though, it's a safer space for the Exile if it gets the sense that the Protector has shifted. It's often the continued harshness or unsafe behaviors of Protectors that keeps the Exiles exiled—that is, tucked away and hidden.

Working with Susan's "Pushy" Manager

Susan had spent years focusing on her personal growth, taking workshops, reading self-improvement books, and seeking counseling. Though she had reached a place of great awareness and understanding, when it came to her feelings, knowing her own truth, and living a creatively expressive, healthy, and joyful life, she had a long way to go.

Part of the problem was that Susan had a Manager/Loyal Soldier part that pushed her to be amazing—the best, most evolved person she could be. This part was always "making" her do things that would help her grow and be spiritually aware. It was inadvertently telling Susan's more vulnerable parts she was "not good enough" as she was.

In her zealous efforts to improve, Susan often missed opportunities to play and nurture herself. Consequently, her forcefulness undermined the very thing she desired—personal and spiritual evolvement along with feeling peaceful and balanced. She came to understand that this pushiness was a behavior—an MO or modus operandi—the role of a part that had positive intentions for her. These intentions were to gain approval, be recognized, and feel appreciated for something that not only *she* valued but her *father* valued, too. He was a respected man with a reputation of high moral integrity. The intentions to be valued in ways even her father would see as wonderful had its usefulness in earlier years, but they were no longer valid. Her interest and goals were still true for her. However, she was compromised by the extreme role of her manager part, which led to the intensity and push she felt. Overall, it undermined accomplishing the balanced evolvement she was seeking.

Susan later learned how to befriend and hence understand, then accept and ultimately transform this demanding part. As the part came to trust the Self, Susan grew to understand and experience that she is valued for who she is in each moment, rather than what she accomplishes. Susan listened to and heeded the desires of her inner self instead of always doing what her "must grow and do something more to be good enough" part decided was best.

After making these shifts, working to honor the feelings and needs of her more vulnerable Exile and practicing other 7 Keys techniques, she approached life quite differently. With the unburdening of her Exile part and the support of a transformed "pushy" part to become a "cheerleader" part, she could finally lead a creative, healthy, and fulfilling life.

Working with Exiles

The first step in working with Exiles is to gain permission from Protector parts that have been both protecting and suppressing the Exile. Ask the Protector:

- *Is it alright with you* (manager/firefighter part) *if we* (you or you and your support person) *get closer to, make friends, and find out more about the Exile* (a vulnerable child part) *now?*

Once you have the Protector's permission to work with the Exile, which it's usually willing to do after being heard and appreciated, it relaxes into its new supportive role. When a Protector has a more positive supportive position, it creates a safer environment that helps the Exile come forth. Also, once the Protector witnesses the process that transpires with the Exile, the Protector becomes more open to dropping its former ways. It trusts that the Exile doesn't need the same type of protection it believed it needed earlier.

Your approach to the Exiles can be quite different than it was with the Protectors. At first, Exiles often need quiet, "no-rush" space. They've came to believe they're flawed in some way (feelings of shame) and often have been suppressed for so long, they feel shy to come forward.

If you close your eyes, thus avoiding visual distractions, it helps you access your right brain and tap into your intuitive self. This is an inner world discovery process, so your attention inward helps. You or your helper would ask, "How do I (you) feel toward the part?" Remember, you need lots of Self present to work with the Exile. When you asked this question dealing with Protectors, you knew Self was present when curiosity was expressed as a main feeling. When working with Exiles you know Self is present when there is a sense of compassion or caring. Exiles especially need the safety of open-heartedness.

Naming and Finding a Physical Feeling in Your Body

Before going too far with words and conversation, go back to Step 3, the Somatic Work, and the section Taking It Deeper. As the part expresses more feeling, you'll think of a good name for it. You can give it a simple name like "Little (your name)" or "Hurt, Scared, or Sad One," even a special name the person had been called as a child. Whatever captures the emotion works.

Finding a metaphoric image may not be necessary; seeing a picture of you as a small child is enough. But even that need not occur. Just feeling its energy is fine. If you've done the somatic work and especially did the Taking It Deeper exercise, you'll be well tapped into this Exile.

Once you have a sense of its presence, invite the Exile part to notice if you (the person seeking to connect) are there. If it doesn't notice you, then ask yourself or have your helper ask you, "Is that okay with you?" If Self is present, it should be fine. If not, then it indicates some other part is present.

At that point, make a statement of intention for Self to be part of this process. The aim at first is to just "be with" that Exiled part in whatever way it needs you to be with it. Giving it your nonjudgmental, all-accepting presence is what it needs at this point. Don't ask a ton of questions yet. Instead, let it know you are here and open to experiencing whatever he/she is feeling. You can hear about whatever it wants to share. Let it all begin organically.

When you get a sense the Exile is ready to share with you, you might start with questions such as these:

- *What do you want me to know about your world? What story do you want to share?*

- *What have you been afraid to say and to whom?*
- *What secret are you hiding?*
- *What feelings have you been holding?*

With this, you might have to remind the Exile not to overwhelm you and to let out emotions in small doses, so you can continue to listen and receive the story. (Review the section on Overwhelm in this chapter, page 242.)

To stimulate more awareness at any point before or during your work with an Exile, look at the list of questions that follows. Either write down the answers if you're working alone or share the answer out loud with another person. It will address where and how an exiled part or parts came into being.

The questions fall into three categories of how an aspect becomes an exile:

1) Lacking Attuned Bonding, Connection or Safety
2) Not Fitting In and Feeling Alone
3) Loss of Childhood due to Need for Early Adulthood

1) Lacking Attuned Bonding, Connection or Safety
- Do you sense there was little or no attunement to your infant/early child self's needs or emotions?
- Were one or both parents "unregulated"—unable to be calm, present, kind, or available?
- Were you traumatized or abused in any way?
- Were you neglected?
- Were you humiliated, denigrated, or rejected?
- Were you directly told you were worthless (or implied)?
- How did you respond or react to these treatments? (the answers to the questions above)
- How did others respond, support, or not support you?
- What did people tell you or make you do?
- What did you come to decide about yourself as a result of these experiences?

2) **Not Fitting In and Feeling Alone**
   - Did you have certain traits or ways of being that made your family uncomfortable or simply did not fit in with them? Or with your School? Peers? Church? Ethnic Culture?
   - How did you respond and what did you do with those aspects of yourself?

3) **Loss of Childhood due to Need for Early Adulthood**
   - Did you need to take over a role of one or both parents? (parentified)
   - Did you play the emotional partner role for one of your parents? (emotional incest)
   - Did you have to shut down any sense of fear or need to have your own needs met?
   - Were you so depended upon that you couldn't allow yourself any emotional vulnerabilities?

More About Exiles

Exiles can threaten your whole internal system (when Self is not leading) because they:

- Are frozen and/or in state of giving up due to trauma
- Carry burdens of despair, fear, shame, neediness, worthlessness, etc.
- Trigger dangerous firefighters
- Have an incessant drive for redemption (to get what they didn't get from key others)
- Make the system vulnerable

At this point in the Dialog Process, the Exile has shared with you, or will be sharing, stories, secrets, and/or uncomfortable or painful emotions. Some of them may not have been told to you before. Yes, you may have had an awareness of a few, but through accessing this part via feelings in the body, you'll have a new level of understanding and empathy for your Exile's experience. Different Exiles would be related to various painful experiences, but they come forth one at a time as needed.

When an Exile speaks to you about a core experience related to an earlier issue, there will often be things that needed to be said that were not, or emotions that were felt that needed to be expressed. Yet back then, there was no one to share them with. These expressions would be like the "shaking off" an animal does after a trauma (as described earlier). "Shaking off" can release trauma from a locked place in the body. Words such as "I am angry, I hate you, I am afraid of you" can be important in the healing, especially when stated with true emotion. Perhaps not all parts of you feel the hatred, anger, or fear. But they are true feelings that vulnerable parts may have felt, even if they also felt love and desire for connection at the same time. Much religious or societal programing says that anger and hate are "bad." But these are part of a range of our emotional palate. To fully shut down any that are deemed "bad" also limits our ability to experience the ones we want to feel.

When we feel anger or hatred easily, then under those the Exile is usually feeling the vulnerable feelings of sadness, grief, core shame and needing to be loved. In this case, the Exile might need to express such words as "please love me, be there for me, be nice to me, see me, want me, etc." *It's extremely important that these statements from the part not be judged by you or a support person assisting you.*

When the most available emotion is sadness, grief, or variations of insecurity, then under this most often is anger. It can be hard for the exile to access this, just as it is hard for the person mainly in anger to access their vulnerable feelings. But revisiting the exiles in this way on a number of occasions can build the trust that you are truly available for all she or he is holding and it will eventually come up.

When they do arise, whether in a session or just in life, please make space for it. This mean come from your observing Self and honor the part that is expressing these feelings, while at the same time keeping it from overwhelming you.

It is these under layers of emotions rising up for expression and loving acceptance, that will free you and shift you deeply.

After an expression of the underlying emotions, (and they don't have to be dramatic or wildly emotional) at some point you will want to complete the process.

Please note that if working with another person, you might speak *for* the part—that is, feeding back to the support person what you hear the part saying or feeling. Or you can do it directly—that is, speaking *as* the part. Just be careful not to "flood" with emotion, that is, going into an overwhelm state. If so, have the helper or the Self remind the part that it has agreed not to go into overwhelm. The part has also agreed to let out emotions in doses that still allow the process to continue. If you cannot stop this flood of emotion, then stop the process. Find an experienced IFS practitioner to further the process with.

> These feelings of both anger and hatred or needing to be loved and cared for are authentic. Once taken out of the realm of the forbidden and repressed, you can find the true feelings of compassion, love, and acceptance that lie beneath. Make a safe space for all the previously judged feelings as they start to surface, knowing they are just a layer in the human cake of emotions.

Sometimes it's good to encourage Exiles to act or speak in ways they couldn't at the time due to the child's age, size, or circumstances. An example might be expressing, "NO, don't do that" and then pushing the person away. Another would be hitting back or running away from someone who'd been abusing or taunting them, or pushing away someone they had witnessed hurting a person they cared about. Though this all happens within the imagination, it creates a new brain pathway, especially when simultaneously experiencing an emotion.

Relative to what was just described, an important question to ask is this:

- *What were there things you needed to say or do but did not or could not?*
- *If you have accessed feelings of shame, then with emphasis and emotion state that you are giving a particular person(s)back the shame, that they instilled in you.*
- *Go ahead and do this now in your imagination or have a helper say some of it for you or support you in this.* (It is helpful to say it out loud but the new playing out of the situation in a way that corrects can occur silently within as well)

Retrieval

Another powerful step that can happen after the previous experience (and sometimes before) is a retrieval. This means a safe, loving person (the Self) will step in and take the Exile out of the situation they find themselves in. Self will ask each Exile:

- *Are you willing to leave this time and situation and come be with me* (the Self of you) *here, now, in this day and time?*

After having been heard and received without judgment in all the Exiles' emotions and stories or secrets, rarely would the answer be other than YES. But sometimes you'd find that child hiding under a bed or behind a rock too scared to step into a big change. If you meet resistance, then give the part encouragement to leave that place and be with you now. You could say:

- *I know this scary or lonely place is familiar, but I am here with Self now. I won't hurt you or judge you and am learning how to be with you in a way that can feel good to you. Things are different here and now, and we* (myself with guidance from my Self) *are able to take care of you in a different way. I will also keep working with that former Protector to teach it new ways to support us, and make sure you feel safe here. It will also help us do what we love and like to do. The former Protector* (name the part) *is excited to start its new job that will make it safer and more fun for you to be here.*

You can be creative with this. Simply close your eyes and wait for your intuition. It will be a combination of your Self and the Exile's impulses and preferences. A way for the Exile to leave the situation to come with you will show up in your mind. It could be as simple as reaching your hand into the scene toward the child's/Exiles's hand. He or she takes it and is suddenly here with you. Or there could be a sailboat that you're on, and he/she steps onto it to go with you. Or something like a magic carpet swoops in and he/she steps into that and comes to where you are. Or a big grey goose shows up. He/she steps onto its back and is brought to you here.

You might see yourself sitting in an environment the child would really like, such as a place in nature, a room he/she likes, or somewhere warm and inviting. However he/she arrives in this place and time, be available with open arms and heart to receive and hold this delicate, vulnerable being.

Reading this in a linear way may sound like make-believe. I promise you, if you go through this process in an open, trusting manner and allow yourself to feel each step of the way, it *does* carve new brain pathways as if you'd truly lived this altered version of the past. Though good things can be accomplished doing this alone, it's helpful to have someone talk/walk you through this entire process while you sit with your eyes closed.

Given what this Exile has experienced, many beliefs and emotions have been deeply anchored into it, and hence into your being. It *is* possible to release these. The more you have let go into this process, the more the changes occur in your brain, ultimately creating different outcomes.

Unburdening

With this next step called unburdening, the Self of you (or your helper) asks the Exile:

- *Are you ready to release the heavy burdens of belief and emotions related to these difficult experiences?*

Assuming there is a feeling of safety and being heard in a loving, open way, this Exile will usually say yes, even enthusiastically. If it happens to say no, then you can ask:

- *What are you afraid will happen when you do?*

Then bring forth reassurances until he/she ultimately agrees.

- *Create a symbol*

Have the Self state out loud the beliefs and/or emotions it will be releasing. Have the person allow a symbol to come forth that represents all that's being released. This can make the process more clear and meaningful. If no symbol comes, then it's fine to simply understand and state what's being released.

- *Use of an Element*

Next, ask of the Self or the Exile to state an element it wants to release this to—the air, wind, earth, fire, light, water, ether. (It can be a combination because as we begin the process in our minds, quite an epic can follow.) Now ask the person to close his/her eyes (if not already closed). Having chosen an element to release into and a symbol representing the burdens, let the release story unfold. Nothing has to be said out loud until completion. When the person doing this is done, he or she retells the story to the helper or writes it down (if there's no helper). Some examples of release stories are:

- "*The burdens all went into a very dense ball that was inside a small wood box. I planted the box in a hole in the earth. Then the earth gave way and it literally ate or took in the box. It went down down down to the center of the earth where the mother's flames were waiting to completely consume it.*"
- "*My belief that I am weak and 'just a girl' took on the shape of a dove* (I think because in my deepest heart I want to bring health and peace to others). *The bird flew up to the sky carrying this burden, then was taken in eventually by the sun. The sun transformed it and it came back down as rain that moistened the earth and became nourishment for new healthy strong growth.*"

These burdens can totally disintegrate or be transformed and then come back as something powerful and positive.

Most often, unburdening is done with the Exiled parts but sometimes a Protector is holding the burden. You'd follow a similar process if it feels right to do this when working with a Protector. Any diversions from the exact process as guided by your intuition are fine. They will show up as you go along. Feel free to be creative with the process.

Recovering Lost Assets

After the unburdening, the part you have just worked with can feel light, happy, and even elated. Yet sometimes, it can feel empty and slightly uncomfortable without the heavy energy it was used to holding for so long. The final step will be to fill that void with something positive and meaningful for your entire system. You will invite the Self to call in qualities, skills, abilities, and characteristics that maybe already inherent, just hidden. After you name some, you can then ask for those you'd be open to integrating more of. Select those that will be supportive on your journey moving forward.

Completion

At some point near the end, ask the Self and the Exile you just worked with to have a conversation between them. In this conversation, the Self expresses its love, appreciation, and intentions for positive change for this Exile part. It states how it intends to further the Exile's safety and comfort, offers space for his/her feelings, and intention of more time for what makes it feel happy, playful, and so on. You would include ideas that would continue healing and counterbalancing what came up in the session. Then have the Exile part respond to what's said. You might need some back and forth for reassurance or negotiation of what's possible and needs to happen.

If you've had your eyes closed most of the time— which is a great way to do this process—you can come out of it by having your helper (or yourself) then count back from 5 to 1 to 0. With each countdown number, it's helpful to say, "I am preparing to step forward in a whole new way." Repeating something that became clear and will be different for each of the 5, 4, 3, 2, 1 counts. Then on 0, open your eyes to this life of new energy and way of being.

And Moving Forward

As you acknowledge the presence of the Exiled parts daily, they gradually open and share with you what they're feeling as well as who they are, including their gifts and joys. Merely acknowledging its presence can open doors to a growing relationship with this buried, frozen, or otherwise missing part of you.

It's in accessing, acknowledging, loving, and accepting everything about these Exiles—including their feelings, weaknesses, and untogetherness—that will breathe joy and vitality back into them. When they come alive, YOU come alive. When core shame has been in the mix, they go from feeling they "are bad' to knowing they are worthy and loveable in the essence of who they are.

You can also use this process when you're confused about making a decision. As the different parts speak about their motivations and fears, you clear the way to see what is the Self speaking and what is one or many of the parts, covering the deeper truth.

Expand the Presence of the Soul-Centered Self

Besides the Full Dialog Process, the other 7 Keys practices greatly support this deeper shift. They help expand the presence of the Soul-Centered Self and anchor transformation into your daily life to become ongoing emotional and behavior change.

After this level of deep work, you might find behavior changes occurring spontaneously. However, consciously adding *intention* to behavior change will assure your transformation is permanently effective. You'll find emotions and feelings will shift organically, making committing to behavior change much easier. All parts of you are supportive of the changes rather than feeling resistance from various polarized parts.

In fact, that's why relapse is common. It happens when the Protector parts, with their good reasons for addictive behaviors have not yet been heard, understood, and accepted. It also happens when they have not yet witnessed or experienced that the vulnerable parts are safe to feel and can be taken care of by the Self. In those cases, no amount of peer support can keep these "hated" parts from acting out.

By doing the 7 Keys exercises, practices and especially the Full Dialog Process, you'll create new deeply held experiences, that create new brain pathways. The resistances within you will have been transformed. At that point, they become supportive of the new rather than fearing or judging it or otherwise pulling you backward.

I encourage you to do 7 Keys exercises and practices and repeat the Full Dialog Process over and over, even in its simplest form, until all parts of you have been felt, heard, accepted, and loved. Also when new things show up in life that require a refresher.

After completing this process with many different parts of ourselves, our Soul Self leads the way over any of the "ego" parts. That's when we move from egocentric to Soulcentric. A Soulcentric life is a Soul Self-guided and fulfilling life. It feels free of obsessions and hurtful behaviors. It's healthy, joyful, and amazingly peaceful. And that's what I hold in my heart and prayers for you.

Visit my website www.drjoyfreeman.com to learn more about my one on one transformational work. Schedule an in person or Skype session to assist you along your way. You can also go to www.selfleadership.org to find an IFS practitioner in your area. Also, please see the Resource page that follows for a list of other suggested therapy modalities and their websites with list of trained practitioners.

One great way to do this work is to create a **7 Keys WorkBook Group** in your area. It is like a book club that goes deeper and makes more powerful connections with your friends or members of your community. Its Free, and Dr. Joy can tell you how to set it up.

If you are interested in setting up a 7 Keys WorkBook Group, sign up at Dr. Joy's web site – Free and Connected:

www.drjoyfreeman.com   or   www.freeandconnected.org

Resources

The following is a list of cutting edge transformational therapy modalities for training Helping Professionals and for finding those trained in each, to work with individuals. This list below offers suggested options for working with Trauma, Attachment Bonding issues, challenged Survival Strategies and one for Nature Based Soul Encounter work. There are other excellent modalities out there but these are ones that I think are some of the best.

AVI Animus Valley Institute *animus.org*
Bill Plotkin, Ph.D: Depth psychologist, wilderness guide and cultural change agent. Author of 3 deeply moving powerful books on humans in relation to, Soul and Nature. Site offers public workshops, wilderness programs and Animus Quests. AVI also offers certifications in nature-based guide work.

Daniel Siegel M.D. *drdansiegel.com & mindsitesinstitute.com*
Forerunner in the field of neuroscience of attachment and child development and author of numerous books. Mindsite Institute offers workshops and online trainings for Helping Professionals and individuals.

EFT Emotionally Focused Therapy *iceeft.com*
Dr. Sue Johnson: relational work based on attachment and bonding science. Trainings and workshops for Helping Professionals, couples, family and individuals. Nationwide and International list of practitioners available (this is not EFT Emotional Freedom Technique, yet that one has some value too).

Gottman Institute *gottman.com*
Drs. John and Julie Gottman: research-based approach to relationships. Workshops for training Helping Professionals and couples. They have developed nine components of healthy relationships knows as the Sound Relationship House Theory. Practitioner references also available.

Hakomi Therapy *hakomiinstitute.com*
Ron Kurtz: Professional trainings in a widely recognized mindfulness based somatic oriented psychotherapeutic approach. This was one of the first somatic therapies and has evolved tremendously since its inception in the 70's. Site contains a list of practitioners worldwide.

Center for Healing Shame *healingshame.com & centerforhealingshame.com*
Sheila Rubin, MA, LMFT and Bret Lyon, Ph.D: Trainings for therapists and Helping Professionals on leading edge work in Shame: a somatic, expressive arts and relational approach. Practitioner list available on healingshame.com.

IFS Internal Family Systems *selfleadership.org*
Richard Schwartz, Ph.D: A rapidly growing therapy modality that honors the multiplicity of the mind and is written about in detail in this book. IFS is considered "evidence based" (A professional research based designation) with trauma and other challenging issues. Professional trainings, certifications and practitioners list available on the web site.

NARM NeuroAffective Relational Model *drlaurenceheller.com*
Laurence Heller, Ph.D: Author of *Healing Developmental Trauma*—neuroscience and attachment theory based approach uses somatic mindfulness and developmentally informed interventions. Site offers Professional trainings and list of practitioners.

PACT Psychobiological Approach to Couple Therapy *thepactinstitute.com*
Stan Tatkin, PsyD, MFT: Author of 5 public books on relationship. His work integrates developmental neuroscience, attachment theory, emotional arousal regulation, with principals of adult romantic relationships. His site offers trainings for professionals and retreats for couples and PACT Therapist Directory.

SPI Sensorimotor Psychotherapy Institute *sensorimotorpsychotherapy.org*
Pat Ogden, Ph.D: SP joins somatic therapy and psychotherapy for healing the disconnection between the body and the mind, especially in trauma The site offers Professional trainings including affect dysregulation, survival

defenses and traumatic memory, attachment repair and more. Site includes a Referral List.

SE Somatic Experiencing *traumahealing.org*
Peter A. Levine, Ph.D: leader in the field of Trauma, author of numerous widely acclaimed books. Site offers Professional trainings and list of approved providers.

Other Important Researchers, Authors and Writings

Alan N. Schore, M.D. *allenschore.com*
As a psychiatrist and researcher in neuropsychology he is a Leading contributor to Affect regulation theory, Developmental neuroscience, developmental psychology, attachment theory, trauma and more—author of four seminal books.

Bessel van der Kolk, M.D. *besselvanderkolk.net and traumacenter.org*
Groundbreaking researcher in the area of post-traumatic stress since 1970s, his work focuses on the interaction of attachment, neurobiology, and developmental trauma. His Book: *The Body Keeps the Score*, is a NY Times bestseller and respected by professionals in the field of psychotherapy as well. He writes about IFS as one of a few therapies he recommends.

Bruce Ecker, LMFT *coherencetherapy.org*[1]
Author of *Unlocking the Emotional Brain* and Coherence Therapy This work is based on the recent discovery of memory reconsolidation by neuroscientists. This allows us to dissolve an emotional learning rather than just do a workaround with a new intentional response.

---

[1] Coherence Therapy:

With neuroscientists' recent discovery of *memory reconsolidation*, it is stated that there exists a form of neuro plasticity that allows an emotional learning or schema stored in long-term implicit memory (that which we are unaware of) to actually be erased, not just over written and suppressed by learning a preferred response.

IFS also integrates the steps that allows this memory reconsolidation to occur.

Bruce Ecker, LMFT, http://www.coherencetherapy.org/discover/ct-reconsolidation.htm for an overview of the research and explanation of reconsolidation read more on the same web page.

Diana Fosha, Ph.D *aedpinstitute.org*
Developer of AEDP Accelerated Experiential Dynamic Psychotherapy for healing trauma and suffering and toward expanding emergent transformational experiences. Trainings.

Dr. Daniel Amen *danielamenmd.com*
In the field of neurobiological science, Dr. Amen and his team have developed a cutting-edge diagnostic system of brain biology for addiction, depression, and other brain conditions. Eight different types of depression and deeper physiological causes of addiction can be identified. The Amen Clinics integrate conventional and new treatments mostly with neutraceuticals, which are science-based yet natural substances. Check out the Amen Clinics across the country at amenclinics.com.

Pat De Young, Ph.D *patdeyoung.com*
Author of Understanding and Treating Chronic Shame: A Relational/Neurobiological Approach. This is an amazing book that takes a very thorough look with great explanations of the many aspects of shame.

Dr. Sebern Fisher *sebernfisher.com*
Author of Neurofeedback in the Treatment of Developmental Trauma: Calming the Fear Driven Brain.

Yes Magazine *yesmagazine.org*
Yes! is a non-profit, ad-free magazine that covers topics of social justice, environmental sustainability, alternative economics, and peace. The magazine is published by Positive Futures Network. It provides inspiration and what is happening on a grass roots level that is extremely positive. It covers news we might otherwise have no awareness of, as normal media does not cover this in depth truth reporting as well as good news.

About the Author

Joy Lynn Freeman, D.C., Ph.D. cand., has been a pioneer in the field of health, personal growth, and transformation for over 35 years as a Natural Physician, Transformational Life Counselor, Speaker, and Workshop Facilitator. In addition to *7 Keys to Connection,* she is the author of *Express Yourself: Discover Your Inner Truth, Creative Self and the Courage to Let It Out,* two music CDs of original songs: *Let It Shine* and *Soul Calling,* and a series of five yoga videos: *Back-care-cise*. She also created and led many transformational workshops and retreats including Quantum Shift Retreats, incorporating expressive arts, deep process, ritual and nature.

As a powerful agent for change, Joy writes and facilitates, both personally and in group with a warmth, zest, and passion that spreads to all whom she contacts. Employing her earnest caring, natural abilities, and extensive skills, Dr. Joy has helped her clients find their buried emotions, deeper truths, and has supported many out of deep and challenging places. She is certified in IFS: Internal Family Systems Therapy, Shame work, and other therapeutic modalities.

Her unique work, both in written word and heartful presence creates an acceptance and safety that assists others in accessing their courage to express their authentic and creative selves, find their voices, speak their truth, and follow their callings.

Dr. Joy can be reached at info@drjoyfreeman.com

www.ingramcontent.com/pod-product-compliance
Lightning Source LLC
Chambersburg PA
CBHW050625300426
44112CB00012B/1668